Real World
COMMUNICATION
STRATEGIES
That

Dear Hillary —
Remember to Live
Human Moments!
Joan Burge
4/05

Insight Publishing Company
Sevierville, Tennessee

Real World
COMMUNICATION
STRATEGIES
That
WORK

Published by Insight Publishing Company
PO Box 4189
Sevierville, TN 37862

Printed in the United States of America

Cover design and book layout by Russ Hollingsworth.
Copy editing by Mitch Moore.

ISBN 1-885640-98-6

Table Of Contents

A Message From The Publisher

Some of my most rewarding experiences in business, and for that matter in my personal life, have been at meetings, conventions or gatherings after the formal events have concluded. Inevitably, small groups of ten to fifteen men and women gather together to rehash the happenings of the day and to exchange war stories, recently heard jokes or the latest gossip from their industry. It is in these informal gatherings where some of the best lessons can be learned.

Usually, in informal groups of professionals, there are those who clearly have lived through more battles and learned more lessons than the others. These are the men and women who are really getting the job done and everyone around the room knows it. When they comment on the topic of the moment they don't just spout the latest hot theory or trend, and they don't ramble on and on without a relevant point. These battle scarred warriors have lessons to share that everyone senses are just a little more real, more relevant and, therefore, worthy of more attention.

These are the kind of people we have recruited for the *Power Learning* series of books. Each title offers contributions from men and women who are making a significant impact on their culture, in their field and on their colleagues and clients. This book offers a variety of themes in the area of Communication Strategies. It is ripe with "the good stuff," as an old friend of mine used to always say. Inside these pages you'll find ideas, insights, strategies and philosophies that are working with real people, in real companies and under real circumstances.

It is our hope that you keep this book with you until you've dog-eared every chapter and made so many notes in the margins that you have trouble seeing the original words on the pages. There is treasure here. Enjoy digging!

Chapter 1

Making Connections:
The First Step in Effective Communication

Cindy Chernow

Networking is and always will be the great equalizer. It is what makes it possible for the mailroom clerk to speak to the CEO. It is what allows people all across the world to provide resources and support to one another in times of crisis. In a world that is becoming increasingly more populated, more competitive and more impersonal, networking can break down barriers, provide resources and even help secure a job.

Since the beginning of time, people have networked, successfully communicating their needs and desires via an assortment of tools—from smoke signals to the telegraph, from letters to the telephone and now, the Internet. Through these processes, we have learned from each other, shared resources, exchanged information and developed skills. But successfully networking with others these days requires new approaches to communication. This chapter will look at some of the new tools that can help people communicate more effectively in the process of making connections and building relationships.

The word "networking" originated with the Greeks during the 14th century, when fisherman would throw out their nets to bring in their catch. The successful fishermen excelled because they knew a net more widely cast would bring in far more fish. They also knew where it was best to cast their nets. Today, the process of attracting individuals into a network works in much the same way; the broader one's net, the greater the return. So in addition to sharing the latest in networking tools, this chapter will show you how to use those tools effectively to reach the greatest number of people.

Indeed, the world has become a "global village," and to be part of that village requires that our networks expand well beyond local communities. Those with whom we feel most aligned and comfortable will remain part of our "core group," but that core will now serve as a safety net while we stretch ourselves to make connections in areas less comfortable. This chapter will also help you learn to identify and overcome some of the challenges and obstacles you might face while trying to network. In turn, you will learn to initiate, expand and increase your networking opportunities.

Networking is an Innate Ability

The need to connect is an innate ability launched in early childhood. When was the last time you watched two- or three-year-olds at play? Their interaction comes naturally and is generally playful, comfortable and unrestrained. Through adolescence and as young adults, the ability to comfortably approach a stranger becomes increasingly more difficult. We have fears of rejection or, at the least, an unfriendly response. "Don't talk to strangers" was the parental rule frequently stated in any adventure in which we would meet new people. With such early shaping of behavior toward strangers, how do we then create a place from which essential networking and relationship-building skills can develop and be enhanced into adulthood? When is it okay to invite strangers into our inner circles? How do you ask strangers for help to achieve your goals?

Practice makes perfect. It starts with baby steps and requires stepping out of your comfort zone. The more you talk with people, the easier it gets.

Everyone is a Potential Candidate for Conversation

If you are the kind of person who only attends events with friends, it is time to change course. Sitting next to a stranger and meeting someone new is the equivalent of an adventure. Just as if you were visiting a new city or country, you learn something you never knew before. I have attended many functions where I thought I knew absolutely no one. It often took a little voice in my head or an imaginary person prodding me to walk up to a total stranger and shake hands. On most occasions, I have been amazed at the good conversations that resulted and the subsequent exchanges of valuable information.

Breaking the Ice

Aren't sure how to approach someone or how to strike up a conversation? If you are feeling stuck, consider asking the other person where he or she was born. The world is getting smaller each day. You can generally make an association with the person's birthplace, or you may have traveled there yourself. For example, if I meet a person from Germany, I mention that our good friends live there and that I have visited them there. Incredible as it may seem, the person might actually know my friends. Regardless, it opens the window to further discussion. Other common factors that bond people might include the fact that you are both married, have children, like the same sports, books or food. Once commonality is acknowledged, people begin to feel comfortable with each other. The conversation becomes less labored, and one conversation leads to another. A bond forms. This is when the real and invaluable information begins to get shared.

Networking is not a One-Time Task but an Ongoing Process

When networking becomes a daily habit, it will become such a natural part of how you talk to others that it will define how you communicate. It is the simplest form of communication that can provide the exchange of information and ideas. If you fear rejection or are generally more timid than most, think of networking as a game of discovery. Experience each new encounter as a stepping stone, and remember that specific networking techniques may feel more comfortable to you than others. Each of us is a unique individual with a style and personality of our own. Use networking skills and methods that work best for you. You may need the help of individuals such as mentors or promoters referred to later in this chapter. These people are among the many who will assist you in making a series of connections with others that will enhance your resources, broaden your perspectives and open new doors.

If You Don't Talk, You Won't Learn

All of us have great stories to share about how a random conversation initiated with a total stranger led to some incredible connection or coincidence. One of those instances occurred when my husband and I were on a night train traveling from Holland to Germany. At 11:30 p.m., there was suddenly a knock at our cabin door. We were joined by two little old ladies who were on their way to volunteer at a soup kitchen in Poland. Only one of the women spoke English. She had previously been to America only twice to visit two people she knew. My husband knew both of the gentlemen, one a professor at the same university where he taught and the other a historian with whom he had done some work. We would never have discovered that coincidence without engaging in a conversation. Another example was when our friend shared with us a cookbook that his sister, now living in Costa Rica, had just written with her friend. Reading the inside cover, I happened to notice that the woman was in the Peace Corps in Kenya during the 1960s when my sister was also there. One phone call to my sister was all it took to get two people reconnected. Keep your eyes and ears open. Always be looking for those possible connections.

Avoid Making Assumptions

Everyone you meet can be a valuable resource. Avoid making assumptions about people that may be inaccurate. Years ago, I was attending a staff retreat when one of the company's new employees approached me and said, "Everyone here says you can make a connection with anyone. Well, you can't make one with me." When I asked why, she replied, "I am Korean and half your age." Her assumption was that I would not know people from her Korean community and certainly not people her age since I was considerably older. As I always do, I began thinking about possible connections I might have with other people she might know. I considered the fact that she was about the same age as one of my sons and remembered her mentioning she had grown up in our area. I quickly asked whether she belonged to the Korean Youth Group in our neighborhood and, if so, did she happen to know a particular young man. Her face paled, and she replied in her "Valley Girl" vernacular, "No Way! How do you know Robert?" When I explained that this young man was my son's best friend in junior high school she responded by saying that her husband was Robert's best friend and had just been the best man at his wedding over the summer. She was stunned when I conveyed to her that we had not only attended that wedding but had been seated at the same table with her, her friends and their high school principal.

A similar situation occurred one evening while I was connecting UCLA alumni together at a workshop in Washington, D.C. I asked members of the audience to make a connection with the people standing next to them. An older alumnus walked into the back of the room late, and the only person left for her to pair up with was a recent graduate. The expression on her face vividly displayed the thoughts she later revealed to the group. She said, "I knew this would be a waste of my time. When I was late, I should have just turned around and gone home." Then she continued, "I could not have been more wrong!" You see, this woman was in a very esoteric field of the arts. Her assumption was that someone so young could not possibly have any idea what she was talking about, and yet this young graduate's entire family was associated with the Smithsonian Institution in her very field of interest. The moral in this case is that every time you make assumptions about the improbability of a possible connection, you leave opportunities on the table. Everyone knows literally hundreds of people who, in turn, know hundreds of people. You never know who is connected to whom.

Listen

As one of our five senses, hearing happens naturally but listening is an art. The real communication that results from making a connection is enhanced when we learn to listen. So much is missed when we talk more than we listen. The average person today is so busy multitasking that communication gets lost. At work, many of us are carrying on telephone conversations while sending e-mails and talking to people passing by our desks. Someone is getting shortchanged. It is far better to stop what you are doing and give your full attention to the person speaking.

The average person speaks 200 to 250 words per minute and listens at 300 to 500 words per minute. Since people think much faster than they talk, you are generally thinking well ahead of the person who is speaking. Do not leap to assumptions about what someone is thinking or about to say. Like most people, you may often find yourself completing someone else's sentence only to find out that is not what she was going to say at all. Learn to be patient. Good listeners keep an open, curious mind. They listen for new ideas and consider each message they hear as an opportunity to gather new information.

George Bernard Shaw said, "The problem with communication is the illusion that it has been accomplished." It is also important to validate that messages are not only being heard but also being understood correctly. All too often, communication becomes nothing more than passing out information. To be a more effective listener, stop to paraphrase or ask questions to ensure that what you have heard or said has been interpreted correctly. If you have problems remembering information, try to focus your attention, repeat information frequently and make associations whenever possible.

Read

Another key ingredient to effective networking today is to read, read, read! Living in such a diverse environment, the more knowledge you absorb about any number of topics, the more opportunities you will have to connect with other people. When you make a daily practice of scanning the morning paper or the Net, you will invariably find that one or more of the topics will come up in a conversation or discussion with people later that day. Your knowledge about most topics may be limited, but you will appear to be well informed and capable of holding a conversation with individuals in almost any situation.

Work a Room

If you walk into a room, don't be intimidated by how few familiar faces you see. Be challenged and excited about the chance to meet so many new people. Take the first step: simply turn to the nearest stranger and introduce yourself. By finding a connection with that individual, the conversation will flow easier. Start with a few simple questions like the ones discussed earlier: "Where were you born?" or "Are you currently working and, if so, what type of work do you do?" These are simple, easy icebreakers. Keep probing. You may need to ask a few questions to find a link. While it is often difficult, you should avoid talking with only one person for the entire time. Your objective should always be to try and meet as many people as possible, especially when the time to network is limited.

If a conversation has turned into a valuable encounter but you want to enable yourself to move freely around to meet other people, simply ask whether you could continue your conversation at a later date. Be sure to ask the person for a business card before you step away. Introducing people to each other is another way to free yourself to move around the room. If you are like me and have difficulty remembering names but want to introduce two people, just ask, "Have the two of you met?" Within seconds they will invariably shake hands and introduce themselves—problem solved.

Passing out business cards is one of the many strategies used to facilitate the art of networking. They are used to identify who we are, what we do and how we can be easily reached. If you do not have a business card, get one! Have business cards made that include at least your name, e-mail and telephone number; your address can be optional. If you are trying to transition out of a particular field, do not assume you have to use your current business card. Have new cards printed and create a title for yourself. Today everyone can call themselves a consultant. The unsavory alternative to not having a business card is to rush around trying to locate a pen and a piece of paper, taking time from your conversation to write out your contact information and taking a chance that the person will think your note is a piece of scrap paper the next day and toss it out by accident.

One afternoon while working at UCLA, I conducted a networking workshop for international students. A graduate student from Columbia who was in the class told me he was hoping to get a fellowship in the entertainment field and stay in the United States. I explained that this was his lucky day. That very evening the Alumni Association was sponsoring Entertainment Night for students. Representatives from all areas of entertainment— including some of the most prominent directors, producers and screen writers (all of whom were UCLA alumni)—would be hosting roundtable discussions. I also suggested he stop by the UCLA Student Union, where there was a machine that made business cards. Later that night, while working this thousand-person event, I felt a tap on my shoulder. The graduate student held up his newly-printed business card and thanked me profusely. He had just come from a table where he met a contact who was willing to provide him with a fellowship. You should always be prepared because great opportunities happen when you least expect them.

Remember, however, that the purpose of networking isn't just to pass out business cards but to make as many connections as possible. So be sure to annotate each business card you receive from others. Note the date, the place and any memorable points about the encounter. All of this information may be valuable for future reference. If you agreed to follow up with that individual in any way or wish to send him something relevant in the future, this information will be essential. If done correctly, you should be able to go back through these business cards years later and remember that individual based on the note(s) you wrote. Imagine how shocked someone would be when you call and remind him that you had met six years previously. I have been able to do this on several occasions.

Networking as a Tool for Employment

"Networking" is only one letter away from "not working." Getting ahead has always been about "who you know, and who knows you." It is almost impossible to break into your career field of choice or move up the ladder of success without accepting a lifestyle that includes networking and informational interviewing. Everyone you know today and will meet in the future is a potential member of your network. You never know who they know or what information they may possess to help you.

Informational interviewing is an ongoing, active method of extending your communication base, and it is easier than you may think. For years, you have been asking others for information to determine the best places to eat, the best movies to see or the best places to get your hair cut. In fact, you have been doing informational interviewing all your life, so applying that same process to the world of work should require very little extra effort. Friends, co-workers, alumni of your university, professional organizations, religious or sports affiliations can all be valuable members of your network. Always build on and broaden your network. Those with whom you have done informational interviews should automatically become part of your network. Remember to say thank you and say it often. Keep in touch with them. Let them know the outcomes of any suggestions or leads they may have passed along so that they will want to continue to help others in the future. It will also remind them to keep you in mind.

Informational interviewing is also one of the keys to unlocking the hidden job market. You never know where an informal conversation may lead once a relationship between two people begins to develop. I once worked with a graphic designer who continuously complained about her job and told me that she was contemplating going out on her own. I suggested she do an informational interview with a friend of mine who had just started his own business so that she could pick up some tips on what might be required. Shortly thereafter, he took her into his company, and the business flourished and became incredibly prosperous. With every connection you make, the process becomes easier. You will be able to turn cold calls into warm calls by saying, "I just had an opportunity to meet with Mr. Helpful, and he suggested that I give you a call." Now armed with new and useful information, you must work to keep the connections alive.

The New World of Work

Many changes are occurring in the workplace; job sharing, telecommuting and flexible hours are just a few. Telecommuting, for example, may no longer be a luxury but rather a necessity to stave off the increasingly long commutes and gridlock that have developed in our urban centers. While telecommuting may appear to be more isolative, it will require greater knowledge of how to network remotely with the resources and the people necessary to help you accomplish your goals.

The success of most businesses depends more than ever on the ability of employees to communicate. The tools you develop today will prepare you for the workplace of tomorrow. Employees will be required to have skill sets capable of meeting the challenges of the 21st century. These changes will include integrated teamwork, globalization and the cyclical nature of work. By 2005, knowledge workers will be assessed not only by what they do, but also by how well they forge relationships and how well they tap into new sources of knowledge. By 2006, it is predicted that 50 percent of the knowledge workforce will work "outside the walls" of their formal workplace. People will use networking to accomplish individual goals and group goals as well as to create bonds and a sense of belonging. Personal and professional networks are not created overnight. Your contacts should be growing daily and be so extensive that you find yourself needing an excellent storage and retrieval system that categorizes all the people you know and the resources you have available to you. This can be a major obstacle for those who have not developed such a record keeping system. Look to technology and database programs or hand held devices to help you in this endeavor.

Building Your Network

Seek out individuals and then connect them to build strategic alliances for mutual benefit and support. Once you learn how to connect names, there may only be a few degrees of separation. As the world expands, so must your network. You must invest in the process and begin to build a web for yourself. Your web should consist of Mentors, Role Models, Hubs, Challengers and Promoters.

Mentors of all ages are a valuable resource during every phase of your life. These are the people who will give you advice. They will help show you the way and provide access, opportunities and guidance.

Role Models will introduce ideas while stimulating preferred behaviors and postures. While we all try to emulate others, we are, nonetheless, individuals. No two people can ever be the same, but role models can help you strive to be the best. Have role models in all areas of your life.

Hubs are a walking referral system. These are the individuals you call when you need to contact someone in a particular area or need to know where to find information. Have hubs in a lot of different fields. The goal of every great networker should be to become a hub for others.

Challengers overtly push you to take risks and challenge yourself. The earliest challengers may have been your parents. They were the ones who encouraged you to study, go out for a team sport or practice an instrument. Most of us will avoid challengers because they encourage us to step outside our comfort zones. They are like the difficult teachers we complained about while in school yet years later wished we had thanked. Find those challengers and embrace them.

Promoters keep you abreast of opportunities and encourage you to be more visible. If you are somewhat shy and timid, promoters are a must in your life. Align yourself with those who will speak out for you. If you are a better communicator than most, become a promoter for others.

Frequently redefine your resources. Identify gaps in your network and find ways to fill them. Your connections with other people and your ability to communicate to get the job done have reached a new level of importance. Often people fail to keep their networks alive. Occasional notes—such as a birthday card or New Year's card—and phone calls are valuable tools to staying connected. A personal retrieval system that might include an index file, Rolodex or computer database is a must. Staying connected will help you update those addresses and phone numbers regularly. Think about ways to contact people on your list at least once a year. Do not let distance become a barrier. Those with whom you connect most may no longer be just the "person next door" but rather the person halfway around the globe.

Volunteer

There are several other ways to be proactive in your networking pursuits. First and foremost, be willing to give as well as get. One of the best ways to meet new people, learn new skills and contribute to your visibility is through volunteering. Pick a charity you feel passionate about or a professional organization where you can meet people with similar interests and get involved. The benefits of being involved with these types of organizations are many. Volunteering is both emotionally and personally rewarding. It provides an opportunity to meet new people in numerous career fields outside the one in which you are currently spending the majority of your time. By doing so, you will be able to develop a new set of friends, resources and allies. You will gain visibility for yourself while gaining recognition as a participant, contributor and leader. Through involvement with professional organizations, you will gain information about new trends, build relationships with peers and develop potential local and global contacts that can lead to future career opportunities. Take on additional responsibilities and take advantage of the exposure as you demonstrate the skills required to implement them.

In the early 1990s, a colleague of mine wanted to transition into development and fundraising, just as it was gaining prominence. Without a previous background in the field, no organizations were willing to hire him. I suggested that he take a year and volunteer to raise money for his favorite charity. At the end of that year, he was able to put on his resume that he had raised approximately $1 million for that charity and was hired almost immediately. Today, he is highly sought after in his profession as a development officer at a prestigious university. His exposure and experience helped him to communicate his skill

Be a Matchmaker

Be willing to give without any expectation of something in return. Networking is an ongoing, relationship-building process that is mutually beneficial. Sometimes you are getting something, and sometimes you are giving. It is like a boomerang—what goes around comes around.

Authors Jessica Lipnack and Jeffrey Stamps wrote, "One person with a need contacts another with a resource and networking begins." It's time to expand on the concept of "we." The world and its people depend on our abilities to help one another. Seldom in life do people succeed on their own. The more you think about helping others, the more natural it becomes and the more people will want to help you.

Conversations inevitably lead to connections. Once a connection is made, other people will benefit from that same connection. Start to look for those connections and be willing to be a resource for someone else. Networkers are matchmakers. They know many people, either directly or indirectly, and they are always willing to share resources. Always introduce people to one another and think about how you can help others get what they need. Those people you help at various points along the way will be indebted and more than willing to return the favor some day when you least expect it.

Staged and selfish methods are easily noticed and will put off most people. It is easy to spot the person who is out for himself or tries to jump over others to get to the top. In managing a personnel agency years ago, I was required to make sales calls to acquire new business. I had tried valiantly, but without success, to connect with the human resource director at a local insurance company. It took more than six months, but I finally received a call back. I asked the director, "Why, after all this time and the numerous attempts to reach you, did you finally decide to call?" Her response was simple—because her receptionist insisted. The receptionist had stopped her one day and remarked that I was the only salesperson who did not simply throw a business card in her face and leave. The receptionist had said to the director on my behalf, "The manager from United always takes time to ask me how my day is going, how I am feeling and how my children are doing. Someone that thoughtful deserves at least a return call." That returned phone call was the beginning of a long-standing business relationship between myself and that human resource director. Do not go over people—go through them.

Everyone you speak with should be made to feel equally important because they are.

A well-developed network acts as a resource bank in your own and related fields, but there are a few essential things to remember: Relationships take time to develop; it is important to treat everyone as an equal; and always give without expecting something in return.

Networking With a Purpose

If you are networking for a specific purpose, be focused and clear about your goal. The truth of the matter is that people genuinely want to help others. My clients who state their goal as "I like working with people" are vague and unclear. Since there is really little opportunity for work that doesn't involve people, they have not shared anything relevant that invites anyone to appropriately offer help, referral or direction. Comedian Lily Tomlin's quote, "I always knew I wanted to be somebody, but then I realized I should have been more specific," is fitting. Help people help you. When communicating your needs and desires, be more specific about your goals so that they can direct you and provide you with the contacts that can help you succeed. Do not leave things to chance and speculation. This is a good opportunity to use what is often referred to as your "elevator speech." Elevator speeches generally involve telling someone, in a minute or less, a little about your past, where you are currently and where you'd like to be in the future. It not only helps to introduce you but provides another opportunity for a connection to be made. Do not be afraid to ask for help or possible leads. If you don't ask, you don't get.

Understanding the Impact of Technology

The computer revolution has provided us with instantaneous communication, unlimited knowledge and unparalleled conveniences. But has the impact of technology contributed to the creation of a more impersonal world? Today's PCs and laptops have more computing power than NASA had the day man first set foot on the moon. It is hard to imagine what our lives were like before July 19, 1969, when Neil Armstrong walked on the moon and personalized the Space Age. How many of us can even remember what life and work were like before personal computers, photocopy machines, cell phones and e mail? In this world of wireless connections, are people truly connecting more?

There is a growing interconnectedness among the world's educated that is being driven by technology—particularly through the Internet and e-mail. People who normally felt uncomfortable networking in person now exchange information freely via the Internet. Information transmitted through technology will be used to enhance the quality of our work lives. However, what is glaringly absent from this new electronic format of communication is the human connection. The major thrusts in wireless technology are small devices with visual capabilities that are designed to mimic or replicate the personal nature that comes from face-to-face communication. The new visual imaging technologies on desktops, laptops, PDAs and cell phones are designed to bring the much-needed human touch to the cold, impersonal world of the computer. These devices are actually being designed to enhance networking by transmitting body language; only a portion of the non-verbal language that makes up ninety percent of communication and which is so important when communicating, especially across cultures.

Until very recently in the "wireless" world, the opportunity for face-to-face communication—the chance to observe one's facial expressions and gestures—had been absent. However, new technology advancements in this area will take a long time to perfect. Computers can only generate information; they have not yet mastered the ability to express feelings and share emotions. In fact, online communication has made it easy to misinterpret the meaning of what has been said, even though the assumption is that the information has been received and understood as it was intended.

Technology can be friend or foe. As technology continues to make quantum leaps, each of us will need to embrace new systems while, at the same time, learning to maintain appropriate levels of communication. With all of these tools, the person 3,000 miles away can become more like your next-door neighbor.

Understand Your Audience

To be effective communicators, we must appreciate and understand our many audiences. No two people interpret what is said or written in exactly the same way. Age, gender, culture, language, education and experiences all serve as filters that contribute to how people interpret the information that is being exchanged. It is why members of the older generation have a more difficult time understanding slang and relating to rap or how in some languages the word "yes" can mean "no". Of the 500 words most commonly used on a daily basis, each has anywhere from 20 to 35 different meanings. Someone who has just become engaged, for example, may hear the word "ring" and think you are referring to a wedding ring while another individual may think you are referring to the "ring" on a telephone. Depending on age, someone may hear the word "forty-five" and think you are referring to a small record with a hole in the middle, while a young person doesn't even know such a record existed and assumes you are referring to a gun. Which meaning someone attributes to a particular word will depend on any number of the filters mentioned above and can be further impacted by a person's values, interests, or emotional state. While these concepts will be covered in greater length throughout the various chapters of this book, it is important to consider the person(s) we are addressing when trying to connect. In some instances, we may need to speak more clearly, more slowly or use different words to clarify what we are trying to say. Different communication styles may also impact the amount of and kind of information we share when trying to connect with others.

Conclusion

In a more global world, it will be incumbent upon you to begin examining your personal bank of resources. To network effectively requires not only a new attitude but a new approach to life. Used correctly, networking will help to celebrate the differences while identifying the common bonds among us. John Demartini said, "Knowledgeable people know facts. Successful and prosperous people know people." It is more than just connecting with others. Networking is a way of life and a commitment to yourself and your goals. The more it is integrated into your daily life, the more natural it becomes. Relationships take a while to build, but each relationship begins with a connection. Our power as individuals will come not from our independence but from our interdependence, our interactions and the way we relate to the people around us. Future survival will require that we divest ourselves of the "Lone Ranger" mentality and embrace the "Concept of We."

Cindy Chernow

The world of work is changing so fast; few of us can keep up. Technology has us more "connected" than ever before, yet we simply are not "connecting." Messages are getting lost somewhere between multi-tasking and interpretation by others whose: age, gender, cultural or work experience is far different than our own. Cindy uses her Cultural Anthropology expertise to guide leaders and employees to rethink how-to re-connect to increase: creativity, customer service, straight talk, and presentation dynamics. Cindy's interesting work with villagers in Chile, India, and Africa helped shape the powerful strategies she shares.

Diverse Clients: Raytheon, Xerox, Universal Studios, AT&T, U.S. Navy, County of Los Angeles, UCLA, Herbalife.

Services: Keynotes • Conference Breakouts • Seminars • Career Coaching

"My sincere thanks for a great staff development workshop (Firing Up Your Creativity). Your presentation allowed me to feel what it's like to step out of the box and feel free again, something I have not felt for some time, but am glad to have it back! I am now rethinking what I do... and how I do it!"
- *Bob Gomez, Assistant Director UCI Career Center*

Book Cindy Chernow for Your Event:

22364 Algunas Rd.
Woodland Hills, CA 91364
(818) 884-3212
E-mail: cchernow@earthlink.net
Website: www.chernowconsulting.com

Chapter 2

Professional Assertiveness

Rhonda Finniss

Regardless of the position we hold, we all have to deal with others in a professionally assertive way. The dangers in not doing so range from losing your job to working with people who either take advantage of you or stab you in the back. Even CEOs of companies are not able to freely speak their minds; they too have to be professionally assertive. In order for us to excel, we have to learn to communicate our ideas, thoughts and plans effectively. To do this, we need to ensure that the correct messages are being communicated, as well as know how they are being interpreted by others.

Communication Styles

We'll start by examining three styles of communication—assertive, passive and aggressive. The style you choose will largely affect how successful your communication will be.

Webster defines "assert" as: "to state positively, declare, affirm. To maintain or defend (rights and claims)."

While I will not criticize Webster, I will offer up a definition that I think is a little better: "To act in your own interests, to maintain your own rights, without violating the rights of any other person."

We want to be assertive in our communication. If we take care of our own rights and act in our own interests, while not infringing on the rights of others, then we will be considered an assertive communicator.

When you are passive, you are protecting the rights of others—putting your own rights and needs aside to ensure that the needs of others are taken care of. The danger in communicating in a passive style is that people will take advantage of you in order to get their own needs met. Continually communicating in a passive style will hurt your chances for promotions and success in a professional environment. It will also cause stress, guilt and damage relationships if it continues over time.

At the other extreme, if you are aggressive in your communication style, it appears as if you are only concerned with getting your own needs met, not the rights and needs of others. You will also not be perceived as a team player. In the long run, people will resent this style of communication, and they will work against you (behind your back, in most cases).

If you were to draw a straight-line continuum of all possible communication styles, passive would be at one end, aggressive would be at the other end, and assertive would sit right in the middle. It is this middle position for which we should aim.

So the question remains, how do we communicate in an assertive manner? How do we say what we mean, still get work done and yet still respect others at work? The answer, unfortunately, is not as simple as we would like it to be. However, this chapter will discuss several ways to communicate in a professionally assertive manner.

One of the main components of professional assertiveness is the intent of our message. Many times when we are communicating at work or home, we are not clearly identifying our intent. For example, let's say you have called a meeting that you want everyone in your department to attend, yet half of the team arrives late. What do you say? How do you communicate your need to have everyone at the meeting on time? In other words, how do you express your intent?

If you were passive, you might not say anything. You may continue to let it drive you crazy and say nothing about it. Granted, not every situation at work is worth speaking up about. But is this one of them?

"Insanity is doing the same thing over and over again and expecting different results." This is a frequently quoted pearl of wisdom, but it certainly would apply if you handled this problem in a passive manner. Do you think that one day everyone would realize they've been chronically late and that it has been driving you crazy? Not very likely.

Not only does being passive not work well, it gives absolutely no intent to your message. No one can be sure what you are communicating when you are not communicating at all. If you don't share your intent, the message may never be received.

Communicating in a passive style is dangerous if it is a habitual problem. Others will learn that you are a pushover and will continue to abuse you and the authority you have at work, regardless of your position. Those who have less authority, responsibility and political power will learn that you are passive and will use that against you by taking advantage of your unwillingness to speak up. In the end, passive behavior will cost you far more than you will gain from it.

The opposite style is aggressive. Should you choose to respond aggressively in the above meeting scenario, you may do something along the lines of reprimanding the straggling department members in front of others: "I called this meeting for 9:00 a.m. It is now 9:15 a.m. If you are late for one of my meetings again, you will find that the door will be locked, and you will not be let in for any reason!"

Yes, that will get people to your meeting on time—only if you have the authority to speak that way to your peers, and very few people have that kind of authority. Even if you did, I wouldn't recommend it. Adults do not like to be scolded in front of others. Can you just imagine the conversations that would ensue in the hallways after the meeting? Intimidation is very aggressive and not a successful communication style in the end. In the short run, it may work, but eventually, the people involved will stop being cooperative, friendly or helpful.

What would be the intent of the aggressive response just mentioned? I would suggest that the intended message is, "If you are late for meetings, you will be locked out." If that is indeed the intent, then I suppose this aggressive statement would achieve its purpose—but not in a professionally assertive way.

But let's say your intent is to have people attend future meetings punctually. How would you achieve that? How could you assertively say what you needed in order to start the meeting on time? There are actually many answers to this question. Here is one example:

"We have a very full agenda today, so I would appreciate it if we could start on time so we may all leave on time."

Beginning a meeting with a statement such as this acknowledges that even though not everyone is there for the start of the meeting, you are going to start anyway. This respects your right to start the meeting on time, and it respects the rights of others by having the meeting end on time.

Remember that being assertive means "respecting your own rights while respecting the rights of others." Would you agree that the statement effectively ensures that the meeting starts on time? Is the message clear to you? Does it reflect your intent to have people attend future meetings punctually?

You could also say:

"I know that not everyone is here yet. Would you all rather wait for everyone to arrive, or should we go ahead and get started?"

This is a little on the passive side of assertive, but it also respects the rights of everyone involved. The intent of this message is to do what the majority of the room wants to do, to be fair to all involved.

The goal of assertive communication is to get the job done and to develop productive relationships.

Following are some other situations (and their appropriate solutions) in which we need to be assertive while respecting the boundaries.

Accepting an Assignment

You've managed to raise your value in the eye of your supervisor. You are finally being considered for the projects you've wanted to get involved in, and the opportunity has finally been given to you! How do you accept an assignment in an assertive way, so that you don't lose the credibility you've worked so hard to achieve? Remember that the manner in which you accept an assignment says a lot about you, so accept it in the most professional way possible.

Here are some hints for accepting assignments:

Be sure to convey the impression that you will work to the highest level of your ability. Not that you would ever give less than that, but be sure to mention that you will give this project your top priority and your extra focus.

If you are genuinely pleased with this assignment, let your boss know it. Don't be giddy and jump up and down, but say something along the lines of, "I am pleased to be involved in the Frazer project. I've had my eye on something of that magnitude for a while. You can be sure that I will give it my extra special attention." Note that in this sentence I have used "I" language to show ownership.

If possible, give yourself some time to think things over before you jump in with both feet. Even if you are pleased to have received the assignment, be sure that you are aware of everything that it entails before you start tackling it. "I am pleased to be involved in the Frazer project. I've had my eye on something of that magnitude for a while. You can be sure that I will give it my extra special attention. Once I've had the opportunity to review the project, I may have some questions before I begin. If you don't mind, I would like to discuss these questions with you tomorrow."

Declining an Assignment

Now let's say the opposite situation has occurred. You've been given an assignment that is not the best use of your talents and skills, and you want to convey the message that you are not the most appropriate person in the office to handle it. Just as the manner in which you accept an assignment says a lot about you, the way you decline an assignment also demonstrates a lot about how you work within the team. You also need to realize that in declining an assignment, you are clear on where your talents and strengths do and do not lie.

Here are some hints on declining assignments:

Review the assignment carefully before you decline. This is not a good time to judge or overreact to the situation either. Are you declining because you are too busy, or is it because it isn't a good use of your time and skills? Be sure you know why you are declining, and don't jump to conclusions too quickly.

Always consider the consequences of declining an assignment. Is it worth the effort? Many times it is not, and people will decline on the basis of principles. Is it worth it to win the battle and lose the war? Only you can decide that, but be sure you consider the consequences.

You can critique the assignment and suggest different alternatives for achieving the same outcome. Critiquing the assignment does not mean that you are criticizing the assignment. It means you are looking it over and giving constructive feedback.

You can also reveal specific reasons why you are not the most appropriate person for the job. "I appreciate that you thought of me. Keeping the best interests of the department in mind, though, it seems that Mary may be best to complete the blueprint."

Handling Put-Downs
Unfortunately, getting put down by others is a fact of life. Put-downs are often made in jest, not intended to hurt us, but in the end, they often do. They are always lose-lose situations, in which it is very hard to be assertive.

Many times it is easier to take the passive approach and pretend that it never happened, and sometimes that is the correct approach (keeping in mind the consequences and the individual situation). Sometimes, though, it's easy to take the aggressive approach and retaliate. So how do we handle these situations assertively?

Begin by using "I" language. State how you really feel about the put-down: "I really feel attacked when you make statements about how I do my job."

You are probably asking yourself what good that will do. In some cases, it will do no good at all. In other cases, it will make the other person aware that he has said something hurtful; he honestly may not have realized what he was doing. However, if you are in a situation where stating your feelings is a waste of your time, then you need to identify for the other person any negative consequences that may result from a continuation of this behavior: "The more comments you make like that, the less comfortable I feel when we are working together."

Or you could respond by asking a question in return (without being defensive): "I am not agreeing or disagreeing with what you have said. Could you give me some examples of when I have been ___?" or "I really wasn't aware that I was doing that. Could you give me a specific example so I can ___?"

How to Say No

Don't you hate it when someone asks you to do something for her, and you really don't have the time? I have a hard time saying no, especially to someone in a more senior position than me. I want to be a team player like everyone else, and I feel that when I say no to a request, I'm not contributing to the team (you know the old expression, "There is no "I" in TEAM"). When I tell someone that I don't have time or that I'm not able to help her, I feel like I'm letting her down. I also feel really guilty when I say no. I feel as if I were the person's only alternative and that I've now left her in a bind. I know this isn't true, but at the time, that's how I feel.

We have to figure out ways to say no without feeling guilty or sounding negative in the process. We also need to communicate the right message, in the right way, without being too passive or too aggressive. Fortunately, I have a great four-step process for doing this, and it works whether you are the boss or not!

1. Acknowledge the Request

When it comes to communication skills, Rule One for the listener is to paraphrase, or give feedback. There are two kinds of paraphrasing. The first one, "para" phrase, means to repeat back to the speaker your understanding of the message using your own words. Let the other person know that you did hear the request and that you did understand specifically what he was asking. Be sure to acknowledge and specifically address the part of the request that you are saying no to.

The other way to paraphrase is what we'll call "parrot" phrasing, or simply repeating the speaker's exact words back to him. This may confirm that you heard the message but not that you necessarily understood it. The only time you should "parrot" phrase is when you are experiencing a hearing impairment or a language barrier. "Parrot" phrase to get the correct sentence, then we move into "para" phrasing to ensure that you correctly understand the request.

2. Decline

This one's simple—use the word "no" in your sentence. If you don't, then some people will think you're telling them "maybe."

For example, take those telemarketers that call each evening at dinner time. Have you ever tried to get off the phone without using the word "no?" It's extremely difficult to do. Similarly, if you don't use the word "no" when declining a request, you've only hinted at your intent, hoping the other person will understand your garbled message. Your intent is important, so don't assume the other person can read between the lines.

3. State your Reason

This does not mean state *all* your reasons. You may have fourteen reasons why you are saying no to this request, but you don't have to give them all. Sometimes one firm but vague reason is far more powerful than twelve soft and scattered reasons. Some people are extremely good at handling objections, too, and if you give them enough information and ammunition, they can convince you that what they need is more important than what you need.

4. Come up with Alternatives

This is where teamwork comes into play. Don't let the team down— help them out by giving them other alternatives that work for you. Don't come up with an alternative that you aren't willing to follow through on, though. If you offer it as another idea, you have to be willing to live with it and all the additional work involved.

Step four is also good for those who are on the passive side. It helps alleviate some of the guilt. If you were to skip steps three and four, it might sounds like this: "You want me to make 4,000 photocopies of this right now? No, I don't think so." In this case, just using the first two steps isn't really going to work well for you, especially if you want to keep your job. It sounds very aggressive without the last two steps. So adding steps three and four helps you keep your job, and it helps alleviate some guilt as well.

Some people consider steps three and four as optional. You don't have to do them if you don't want to, but I would strongly recommend that you at least use them at your job. Should you decide to drop these two steps at work, you may be seen as very aggressive and not a team player. Of course, how you choose to be seen outside work is up to you.

Now let's walk through the four steps. Let's assume that it is 3:30 on a Friday afternoon and that it's your birthday. At 5:00 that afternoon, your best friend is taking you out to dinner to celebrate. You've been planning this for weeks, and you are very excited. He/She is taking you to the nicest restaurant in town and is even picking up the tab! At 3:30 you are counting the minutes until you can go. That's when your boss comes into your office and says, "I know that this is last minute, and I know that you probably have plans, but the CEO just called me and asked me to make a presentation first thing Monday morning, and I don't have anything ready. I know I'm really late, but can you please work overtime tonight and help me out?"

Tough dilemma if you and your boss work really well together and you really want to help him out, isn't it? If you are going to say no, you need to follow the steps.

Step one is to acknowledge the request. How do you accomplish this? You could say, "I realize that this is last minute and you need me to work overtime, but no, I can't. It's my birthday, and my best friend is taking me out to dinner at the nicest restaurant in town."

This doesn't sound too bad, but there are a couple of things wrong with it. First, while you've acknowledged part of his request, you have not accurately clarified what you are saying no to. In the reply above it sounds like you are saying no to working overtime. But is that really what you are saying no to? Or is it "working tonight" that is the problem? You have to clearly communicate what you are saying no to, or you may not be seen as a team player. The boss may hear that you aren't willing to work overtime, when that isn't the intent of your message at all.

Change the first part of the sentence to clearly acknowledge the request. The request you are saying no to isn't working overtime but to staying that particular night to work late. Then your response might sound something like, "I realize that this is last minute and you need me to stay tonight to work, but no, I am unable to stay tonight." This clearly acknowledges what you are saying no to.

This sentence also has the word "no" in it, which is good. If you avoid saying the word, then you have also avoided turning the other person down.

Thus far, we have completed steps one and two. Now let's move on to the second part of the sentence: "It's my birthday, and my very best friend is taking me out to dinner at the nicest restaurant in town." This is fine, but ask yourself if it's really necessary. Is it potentially taking the response and making it a little more passive than you intended? Are you sending the wrong message? What is the intent of this?

I was teaching this concept to some clients in Washington, D.C., a few years back, when a woman in the audience said that she had tried this very excuse on her boss the previous year when she was asked to work overtime. The response she got was, "Well, how about if you work overtime for me now, have your friend come here and wait, and when we are finished, I will pick up the tab for the both of you for the rest of the evening." Sounds like a generous boss, right? No, not really. This woman wasn't paying for dinner anyway, so all she was doing was shortening her evening, inconveniencing her friend and getting the work done when what she really wanted to do was go out and celebrate. If you give too much information, some people will solve your problem, and then you have nowhere to go. You've been boxed into providing the solution that you didn't want to provide.

Instead of stating all the reasons why you can't work overtime, try something like this: "It's my birthday, and I have plans that cannot be changed." You are not lying; you are stating a reason, and your reason is vague enough that someone could not "fix it" for you. Even the "It's my birthday" part could be considered optional and not really necessary.

The final step is to provide alternatives. As stated above, only provide alternatives on which you are willing to follow through. Here are some possible responses:

"I do have time tomorrow afternoon to help you out, though. Will that work for you?"

"What I can do is take the next hour and a half and get quite a bit done so there won't be as much to do later."

"We can call our temp agency and have someone here within the hour, and I can spend some time with that person before I leave."

"I can come in early Monday morning and finish up anything that doesn't get done today."

Then the trick is to wait for a response. Many times we feel the need to jump in and fill the silence by offering more and more. This is an instinctive reaction, and many times we wind up doing what the person asked for in the first place, even when we wanted to say no.

A few years ago I read a tip in a book that has saved me many times. It is simple, straightforward and almost always foolproof. When someone asks you to do something, and you want to say no, just ask for two minutes of time to see if it will work out for you. In response to the overtime request we've been using as an example, you could say:

"You need me to work tonight? I do have plans for this evening, but if you give me just two minutes, I will see if anything can be arranged. I'll come into your office as soon as I know what I can do."

This response utilizes a couple of the steps mentioned previously, but it has not committed you to a yes or a no in either direction. What it does is buy you some time to walk away and figure out what you can or can't do, without any other pressure. You can assertively decide how to respond without feeling like you are trapped into solving the boss's problem for him. What usually happens is the boss will then move onto the next person on the list, and before your two minutes are even up, he has solved the problem by utilizing someone else.

Treat any yes-or-no question as if the other person is holding out a big balloon in his hand. The balloon represents the problem. He just wants to give the balloon away. He wants to find someone he can trust to deal with the problem so that he doesn't have to. If he is used to you always taking the problem from him, then you will always be the first person he approaches to take care of it. Imagine they are holding the balloon out, just looking for someone to take it. Don't take it!

I'm not saying that we shouldn't help people out. In many cases, that is what our jobs are about—doing things that others need. What we need to do, however, is communicate what we can and cannot do.

Confident Communications

Sometimes saying things that are difficult is harder on us than it is on the person at the receiving end. For whatever reason, we feel guilty about it. Why? Often, it's because our passive side is shining through.

We will now look at some of the things we say and do that take away the appearance of confidence. After all, words, and the way we use them, have a big impact. Below are some tips on word usage that can make us sound professionally assertive and confident, giving our voice the authority it occasionally needs. Listen to yourself the next time you are in a meeting and try to notice if you hear yourself in any of these examples.

Avoid "absolutes." Any time you use words like "always" and "never," you are using absolutes. You will lose some credibility by using them. It almost sounds like a child having a temper tantrum, screaming, "You *never* take me to McDonald's," when in fact, this is not true. Whenever we use absolutes, we make the receiver defensive, which puts barriers into the conversation. We may not even realize that we sound aggressive to the receiver.

Keep it simple. Words that are monosyllabic (those with one syllable) are the most forceful words in the English language. Think about some of the great speeches of our time: John F. Kennedy's, "Ask not what your country can do for you—ask what you can do for your country," or Martin Luther King's unforgettable words, "I have a dream." This is powerful stuff.

Along the same lines, don't cloud your message with big fancy words. Professional communication requires that the person you are speaking to understand the meaning of the words you are using. Using fancy words from deep within the dictionary makes your message sound condescending and aggressive. Simple, one-syllable words are easy to understand, easy to remember and have an assertive feel to them.

We all have our own favorite phrases that we use over and over again without even being aware that we do it. You can be sure that the person who works in the cubicle next to you knows exactly what yours are, the very same way you can tell her what her favorite expressions are. When you don't use a particular word or phrase, you become very aware that the other person uses it constantly.

A great example of repetitive phrasing is using "eh" at the end of a sentence (as in, "The author of this chapter is from Canada, eh."). Most of the time the speaker is totally unaware that he or she is using "eh" frequently in speech. It becomes a vocal habit. Similarly, many people use "okay," "um" and "ah" to transition from one thought to the next.

Also avoid overused, "trendy" phrases such as "yada, yada, yada" (from our *Seinfeld* days) and "24-7." You will find that some people use these phrases excessively, even in situations where they don't apply. The danger is in the unprofessional appearance or flavor they give your message. They are definitely not what you hear from most CEOs and senior level managers (or at least, they shouldn't be). These habits will take away, not add, to your credibility.

Pausing can have a great impact on your message as well, in both a positive and a negative sense. If you pause too much, it looks like you don't know what you are going to say, and you lose impact. Appropriate pausing can make you seem very deliberate and strategic in your word choices and, therefore, lend you some credibility.

Rushing through words with few pauses can make you sound scatterbrained, overly excited and wound up like a top. Conversely, rushing a message just a little, and in the right places, can make you come across as enthusiastic, energetic and excited about what you have to say.

So where is the perfect balance? In the one-two dance step. Anywhere in a sentence you would find a comma, a semicolon, a period or similar punctuation, think to yourself, "One-two," at about the same tempo as a waltz step. Pausing long enough to think "one-two" will space your phrases out at just the right pace. Just remember, "Speak-one-two, speak-one-two."

"Soft" words and phrases—those that are intended to soften the impact of a message—really work against us when we aren't in charge. Without our realizing it, they can take away any credibility we may have established and make us appear far more passive than perhaps we were even aware.

For example, the word "try" is one of the biggest culprits when it comes to soft words. We use "try" when we aren't sure what we can or can't do. Let's say someone comes up to your desk and asks if you can get a report done by 5:00 p.m. You are really swamped with work, but you really like this person and want to help her, so you say, "I'll try." In your mind you are thinking, "I really doubt that I can help you, but because I don't know what else to say, I'll tell you that I'll try to get it done. But don't expect that it will get done." The other person, however, has heard, "It will be done."

This is a classic mistake in communication. Don't tell people what you'll *try* to do—use an assertive, confident tone of voice and tell them what you *will* do. This way, you won't be seen or treated as passive and subsequently lose the respect of your co-workers.

Another soft phrase is "I'm sorry." I know, we use that phrase to be polite. The problem, however, is that "I'm sorry" is perceived as taking responsibility for something. If you could have avoided a particular situation and chose not to, then "I'm sorry" is appropriate. But it is not appropriate to say "I'm sorry" when you are bumped into by another person, when you are asking someone to repeat what he or she has said or when you cannot do what the other person wants you to do. (Interestingly, the higher up the corporate ladder people climb, the less likely they are to use the words "I'm sorry.")

Let's say you are busily working at your desk on a high-priority task, when a supervisor comes up to you and asks you to take care of a different task for her. Should you say, "I'm sorry, I can't help you right now?" Only if you really are sorry, in which case you should say so. If you're not truly sorry (and chances are you're not), you would be using the wrong words in your effort to be polite.

In another example, a co-worker asks you to attend a meeting for her. Instead of saying, "I'm sorry, I can't go today," be polite and say, "Thank you for asking me. I am unable to go today."

Another word that will work against you is "can't." Someone once shared with me that "I can't" is a great acronym for "I Certainly Am Not Trying," because there are very few things that you cannot do. There is much that you *choose* not to do, but it is rarely because you are not actually *able* to do so. For example, I *can* embezzle millions of dollars from my company; however I *choose* not to do it.

Before saying that you can't do a particular task by a certain deadline, you have to first decide whether you really, in fact, cannot do it. In other words, if you didn't do anything else for the rest of the day and focused on that project only, would you physically be able to get it done? If the answer is yes, then the words "I can't" do not apply. The truth is that the other demands on your time take precedence, and you choose not to do the task. In such situations, what you need to say is what you *can* do, not what you *can't* do.

The words "I wish" are also soft words; they give the impression that you don't know what you can and cannot do, which makes you appear passive. People who are assertive or even aggressive are very clear on what they can and cannot do; they don't use the words "I wish."

In summary, we've learned that to be professionally assertive, we have to be able to say what we mean and stick to our guns.

Choose to communicate assertively rather than passively or aggressively.

We have to ensure that our communication is clear.

> Make the intent of your message obvious.

We have to make sure that the words we use are not working against us by softening our message.

> Avoid phrases such as "I'll try," "I'm sorry," "I can't"
> and "I wish."

We must be aware when we are using extreme and forceful words.

> Avoid absolutes such as "always" and "never."

Be conscious of the pacing.

> Use the "Speak-one-two" dance step.

Stay away from trendy and repetitive phrases.

> Ask your work buddy what your favorite phrase is,
> and work on reducing the number of times you
> repeat it.

By implementing these simple steps, you will be able to expand your own professionally assertive communication skills. Then you will get the work done that needs to get done by clearly and effectively communicating with others.

Rhonda Finniss

Rhonda Finniss is a professional speaker, trainer and author based in Canada, who has spoken to tens of thousands of people in seven different countries with her humorous and approachable style. Rhonda is the 2004 President of the Canadian Association of Professional Speakers (CAPS).

Rhonda uses her interactive style and contagious sense of humor to keep everyone involved in all of her keynote and training presentations. She has an uncanny ability to look at the normal and see something quite different. You will find that looking with Rhonda will unlock many thoughts that you enjoy and benefit from both personally and professionally.

Rhonda specializes in training for non-management staff. She gives them the tools and information they need to get the work done professionally and effectively. These strategies will not only keep your work team happy and sharing their positive attitudes with all your customers (internal and external), it will increase your bottom line!

Rhonda has received her CSP (Certified Speaking Professional) designation. It is the highest speaking designation *in the world* that can be earned. When hiring speaking or training professionals, you should always look for the CSP designation - it guarantees you are getting a proven professional.

Contact Rhonda at:
ON THE RIGHT TRACK - Training & Consulting
www.on-the-right-track.com
Rhonda@on-the-right-track.com
or call toll free, 1-877-213-8608

Chapter 3

Are People Getting More Difficult, Or Is It Me?

Donna Steffey

Do you remember the last problem person you had to deal with?

For Diane, a twenty-year real estate veteran, it was the client who overreacted to a simple e-mail and threatened to cancel a deal at the last minute.

For Dave, a supervisor at the post office, it was the employee with two years left until retirement who spent more time complaining then contributing.

For Paula in pharmaceuticals, it was a double whammy: a manager who refused to step in and settle disputes and a new employee who was creating a dispute by trying to take over, even though she lacked the competence to do the job.

Problem people aren't limited to our work world either. For instance, when was the last time your significant other came home from work with a bad attitude? Or a teacher embarrassed your child in class? With daily opportunities to exercise your conflict resolution muscles, you may wonder, "Are people getting more difficult, or is it me?"

The answer on both counts is "yes." People are getting more difficult—and yes, you are probably becoming more sensitive and difficult as well. Take all of our daily routine stresses, and then add current events such as high unemployment, unethical business practices, a poor economy, multicultural and generationally diverse workforces, global competition and threats of terrorism. Is there any wonder why today's businesses are especially vulnerable to conflict? We are like cans of soda being shaken by current events, rattled by less time and greater demands and rolled by constant change. When strained and confined to work together for eight hours a day under these conditions, the pressure in our "internal soda can" is so great that even what appear to be minor "people problems" can cause us to explode.

[1] Research shows that increases in workplace changes are linked to increased incidents of workplace aggression and even violence. The United Nations' International Labor Organization has stated that conflicts in the workplace will be the biggest challenge facing both employees and employers in this new millennium. The cost of workplace conflicts to individuals is felt as low morale, anxiety, dissatisfaction with work and even physical or psychological illness. The cost to employers may be reduced productivity, increases in litigation expenses, employee turnover and stress-related medical claims.

To what extent are you experiencing increases in workplace friction and a decrease in the ability to tolerate frustrations? To gain some insight into your present level of workplace stress exposure, take the following quiz.

	Mostly True	Mostly False
1. Most days I am surrounded by negative attitudes and find myself contributing to the negativity.		
2. There are frequent unresolved misunderstandings that result in arguments or silence, and I am part of it.		
3. I do not like going to work some days, and I dread Mondays.		
4. I could be more cooperative with my team members if they were only more cooperative with me.		

[1] *Workforce Magazine* article, August 1998, Dr. Jim Wickerson's, "Link Between Workplace Violence and Workplace Change"

	Mostly True	Mostly False

5. People talk about others behind their backs; I have been known to be an active participant and good listener in these discussions.

6. I have noticed that customers have become more "demanding" lately.

7. I have experienced lots of changes at work the past few months.

If even some of your answers were "mostly true," you may be wondering if it is possible to learn to navigate through conflicts more effectively, reduce your tension and improve relationships during these challenging times. While there is no quick fix, there are techniques that can help. As a consultant and trainer for the past twenty years, I have seen many individuals and organizations thrive under pressure. We can't change the compressing events, but we can survive their assault.

This chapter will help you identify your options when confronting difficult people or situations. It will help you examine human behavior to identify the payoffs and consequences of being difficult so you can relate more strategically. It will help you determine the best course of action, depending on the nature of the problem and its urgency, your relationship with the problem person and your power to influence the situation. It will not tell you what to say or do to manage difficult people and situations, but it will offer guidelines and strategies so that you can figure these things out for yourself.

Puzzling People

People's behaviors come in all shapes and sizes, just as people do. But did you ever try stepping back and analyzing the behaviors of others before reacting to them? As Steven Covey says, "We are a product not of our environment but of the choices we make between the stimulus and our reaction to our environment." Surprisingly, there is an enormous amount of time between the stimulus and our reactions. We often think our responses are automatic: "She made me so angry, I couldn't help myself!" The truth, however, is that we have plenty of time in that moment. It is filled with rapid self-talk. Do you know what you are saying to yourself in that moment? The way you and others react in that moment is influenced by typical behavior styles, situational stresses, deeper personality needs and, sometimes, serious clinical problems.

The first step in improving a difficult relationship is to step back and try to understand the other person. What type of behavior is he or she displaying? If you can analyze that correctly, your insight can serve as a guide for deciding how to react in a way that reduces tensions and improves your relationship. Let's take a look at some common behaviors.

As the name suggests, Different Behavior refers simply to behavior that is different than yours. History supports the divisions of human behavior into four fundamental categories. As early as the fifth century BC, Hippocrates linked what he called the four temperaments of body fluids. Modern scientists today describe similar groupings of characteristics identified through brain and biochemical studies. One category is not better than another, simply different.

Whether you look to Aristotle, Jung, Meyers/Briggs, Physiognomy (the study of personality through face shapes) or DiSC, you will find a similarity of groupings. The four categories are usually described as follows:

Direct, dominant, driver, decisive - fast-paced, task-oriented, independent, goal-centered. Can be authoritative, aggressive, pushy, arrogant and controlling under pressure.

Influential, innovative, idea-centered - adventurous, energetic, adaptable and optimistic. Can be impulsive, unfocused, scattered, forgetful and superficial under pressure.

Stable, sociable, supportive - good listener, team player, patient and process-oriented. Can be shy, nonassertive, easily hurt, slow and passive/aggressive under pressure.

Comprehensive, cautious, consistent - analytical, quality-centered, detailed and focused. Can be perfectionist, inflexible, critical, a loner and narrow-minded under pressure.

Which are you? Which is the person you're dealing with?

These differences can be the source of much conflict. I like to refer to them as different languages. If you consistently speak a language to co-workers, bosses or customers that differs from their own, the frustration builds. There is misunderstanding, judgment and perhaps some negative behaviors displayed due to the other person's feeling pressure. To reduce conflict, recognize the differences and stop labeling the other person as "difficult." Then, adjust your "language style" to match the other person's. Match the person's pace and level of animation, and you will become "style multilingual."

I remember making a sales call to the financial service industry. I got to Harold's office and, even before I sat down, he started bombarding me with questions. We volleyed back and forth with rapid speed for ten minutes until it was time to meet with his supervisor. His language style was direct and comprehensive. My style is influential, but I was able to speak his language. His last question was, "My supervisor wants a trainer who is fun, energetic and enthusiastic. Can you do that?" I replied, "Can do. Let's go." He stopped me and commented that I hadn't demonstrated any of that behavior thus far. I replied, "You didn't want to see any of that behavior. She does and will." As we passed over the threshold, I reverted back to my natural style of fun, energetic and enthusiastic, and I landed the account.

Learn as much as you can about the way each style thinks and acts, and practice imitating each style.

Beyond behavior styles, some people have special problems that can throw a monkey wrench into your interactions with them. These problems include distressed, needful and clinical behavior.

Distressed behavior may be the result of experiencing one anxiety-producing situation after another. Our fuses are shorter. We are more impatient, more sensitive to irritants from others. We may feel depressed or anxious. According to Dr. Robert Eliot[2], "Your body finally rebels against being uselessly switched on and off by remaining stuck in the 'on' position, ready for flight or fight." This is not our normal behavior state. Distressed behaviors should be viewed situationally. If someone seems distressed, you can usually help bring the person back to a more civil state by looking beyond his or her negative behavior and empathizing with the person's underlying stress level.

Needful behaviors are usually more habitual. A person can have a need for recognition and reassurance or a need to feel superior or to feel needed. These needful behaviors are often tied to a person's ego and are

---

[2] From Stress to Strength, Bantam Book, 1994

deeply ingrained. They can explode like land mines when we attempt to proceed with the relationship.

Behaviors such as drug abuse, alcoholism, chronic depression and other clinical illnesses are best referred to your HR departments. If you suspect any of these behaviors, avoid confrontation and seek confidential counsel.

Three Choices

In any difficult situation or relationship, there are really only three options: enrich it, endure it or end it. To enrich a situation you can create a plan, strategizing and scripting what you will say and do. Sometimes your only choice is to endure a situation, as long as it is not mentally or physically abusive. Other times, all the enriching and enduring are not enough. You just have to end it. Ending the relationship may be your choice or someone else's.

Over the next few pages I will share with you how to enrich the seemingly bankrupt relationship, how to endure the relationship when life's circumstances call for it and how to prepare yourself for an ending, whether it eventually occurs by your choice or someone else's.

Let's start with techniques for enduring a difficult relationship or situation, since enduring will be needed for most of life's challenges.

Endure It

Endurance was the name of Sir Ernest Shackleton's ship on his astounding voyage to Antarctica in 1914. The purpose of the expedition was to cross the icy continent by land. A month into the journey, his ship became frozen in ice like the stick of a popsicle. He and his twenty-seven men survived the Antarctic cold and darkness for almost two years. As captain of his ship, Shackleton refused to succumb to the hardship and misery they faced. The lives of his men were at stake. He focused on his new goal: keep everyone alive!

History has given us hundreds of stories of endurance. They can be sources of inspiration and ideas during difficult times when you don't have an option and have to endure a difficult boss, co-worker, job or customer account. It might be that you are a single parent, employee nearing retirement, unskilled laborer or employee in golden handcuffs. If the work relationship is "difficult" and not dangerous, you may feel that you must stay. Reading biographies and autobiographies can help you to endure.

Focusing on your goals can also be helpful. To do this, ask yourself:

1. What are the important things in my life?

2. Why am I earning this money?

3. What things of value is it buying me?

4. How will this situation help me build character?

5. What can I learn from this person or situation that I can use in other areas of my life?

6. What are my short-term goals?

7. What are my long-term goals?

8. What is going right in my life?

Yet reading inspirational stories and counting your blessings won't work in every situation or all the time. Sometimes you need more than inspiration! You need techniques for survival.

One technique, the Intelligent Self-Management System, can be used to diffuse your feelings in a tough situation before you say or do anything that might further complicate the problem. Whether you are the type of person who talks first and thinks later or one who thinks first and only wishes that you would say what you are thinking, the system will help you determine the best course of action. And it's as simple as learning the ABCDs.

Learn Your ABCDs

The Intelligent Self-Management System is a tool for altering our perceptions, attitudes and behaviors that was pioneered by [3]Dr. Albert Ellis, internationally recognized as the father of Rational Emotive Behavior Theory. Ellis's great contribution to twentieth century psychology was his insistence that we can modify and change our feelings by means of logical and deductive reasoning, instead of allowing our feelings to get the better of us. His work is a major part of the foundation

---

[3] *Albert Ellis Reader, a Guide to Well-Being*, by Albert Ellis and Shawn Blau, a Citadel Press Book,1998

of the Emotional Intelligence movement popularized in 1995 by Daniel
Goleman in his book, *Emotional Intelligence.*

Let me identify the elements of the ABCD system:

A – Activating event: Identify the activating situation that is
causing you to be upset or angry or to feel uncomfortable. Write
it down and describe it in detail. Act as if you are a video camera
recording the event, and leave out the exaggeration and
judgments.

B – Beliefs: What beliefs do you have about this event? What
are you saying to yourself? Your beliefs are your silent self-talk
that you engage in throughout the day. They are almost
imperceptible and easily overlooked. See if you can identify what
went on in your mind immediately after the activating event.
Write it all down. Don't leave anything out. Even those
"automatic negative replay tapes" have to be recorded.

C – Consequences: What are you experiencing as a consequence
of your own beliefs? Write down what your unpleasant feelings
were and what behaviors accompanied them.

D – Dispute: Most rational thinking systems will take you
through the ABCs. It is the D that is so important. You must
debate, dispute and discard your irrational thoughts that give
rise to your consequences. Dr. Albert Ellis identifies some major
illogical philosophies held by most people. They are:

> I must be loved or approved by practically every
> significant person in my life or I am worthless.
>
> I must not make errors or do poorly, and if I do, it's
> terrible.
>
> People and events should always be the way I
> want them to be.
>
> Life should be fair, and if it is not, that is horrible.

Do any of these irrational thoughts go through your head when you
are upset? Let's begin to dispute them. Look for evidence and use logic.

It's definitely nice to have people's approval, but even without it, I can still
accept myself.

Doing things well is satisfying, but it is human to make mistakes.

People are going to act the way they want, not the way I want.

Life isn't fair, and I shouldn't expect it to be fair for me either.

Let's do an example with the ABCD system.

Dan sold ads for a small radio station. This was often a frustrating job. Commission was only paid after the client paid for the ad, not when the ad was sold. It had been a particularly bad month. The boss was on everyone's case to sell more, the economy had slowed down, and Dan's car needed repairs. Because of the bad economy, the clients were paying their bills more slowly. Dan had to do something. What did he do? His behavior was to call one client on the phone and leave a message, including a few "choice words" about the client's tardiness at bill-paying.

Any surprise that Dan's boss chose to "end" the relationship? Regardless of whether the customer was right or wrong, what are the consequences of Dan's own behaviors and beliefs? What must Dan have been telling himself to make that phone call?

A – Activating Event

There were a number of events we can analyze. Let's use the client not paying his bill as the activating event.

B – Beliefs

What was Dan telling himself? Probably, "That's not fair. I sold this account. He should pay his bill. The client is a jerk. The company shouldn't have such a stupid rule. Why did I take this job in the first place?"

C – Consequences

What are the consequences of that thinking? Dan feels bad about himself, the job and the client. He works himself into a frenzy and then calls the client and says some nasty things.

The point of the ABCD system is to help you stop yourself and think before you take action. Dan should have moved to D and begun to dispute his beliefs before he took action.

D – Dispute

"Life isn't fair. I took this job knowing the rules, and I agreed to them. Most of the time the rules work well. It would be worse if I got paid and had to return money if the customer did not pay. This customer has the right and the freedom to do what he wants, not what I demand that he do."

E – Emotionally Intelligent Plan

Building on the ABCDs above, I have added one more step to this system, letter "E." Only after you calm yourself down should you begin to make up a plan of action. Ask yourself, "What are the five most important things I can do to make this situation better?" After you have done your ABCDs and are thinking rationally, you can trust your judgment in answering this question. Then list the roadblocks you suspect might prevent you from doing those five things, and watch out for them as you proceed.

By the way, if Dan had calmed himself down, do you think he would have chosen the same plan of action to call the customer? Fortunately, Dan did eventually learn the ABCDs and now avoids pushing his self-destruct button at the new job he enjoys.

Using the ABCDs as soon as you are in a difficult situation, you will be able to calm down and make intelligent decisions to enrich, endure or end a situation.

Intelligent Self-Management System

Analyze your own feelings, dispute your irrational beliefs, and then problem-solve. Feel free to jot down your responses under each section below.

A. What is the Activating Event that triggered an emotional response? What would a camera see?

B. What are your Beliefs? What are you telling yourself? These beliefs pass through irrational filters of "shoulds" and "musts." This usually results in the irrational process of "awfulizing" or blowing events out of proportion, leading to frustration, impatience and judgmental thinking.

C. Consequences. What are your unpleasant feelings due to your beliefs, and what behaviors accompany them?

D. Your next step is to debate, dispute and discard these self-defeating beliefs. 1) Look for evidence to prove that life should be... 2) Use logical, cause-and-effect analysis. 3) Is this belief really helping you achieve your goals?

E. Emotionally Intelligent Plan. Write down your new rational beliefs and any ideas for a solution.

End It

"You guys go ahead, and if I can't see in thirty minutes I'll stop and go back. I will end my climb to the top." Those were the words that [4]Beck Weathers spoke on May 10th, 1996, the deadliest day on Mt. Everest. Nine climbers perished in a blizzard on the mountain that day, and Weathers' decision to end his climb probably saved his life.

There are many stories of people who faced all odds and courageously continued on a dangerous path, but there are equally many stories of people who had the courage to call it quits. Sometimes we are better off stopping on the path and saying, "You guys go ahead."

---

[4] *Left For Dead*, Beck Weathers, Villard Books, 2000

When the best thing to do is to end it, call it quits, say good-bye, give it up, dump it, throw in the towel, resign, withdraw or any other of the fifty ways to leave your trouble, then do it—BUT prepare yourself first. Preparing yourself to move on, while still enduring, is a good idea. We must prepare ourselves in at least three ways: emotionally, mentally and financially.

Emotionally – Start with your ABCDs again. If the activating event is "ending it," what do your self-talk and behavior sound and look like? What are you telling yourself that the consequences of your behavior will be? Are they rational thoughts? Dispute them and check the four categories to see if you are being irrational about your demands. I also recommend that people seek professional help from a qualified counselor or coach. Your ABCDs and counseling can help you endure until you are emotionally ready for the end.

Mentally – How does your resume look? Is it updated and ready to go? Have an updated resume at all times. According to [5]Daniel Pink, author of *Free Agent Nation*, the evidence overwhelmingly suggests that you will probably be needing it shortly. Pink says that median job tenure in the state of California, for example, was only three years in 1998. In 1999, according to *U.S. News and World Report*, approximately seventeen million workers quit to take other jobs, up six million from five years earlier. And in 2001, thirty percent of the American workforce held nontraditional jobs as independent contractors, self-employed professionals or part-timers.

How does your resume look? What skills do you have or need? How can you beef up your resume? Until you are mentally ready to end it, you don't have the freedom to end it.

Financially – Are you set, financially, to make a change? Is now a good time? Can you endure your current situation and look for another job at the same time? Does it make sense financially to end your current situation, or would using the ABCDs to endure make more sense now? If you are thinking of making a move, contact a financial advisor and make a rational decision.

---

[5] *Free Agent Nation*, Daniel Pink, Warner Books, 2001

Ginny is in commercial sales. She has two children and was married to a nonviolent alcoholic. She had endured her marriage for years but wanted to end it. To prepare herself for leaving, she did her ABCD work daily and sought counseling and self-help groups. She looked at her skills and decided she was worth more than she was getting paid. She prepared herself to change jobs first, so that financially she and the children would be okay when she was on her own. By the time Ginny was ready to negotiate a base salary with the new company, she had plenty of confidence and secured the highest base salary the company offered. She had done her prep work mentally, financially and emotionally and secured a new job, giving herself the freedom to seek a new life for herself and the children.

Then there was Patrick. I met Patrick in a workshop for fast-track accountants at a sporting goods manufacturing company. Patrick was good at his job, but knew he had another calling. We talked most of the week, and I encouraged him to look for real fulfillment in his work. A few months later, I received an e-mail from Patrick saying that he had decided to see Mt. Everest and do volunteer work in Tibet. He ended his job in a big way.

Patrick and Ginny chose to end their relationships, but sometimes we don't get a choice. Someone else ends it, or we are forced by circumstances beyond our control to end it. Regardless of how it happens, it is always better to prepare for endings so that, if and when the time comes, we will land on our feet.

Enrich It

To enrich or improve a situation, there are three possible targets for change: yourself, the other person or the system. How do you determine which point to target for change? Changing ourselves isn't the least bit easy, but imagine how hard it is to change others or to change the system! That's why it is usually best to target yourself for change first, starting again with the ABCDs. You can then move on to E and envision and execute a plan for change.

I remember a few years ago I had a "problem" with a client named Kathy. It took ABCD work on my part to calm down and rationally accept my responsibility in our misunderstanding. I decided to write out a plan for mending and enriching the relationship. I identified the five most important things I could do over the next three months to make a difference in this relationship. It included getting assignments done early instead of simply on time, being patient when I wanted to "expedite" the conversation, visiting when I was on site, and probing and paraphrasing for clarification on projects to eliminate misunderstandings. Next, I identified three or four roadblocks to success. These were the habits of thinking or acting on my own part that might prevent me from taking the actions I planned. My roadblocks were lack of time, poor prioritizing, lack of patience and weak listening skills. In order to achieve my plan for improving the relationship, I had to overcome these habits. As hard as it is to change habits—and it was hard—it is still easier than changing others! And yes, my relationship with Kathy is great now. It has resulted in many laughs and more income.

Targeting others to change

Targeting and influencing others to change starts with analyzing the source of difficult behavior. Are they displaying different, distressed or needful behavior? What is motivating them to behave this way? Is it a combination of behaviors?

Gabe is a football coach, and his boss, Fred, has a dominant style.

"I think I've found a way to resolve our personality differences."

Fred is authoritative and aggressive under pressure, with an ego-based need to control. The school had a losing team, and everyone felt pressured to win. When Fred decided to fire Gabe's assistant coach, Gabe felt angry and decided to confront Fred. Considering these variables, Gabe needed to do his ABCDs to calm himself down, then plan out his dialogue carefully to influence Fred to change his mind.

Gabe also needed to figure out what the payoff was for Fred's behavior. People demonstrate behaviors that get them the results they are looking for. What did Fred want? In this situation, Fred had a need for control and a desire to win. Should Gabe try to eliminate Fred's payoff or feed it? "Why try to eliminate Fred's desire to be in control?" he reasoned. Gabe decided to go to Fred with an approach that left Fred in charge, feeding his need instead. Gabe did not win back the job for his assistant, but he did earn more respect from Fred as well as more freedom to experiment with different plays for the team.

Let's review the steps for attempting to influence a difficult person:

1. Do the ABCDs first to diffuse yourself.

2. Analyze the source of the difficult behavior from others. Is the person a different style, distressed or needful?

3. Determine the payoff the person is seeking through using difficult behavior.

4. Decided if you want to eliminate or feed the payoff.

5. Decided what to say and do. Be sure to match the problem person's style during the conversation.

More Tips for Understanding Others

Manipulators engineer situations to benefit themselves. They plot and scheme and cause other people to feel tricked. Director and influential types often utilize this technique to get what they want.

Payoffs: They get their way, temporarily look good, and some people probably believe that that is the way the game is played.

Options: Call their bluff and confront them with their deviousness. Discuss their behavior using the BAKE strategy, which you will learn shortly.

Examine the system at work. Remember, the system is the other point of change. Perhaps things are too complicated, and finding a way to simplify the red tape so people don't need manipulation to succeed is a good way to dilute that behavior.

Martyrs are self-sacrificing and try to make others feel guilty and indebted to them. Stable style people often utilize this technique. They want to be liked and are afraid of conflict, so they say "yes" when they prefer to say "no" and then feel overwhelmed.

Payoffs: They feel good about themselves, get the attention and praise they need, and others feel guilty and stop asking them for favors.

Options: Provide plenty of unconditional positive praise and thanks, therefore feeding their need.

Change the system by creating a reward system for all employees so everyone feels valued. Be sure that employees are delegated to fairly and according to skill and desire levels so no one feels overly burdened.

In these examples we are analyzing interactions, not just reacting at a gut level. With most situations, it is best to react within the first twenty-four hours of the event.

For those that talk first and think later, use...W.A.D.E.
- Walk away
- Analyze the behavior
- Diffuse yourself using the ABCDs
- Execute a plan within 24 hours

For those who don't talk, use... L.A.D.E.
- "Let me get back to you."
- Analyze the behavior
- Diffuse yourself using the ABCDs
- Execute a plan within 24 hours

Communication Strategies

How can you confront negative behaviors and still enrich the relationship?

Ken was new in his position with the government. With this promotion he was in charge of many projects. At weekly team meetings, one of his colleagues constantly monopolized meeting time, preventing Ken from having sufficient time to present his project findings. Even though Ken was new, he needed to confront the negative behavior. He tried a number of approaches. He made a few jokes about it, mentioned it to his colleague in passing and tried to ignore it as long as he could. But none of these approaches solved the problem.

Ken did not like being manipulated, and he did not want to play martyr. Luckily, he learned about the ingredients in the BAKE dialogue strategy and decided to use it to confront the situation directly.

BAKE Dialogue Strategy

Behaviors: Identify the behaviors or activating event, just as you did with the ABCDs. Remember to describe them in detail without exaggeration and judgment. Write this down and read it back to yourself to check for accuracy.

Affect: Next, identify how these behaviors affect you, the team, the organization, the customer, profits, productivity and even the individual committing the offending behavior. Remember, you have twenty-four hours to respond—plenty of time to analyze and plan your communication.

Konsequences: (Okay, I cheated on the spelling) Ask yourself what the konsequences of this behavior are. What could be an end result if the team were not sharing information? What kind of impact would that have on profits? What could be the konsequences to an individual's career if he or she continued this behavior? Remember, some people don't care how their behavior impacts others, but they do care about themselves. When Ken began to analyze the konsequences, he thought about how the behavior of monopolizing the meeting could have impact on national security if superiors did not receive all the information available. When he identified the possible konsequences, he recognized the need to confront his colleague. His style was the stable/ cautious style, so this analysis helped arm him with the information and confidence he needed to communicate with his colleague.

Expectations: What is expected of someone on the job? Paint a picture of the relationship and tasks. Remember, some people are motivated by rewards, and others are motivated by fear of consequences, so include both.

You have all the ingredients laid out for the BAKE discussion. It is time to cook up a conversation.

Set up time for the discussion.

After a polite greeting, say that you want to talk about the behavior or activating event that occurred within the past twenty-four hours.

Describe the event without exaggeration or judgment. In Ken's situation, he might say, "On Friday, during the thirty-minute meeting, your report lasted twenty-five minutes, which only allowed five minutes for my report..."

Tell how it affects the different entities you identified. Choose these items carefully. Some people don't care how things affect you, while others might be threatened if you talk about how it affects them. This is why I can't tell you what to say. You must analyze the nature of the person and problem, the urgency of the situation and your relationship to the problem person. You might want to role-play this conversation before you try it with the person.

Paint a picture of the possible consequences. Again, choose your words carefully to motivate and not threaten the person.

Give the person a chance to respond.

With the proper preparation, you will feel calm and confident in this discussion. You have chosen the ingredients for your conversation carefully, and you are prepared if the conversation calls for additional affects and konsequences.

Verbal Judo

What if this first conversation doesn't work? George Thompson has taught "Verbal Judo" to thousands of cops in nearly 700 police departments and to thousands more in corporate and retail America. His book, Verbal Judo, The Gentle Art of Persuasion[6], describes what he calls the Five-Step Hard Style. I have taught his system to thousands of participants over the years.

1. Ask for new behavior. He calls this the ethical appeal. The BAKE discussion serves as an ethical appeal. This will not always work, or it may work temporarily. In those cases, go on to the next conversation.

---

[6] Verbal Judo, the Gentle Art of Persuasion, by George J. Thompson, PhD., First Quill Edition, 1993

2. Use a reasonable appeal. Remind the person of the reasons, policies or benefits of doing things as discussed earlier. Again, do this in a positive, non threatening way. This will work for most people. For some it will work temporarily.

3. An optional appeal may be a little more threatening. You present the next move as the person's choice. "If we do X, then here are the positive effects. If we continue to do Y, here are the possible negative consequences. Which do you want to do?" You are painting a picture and giving choices.

4. A personal appeal may be necessary. I love Thompson's dialogue, and I do recommend using this line verbatim, "Is there anything I can say or do at this time to earn your cooperation? I'd sure like to think there is." At this point, you may have had four behavior-focused conversations with the problem person. You have used flexibility and variety in your approach, showing strength in your convictions. This line may be exactly the question that finally opens a dialogue. If it doesn't, then you must follow through on the next step.

5. Act. I can't tell you what that means for your situation. If you have used the ABCD Intelligent Self-Management System to calm yourself down; analyzed the behaviors, payoffs and options for dealing with the problem person; scrutinized the effects and consequences of the negative behavior; and then had four conversations about it, I think you will agree that it is time to act! In a work situation, that usually means reporting the behavior to a higher authority. Consider inviting the person to go with you to discuss the situation with the higher authority.

When you get there, remember that you will have done your prep work and calmed down using the ABCDs and will be equipped to have a behavior-influencing conversation.

The bad news about learning to apply the sophisticated techniques of ABCD, BAKE and Verbal Judo is that self-training in these skills will take a long time and a whole lot of determination, self-discipline and energy. The good news is that they work! And because problem people have developed their difficult behaviors over a lifetime and are not likely to change too soon, they will offer you all the practice you'll ever need to achieve skill mastery.

About The Author

Donna Steffey

Donna Steffey is an energizing consultant, facilitator, radio personality and sought after speaker who has helped improve motivation, performance and output on four continents. Global organizations in the US, UK, Australia and China have found employees were more productive, customer service driven and mindful of their communication approach after attending one of her programs. She is founder and president of Vital Signs, a training and development firm that Vitalizes People, Performance and Profits with award winning programs in a variety of industries including printing, financial, telecommunications, and government. Donna balances each training session with just the right blend of information, activity and humor and has a powerful philosophy. She believes we have three choices in our relationships. We can enrich them, endure them, or end them. When it comes to customer services or workplace relationships she helps participants learn the skills to enrich them, the fortitude to endure them, and the intelligence to know how to end them professionally. Donna is a member of the National Speakers Association and winner of the Speaking Professional Award from NSA Illinois. She has also been on the board of the Chicago Chapter of ASTD since 1998.

Donna Steffey
Vital Signs
40 Delburne
Davis, IL. 61019
Tel: (815) 248-3104
Fax: (847) 991-0217
Email: itrainum@earthlink.net
www. VitalSignsTraining.com

Chapter 4

Choosing the Right Tools
for Effective Communication

Joan Burge

A broken relationship, a lost sale, a hurt co-worker, an angry boss—all are the results of not choosing the best medium through which to communicate. Communication links us together. It is the vehicle by which we make things happen—or not happen—in the workplace. Everything we do connects to someone else. We do not work in isolated boxes, without any contact with the outside world. Even when we simply file a piece of paper, that file can be pulled by someone else who will need that information. If we place an order via the Internet, a person will have to receive that order and process it. When we mail a meeting agenda, the attendees will view it and make decisions based upon it.

Look at the chain of communication: We receive something, form an opinion about it, make a decision as to the next step we will take, possibly add our own two cents and send our response to another person or place. If we do not do our part correctly and effectively, our actions will have a negative effect on the receiver. We will be the weak link in the chain of communication.

We use a variety of media to communicate information—technological (e-mail, voice mail, computers), written, verbal—but the key to not being a weak link is to select the best medium. One might know what to say and how to craft the message but select the wrong medium; or choose the right medium but not use it correctly; or use the right medium and a well-crafted message but still not be effective in communicating to the recipient.

I'll illustrate with a recent experience I had conducting training workshops in Illinois. My hotel provided shuttle serve to the training site on a daily basis, and the shuttle driver was scheduled to pick me up every morning at 7:00. On Wednesday night, I realized I would not need the service the next morning (I had other transportation available), so I called the valet service to inform him of the change. The next morning, however, I received a call from the front desk at 7:05, asking me if I was coming down to get on the shuttle! I informed them that I had called valet the night before to cancel. Obviously, the valet had been the weak link.

Here's another good example: One of my clients, a large corporation I work with regularly, once failed to inform a group of workshop attendees booked for an upcoming class that the dates had been changed. When the client and I had first discussed possible workshop dates earlier that year, we had initially looked at September 10 through 12. After they surveyed the attendees' availabilities, the client said they needed to change the dates. So we changed them to September 17 through 19. They surveyed the group again, only to go back to the original dates.

When I showed up for my August training sessions at this corporate location and told the participants I would see them again September 10 through 12, I got blank looks. Some of them said, "I thought the next class was September 18." What is unique about this story is that this particular group was at an advanced level of training and had to attend several four-day workshops over a four-month period in order to graduate. If they missed even one class, they would have to wait another seven to nine months before that class would be offered again. Needless to say, the scheduling snafu created much chaos. I could not move the dates because I already had other speaking engagements booked around the 18th. Obviously, someone at this client's corporate university was a weak link. He or she did not communicate the scheduling changes, which had a major affect on the lives of sixteen people!

Communication has such a huge impact on our ability to be productive. It also has a huge impact on the types of relationships we have with others. Communication is at the very core of our relationships. Think of any relationship: wife/husband, parent/child, sales person/customer, manager/employee, pilot/passenger. What occurs in each of these relationships? Communication—even if it is silence (silence can communicate that we agree or disagree or that we are hurt and choose not to speak). All day long, we are communicating with others inside and outside our organizations. We not only need to know how to say something (correct grammar, punctuation, etc.) but we need to know the most effective tool for saying it.

If we can better understand the different media and their positive and negative effects, then maybe we will do a better job of choosing the right one. If so, then we will experience more rewarding relationships, increase sales and productivity and reduce rework.

The Hazards of E-Mail

Ah, e-mail. We love it. We hate it. We can't live without it. We can't live with it. When we are supposed to be working on a project, it pulls us in with that elusive phrase, "You've got mail!" We are drawn in, and before we know it, we've lost track of our thinking and can't finish our project.

E-mail is an absolute wonder. What did we ever do without it? How did we ever manage? Just think of all the wonderful things it does for us:

- Allows us to communicate with others at any time, regardless of time zones
- Keeps information flowing
- Provides those who travel with the ability to communicate to anyone at any time
- Allows for frequent communication with friends, family and business colleagues, thus reducing long distance phone bills
- Reduces the costs of printing and postage
- Helps transform organizations into "networked" forms
- Lets senders keep records of their correspondence
- Is used to organize meetings and manage virtual work teams

John Bowie, an information engineering executive, says, "E-mail has transformed interoffice communication. Sending messages electronically is painless, instantaneous and reliable. It's so easy, anyone can do it. And that's the problem. With the explosive growth of the Internet over the past few years, e-mail has become the business world's communication vehicle of choice. E-mail is popular because it is fast, cheap and makes it easy to dash off a message and sent it to one or a hundred people."

As much as e-mail provides numerous benefits for us, it also presents us with many challenges and has its share of downfalls. For example, here are several ways that an e-mail receiver can contribute to a negative communication experience:

- Misinterprets the message because the sender did not provide enough information
- Is offended because he cannot tell the tone in which the message was delivered
- Thinks worst-case scenario because the sender did not deliver the message as intended
- Burns bridges with co-workers because of misinterpretation
- Is less productive because the sender did not give enough detail; therefore, the recipient cannot move forward on the project or task until he gets the information he needs.

Here are some additional ways that e-mail can create a bad communication environment in general:

- Makes it harder to resolve disputes
- Takes away the opportunity to immediately confirm what the recipient thought the sender meant
- Enhances biased perceptions of the other party
- Reduces feedback and social cues
- Allows for excess negative attention to be focused on statements made

"We're expecting far too much communication from e-mail," says Quentin Schultze, a professor of communication arts and sciences at Calvin College in Grand Rapids, Michigan. "There's a tremendous over reliance on e-mail, which is leading to a lot of confusion, misunderstanding, anger and frustration."

I see this happen all the time as I work with companies nationwide. I also see this in my own business when working with vendors. While traveling in Minnesota recently, I experienced my own case of misinterpreted e-mail. I got a telephone call from my husband, who told me about an invoice he had received from my accounting firm. My husband was concerned because he thought the amount was much higher than what I had been quoted. Since I would not be home for three more days, I e-mailed my accounting firm about the invoice. I thought the e-mail expressed surprise and my desire to reconcile the invoice with the quote I had been given. The following morning, however, I received a voice message from my accountant, who thought that I was upset with him. I called him immediately to clarify that I was not angry but shocked. See what I mean? E-mail can be hazardous to your relationships!

The other day I was conducting a workshop in which I was discussing some of the pitfalls of e-mail with the attendees, one of whom belonged to an Internet professional group. She had been receiving information that was not relevant to her, so she had replied to these e-mails, asking that they be discontinued. She did not realize that her reply had gone out to hundreds of people until she started receiving nasty e-mails from people in other companies across the country, who had read her requests to stop writing. What started out as a simple request escalated into hateful comments that I won't repeat here.

Another hazard of e-mail is that it slows down productivity for people who have not yet embraced this wonderful technology. Two years ago, I was working with the vice president of a large corporation in Kentucky and his administrative assistant. I was hired to provide consulting services to improve their team productivity. Part of my job was to observe the assistant's work habits and processes as well as how the assistant and executive interacted. I was amazed to see that the executive had his assistant print every e-mail he received! Then he would go through each one and write his comments. In turn, the assistant would e-mail her boss's comments back to the author. The day I visited, this process took half her day!

When I asked her why her executive was not managing his own e-mail, she said he just didn't want to, that he was not quite comfortable using e-mail. That was unfortunate because this was not the best use of the assistant's time. There were so many more important things she could have been working on. Of course, my first recommendation was that the executive learn about e-mail, practice using it and gain a comfort level with it. I pointed out the benefits of making this change and how it would increase their team productivity. While many assistants filter their executives' e-mails because of the volume received, executives should still communicate their own responses.

Another pitfall of e-mail is that we often can't read between the lines. This is difficult when trying to provide good customer service. Let's say a well-established client of yours e-mails you regarding a particular service or product you offer. To better serve your client and keep them coming back, you need to truly discover what they are trying to accomplish (unless you just sell widgets, books or household items). Possibly another product or service would better meet their needs than the one they are inquiring about. Rather than responding by e-mail, you should pick up the telephone and learn more about what they are trying to achieve. You might send them a brief e-mail telling them you are going to call, but then follow through by phoning them.

Think about it for a moment. True customer service is learning a customer's needs and then trying to determine what we have to offer that will help meet those needs. It's not just about selling a product or a service. If that is all you think, then you probably will not have that customer long term. The best way to meet those needs is through immediate back-and-forth dialogue. Who knows? You might turn a $3,000 sale into a $24,000 sale, just as I have done.

A few years ago, I had a potential client call me requesting a seminar on attitude for their employees. Through verbal questioning and clarifying, I learned that the reason attitudes were bad at this company was because numerous changes were taking place; employees were feeling frustrated and worried about job security, and they were concerned about several changes in their benefit plan. I recommended that I conduct a program on change first. We did that with much success and later did conduct a workshop on attitude.

One of the greatest pitfalls of e-mail, however, is that it denies us what I call Human Moments. I do love e-mail; don't get me wrong. I use it all the time in my work, and it is a blessing when I'm on the road. It does keep things moving. But Human Moments are important. As I travel across the country, going into all types of businesses—mostly large organizations—I see how much employees are losing the human touch. In some instances, I watch employees in their cubicles, and they almost look robotic—sitting at their computers, glued to the screen, sending and reading hundreds of e-mails in one day. They are so crunched to get the work done and get things moving that many don't make time for face-to-face communication.

Imagine this scenario: You wake up in the morning, turn on the news and power up your cell phone. Before you know it, you're listening to voice messages that had been forwarded from your office the night before. Soon you're in the car on your way to work and back on the cell phone. You drive to the office, go to your private work area or cubby, power up your computer and hear a robotic voice say, "Good morning." You open your e-mail service and find twenty-five messages from the afternoon before. You then make ten phone calls to potential clients, current clients and vendors only to get eight voice mail boxes. In the meantime, you have eight new voice mail messages of your own that came in while you were on the telephone trying to reach other people. Your stack of e-mails grows, and now your cell phone has a dozen new voice mail messages. While all of that is happening, you sit in front of your computer trying to get work done.

But where is the human interaction in all this? And we wonder why we are more stressed than ever before. Technology was supposed to make our lives simpler, more productive and paperless. But it hasn't; it has made us lose our human touch and become less tolerant and less understanding. For people who are task oriented, don't like to handle confrontation or don't know how to express themselves, technical communication has become a crutch.

I went into one organization where an employee sent an e-mail to a co-worker in the next cubby rather than get up and walk six steps to ask a question. Have we become so lazy as a work society that we can't even take a few steps to ask someone a question or give her the bit of information she needs? Or maybe we are just trying too hard to be really efficient.

From the employer's perspective, this is great news; if employees don't get up and talk to each other about work, then they won't chitchat. But Human Moments allow us to be in the same surroundings and see what other people are doing and looking at. We can pace our words and phrases for impact and time them with precision. We can express ourselves through our tone of voice. We can send and receive information at once. We can give and get immediate responses. And we can express agreement or disagreement immediately.

The following narrative, which I jotted down while on a recent business trip, provides a good illustration of the Human Touch at work.

"I'm sitting at The Camberly Brown in Louisville, watching a table of four men waiting for their dinner to be served. I'm wondering, 'Why are they here? Are they attending a conference? Are they just good friends getting together for a holiday dinner?' But I'm also watching gestures and facial expressions. I see nods, smiles, arms resting on the table, another man sitting back casually in his chair. The Human Moment—there is nothing like it. I just heard group laughter. While they are talking business, they are interjecting personal stories. All of a sudden, one man raises his voice above the rest to gain attention. Another laugh. Clarification. The conversation continues."

When we interact, we often look for clues as to how the other person will react. Let's say you are negotiating a new contract with a long-time client. You have kept your fees the same for two years, but now they are rising substantially. It would be far better, if possible, to discuss this increase with your client face to face. You would see how he reacts to this increase. Facial expressions are important to understanding emotional states. Think about a television show or even a newscast you frequently watch. Think about the facial expressions and how critical they are to gaining a sense of how the character really feels. But what if the client is basically an expressionless person? Then you could listen for his tone and the words he uses. In either case, you have an opportunity to immediately explain your reasons for the fee increase, if there is any resistance.

"We learn about others by interacting over time. Such learning is more successful the more there is ongoing interaction and feedback. If feedback is limited, a person is prevented from developing clarity and confidence." [Powell and O'Neal, 1976] While that passage was written more than quarter century ago, it still holds true. Speaker and author Dianne Booher delivers a similar message: "People long for human interaction. In such a world of emotional disconnection, there's a growing sense of discontent."

Another challenge that e-mail presents is not being able to gauge a person's reaction. We can't hear his voice or see his demeanor or expression. We are at a disadvantage in knowing how that person initially reacts to our message. Or, conversely, we might over gauge. In other words, based on the information we receive back, we might think the sender is upset with us when in reality she is not.

With e-mail, communication is more task-oriented and depersonalized. It has characteristics that make it highly susceptible to conflict escalation, as stated in a study by Raymond Friedman, associate professor at the Owen Graduate School of Management at Vanderbilt University in Nashville. Friedman did an extensive analysis, along with Steven C. Currall from Rice University, on the limitations of e-mail. The focus was on how disputes that began as small differences between parties ended up in full-blown arguments—all because they communicated via e-mail. The study is posted on Vanderbilt's web site (www.mba.vanderbilt.edu/ray.friedman) and points out some very interesting insights.

On the other hand, we also need to think when we do speak. Just because we decide verbal communication would be better than e-mail, it doesn't mean we won't hurt someone's feelings or be misunderstood. Verbal communication is not a guarantee that we will persuade a potential customer. We need to choose our words carefully, provide enough detail and clarify what we mean, or we could create the same effect as an ineffective e-mail.

E-mail, Face-to-Face or Telephone Communication—Making the Right Choice

How do we balance the use of electronic communications and Human Moments? That is an interesting challenge. Recently I conducted a time management workshop for AAA Nevada. I touched on the subject of hallway chitchat, pointing out how many minutes it can rob a person of in a day. I was telling the group how they needed to reduce the amount of time they spent on chitchat, when a woman from Human Resources questioned my idea, saying that part of her job was building rapport with employees. She was concerned that cutting back on chitchat would make her appear unapproachable or abrupt to employees.

I understood perfectly what she meant and pointed out that her situation was similar to mine when I conduct a full-day workshop. I have certain topics, goals and objectives that I must accomplish by the end of each day. That is what I am hired to do. But often, attendees will ask questions and want to know more about a topic or ask something unrelated to our program. I have to know when to limit discussion time and when it is important to address the question or comment. While the Human Resources woman needs to maintain good relations with employees, she may also need to use a combination of electronic communications (to be more productive) and face-to-face communications (to build rapport).

We need to know when the Human Moment is critical. How do we know that? We have to be good decision makers. Here are some questions we can ask ourselves during that decision-making process:

- Could the message I'm delivering be misconstrued or misinterpreted in any way?
- Could the information I'm communicating be taken as hurtful in any way?
- Could I come across as being prejudiced or bias?
- Is this bad news for the recipient?
- Because the receiver can't hear my tone in an e-mail, will she know I'm just joking?

While we won't always make the best choice, we can at least try to make better choices more often. For example, upon receiving one particular e-mail recently, I decided it would be better for me to call the sender rather than e-mail my reply. I wanted to make sure that I did not come across as offensive. I also wanted to ensure that I did not hurt this person's feelings. Another important reason for my decision to use the telephone was that it would help me better explain the areas he needed to work on and demonstrate my comments about tone and inflection. Additionally, I could immediately answer any questions he might have in reaction to my comments. I made the call, and it went very well. This vice president was very appreciative of my taking the time to speak with him, as opposed to just jotting down some quick ideas in an e-mail.

```
Hi Joan

You have had the opportunity to see me in
action (making presentations) on two
occasions. The first one formal, today "off
the cuff."

If you would be so kind, I would appreciate
any feedback you may have on my presentation
style and/or content. I am particularly
interested in how I can have more impact on
the audience.
```

```
Thank you.
```

Cultural differences might also dictate that we make a telephone call instead of using e-mail. I have been doing extensive consulting and training work within a large organization that has several multicultural employees. Once, I needed to gain some insight from one of those employees, but rather than exchange e-mails with her, I suggested we schedule a conference call prior to the program. This was a much better choice of media. I was able to immediately clarify what I thought she was telling me. She was able to carefully select the words she felt would best convey the problem the employees were experiencing. This also gave me an opportunity to bond with this individual. She was a key piece in helping us put together the pieces of the puzzle. Because she was one of the employees (although at a higher level within the company), she had knowledge of the other workers' frustrations and concerns. She was a valuable asset to me in writing the customized workshops.

Sometimes, we can select the right media and still get the wrong answer. An executive assistant who works in a large Fortune 250 company sent an e-mail to a woman at another company. That e-mail is presented below, followed by the response the assistant received. I have purposely left out names per the assistant's request.

```
Left a couple of messages for you and haven't
heard back, but realize you are probably busy.
Thought you might have a better chance of
checking your email, so thought I would try
that way. Have a couple of questions.

#1 - Jeff has asked that I send out the
information below via email to all
persons. Can I get approval to do so? (Rick
has not responded to my inquiry below).

#2-Not sure where to send the balance that we
owe. Should it go to the PO Box, should it be
left in your box at the rink, or should I just
bring it to registration? (Registration will
probably be faster...)

#3 - Two or three parents have asked me (given
my prior history with being Commissioner,
Newsletter person, etc.) what amount they
should pay at registration, i.e.: They are
going to try out for a travel team, with the
hopes that there will be a second travel team
```

```
(but none has been announced at this point),
so if they don't make the team, they will be
back in the house. (The likelihood is that
they won't make the team; several don't want
to play that many games). Should they pay the
$150, or should they pay $100?

#4 - Will Graham be getting a
scholarship? Shelley is stressing that she
needs to come up with money this weekend for
registration, and I told her to hold tight and
let me talk to you. Can you let me know so I
can quiet her mind a little on this one?

#5 - Has a final fee for house been decided
yet?  I know that it is $100.00 registration,
but what will be the monthly payment so that
folks can figure out the final total for
budgeting purposes? (Again, I have had 4-5
folks call me and ask me, and I have told them
"Not sure, ask the board.")
```

Now here is the response from the recipient of the previous e-mail:

```
No.
```

I'm certain you can see the problem with the recipient's e-mail. It left the assistant wondering:

- Was she saying "no" to my idea?
- Or was she saying "no" to all the questions?
- Or did she mean "no," that she doesn't want to even answer my questions at all?

What did she mean by "no?" The assistant was forced to pick up the telephone to call the woman and clarify her comment. She said they spent forty-eight hours playing phone tag! Imagine two people taking two full days to reach each other, just to clarify something that should have been explained clearly in the first place.

Voice mail also has some gray areas. While many experts tell us to always leave an explanation for our call, it is sometimes better to personally deliver a message. Even a voice mail message can offend someone or ruin a potential sale.

Voice mail should not be used to:

- introduce yourself to someone

- offer condolences
- convey confidential or critical information
- negotiate
- criticize someone

The purpose of voice mail is to convey information quickly, reach someone you may not normally have access to or keep communications more personal than e-mail or fax. It also is a great tool when working with people in different time zones, a challenge that hit home with me when I moved from Michigan to Nevada two years ago. Most of my clients are in the East or Midwest; therefore, if I have to communicate something that comes up late in the day, most of my Central and Eastern Time clients have already left work. That makes voice mail and e-mail great since these people can get my messages early the next morning when they get back to work. If I feel that my message really needs to be communicated via the telephone, then I will wait until the next morning and call when I arrive at my office.

What is interesting is that we can still have a communication crisis even when we think we've used the right medium. Communication crisis is defined as a conflict occurring between two or more people that is based around communication problems such as someone not listening, not giving enough information or not clearly stating expectations. However, a closer look shows it has more to do with:

- personal opinions
- prejudices
- personal goals
- power (one person wants or has power over another)
- an "I want to win" and "You have to lose" mentality
- hurt feelings (that aren't expressed)
- past events (your previous interactions and outcomes with this person or group of people)
- stubbornness
- timing (this is just not a good time for the other person for personal or professional reasons)

Any of these could create or lead to a communication crisis.

Communicating In Style, With Style

Our word "communicate" is derived from the Latin word, *communis*, meaning "commonness." When we are communicating, we are trying to establish commonness with others. We are trying to share information, encourage or inspire others, provide direction, persuade someone to make a change or see our point of view, build rapport, connect with someone in some way—all of which lead to establishing commonness.

In the workplace, whether you are a salesperson, a high-level executive or a systems analyst, you have to communicate in order to make things happen. The salesperson or account executive is trying to get the customer to purchase her product or service. The high-level executive is trying to persuade her staff to implement a new process or provide direction and encouragement. The systems analyst is trying to help an employee who is having difficulty with a new software program. In all of these situations, these people will only be as effective as the styles in which they communicate. You do have to take other things into consideration, such as timing and product knowledge; however, communicating in a way that is most favored to the recipient opens the door to your getting to talk about your product or service.

Most people like to communicate in the way that is most comfortable for them. Some people are detailed thinkers and like to communicate lots of details. While they may think they are being effective with the receiver, the receiver might be thinking, "Information overload! Please stop!" Actually, that would be my reaction. I am a big-picture thinker. I only think of the details when I need to. I so much favor big-picture thinking, that in the past, I have not bought something—even though I needed it—because the sales associate gave me too much information. A better approach would be to first give me the big picture or overview of what the product or service is and what it could do for me. Then, as I express some interest in learning more, fill in the details.

Others prefer to communicate in my favorite way. They want to provide an overview, a vision, a plan, but without much detail. But if the receiver in such a case is the kind of person who needs more details, he might have a hundred questions going through his mind. And if the receiver is an employee, he might move forward with a task that was given to him in big-picture style, only to realize later that he has wasted his time. Why? Because the employee thought he understood what his manager wanted, went back to his work area and followed through. But because he didn't have enough details or ask enough questions, the project did not meet his manager's expectations. Thus, the employee has to go back and spend more time on the project or trash it entirely.

Another great example is the vendor who misses out on a great sales opportunity because she speaks in the fashion she prefers rather than taking time to learn how the potential customer needs to be spoken to. The potential customer is turned off by the vendor and selects another vendor who takes the time to communicate in the style the purchaser needs.

Granted, when you make that first call to a potential customer, you aren't going to immediately pick up on whether he has a preference. If you listen carefully to his words and depth of information, you might get some initial insight. In written correspondence, it is easier to tell whether the author has a preference. People with a preference for detail will usually have lengthier letters or e-mails. People like me, who prefer the big picture, tend to write correspondence that is shorter and more to the point, unless it's something like a proposal. But even then, the proposal might not be very detailed. It might be a big-picture proposal for which the writer chooses to explain the details verbally.

Some people can rely on either front or back-brain thinking when taking in information and providing information to others. These people have what is called a "focused profile." This doesn't mean they don't use the other parts of their brains. We all use all parts of our brain regularly. However, those with focused profiles have preferences and enjoy work activities that involve one specific kind of thinking.

Elaine Biech, an author on creativity, explains it this way:

> Regions are differentiated in the brain, but the activities are integrated. We need to understand that there are two ways of thinking that can be called front brain (big picture thinking) and back brain (detailed thinking). We cannot do both types of thinking at the same time, and we shift from one part to the other constantly. And in many people one part is more active than the other. The most successful people are those who can easily shift from one thinking to the other

Other people access both parts of their brains for taking in and giving information. These people have a "balanced profile." This does not mean they are more mentally balanced than those with focused profiles; as I said, we all access all parts of our brain throughout the day. It just means that some people can have strong preferences, or no preferences, when it comes to communication style.

Colors are one way of identifying characteristics that relate to the different ways in which people prefer to receive communication. This information is not meant to offend anyone; it should be used to better understand other personalities and know how to communicate with them successfully.

Identifier	Characteristics	How to Communicate
RED	Action-oriented. Wants to know the short-term objectives of a project. Does not like indecision. Take charge type. Likes to be in control. Does not like advice. Risk taker, concrete, and impulsive. Uninterested in personal feelings.	Be supportive of their goals; be business like. Avoid trying to get personal. Be short and to the point. Give facts and documentation where possible. If you disagree, argue the facts, not feelings. Be precise, efficient, and time-disciplined.
YELLOW	Empathetic, personal, intuitive. Emphasis on human relationships and feelings when communicating. Enjoys friendly, informal relationships with everyone. Dislikes telling people unpleasant things; seeks harmony.	Don't hurry the discussion. Emphasize feelings. Try to avoid arguments, but look for alternative solutions. Be friendly and personable. Don't let them stray from the subject. Be supportive of their opinions and ideas.
BLUE	Introspective, creative, conceptual. Enjoys expressing ideas. Ask questions for understanding. Good listener. Can take small pieces of information and form a whole.	Try to show that you are interested in him/her as a person. Make certain you find out what he/she really wants. Be informal, casual. Avoid dictating to Blue. Be supportive of their feelings and idealism.
GREEN	Precise, analytical, impersonal. Prefers clear procedures, rules and regulations. Wants guidelines and structure. Needs to know deadlines. Principled, cautious, prefers working alone; likes problem solving; unemotional.	Be systematic, exact, organized and prepared. Provide solid, tangible evidence to support your idea. Stress principles, logic, theoretical, and proven ideas. Be supportive of their organized, thoughtful approach.

As you can see from the chart, Reds and Yellows are quite different in their characteristics as are Blues and Greens. If a person strongly favors the red style, he should consider how to soften his e-mail when corresponding with someone with strong yellow characteristics. It may be even better for the person with the red style to telephone the person with the yellow style, although he would still need to be careful with his words and tone. The important thing with styles is to remember not to categorize people.

Now that you have a basic understanding of these communication styles, you can use this information to:

- market yourself or an idea
- build rapport with co-workers, superiors, vendors and customers
- complement others' styles of communication in the workplace
- increase productivity
- improve teamwork
- reduce conflict
- increase sales

For example, I have one client who is very much a get-to-the-point person who doesn't like social chitchatting. So when I get on the phone with her, I get to the point. We're done in five or ten minutes. Another client, with whom I've worked for five years, loves to talk about everything from what is going on at work to family matters. Because I care about this person and our business relationship, I will let her talk, and I will ask questions related to the topics she enjoys. Once we get the socializing done, we then move on to business. It's not that I'm being a fake. I truly care enough about my customers to communicate in a fashion that they like or need.

Since 1990, I have used the above model with hundreds of employees, from all types and sizes of businesses, to improve work relationships and build rapport with colleagues. I recently had the opportunity to work with the research and development department of a large company that had fifty-four food technicians, food technologists, culinary and sensory workers and administrative staff. One of the key goals of our workshop was to improve communications within the group. We discovered that the majority of the attendees were Yellows and Blues, with fewer Reds and even fewer Greens. By understanding their peers' profiles, some could then see why they seemed to have such a difficult time communicating with their colleagues.

One attendee who embraced the yellow characteristics admitted that she used e-mail to avoid face-to-face contact with a co-worker regarding a potentially confrontational situation. She said e-mail made it easier for her to express views that might be different from someone else's or to critique someone. While she considered e-mail to be a real benefit, I pointed out that she was using e-mail as a crutch and that she would not develop conflict resolution skills, improve her communications and learn to express herself in a professional and assertive fashion by continuing this habit.

As a result of my using this communication model with this group, the employees returned to work with a better understanding of each other. They also had tools to help them better communicate with each other. Because they improved communications, they had less rework and higher levels of productivity. They reduced conflict and stress because they knew how to better communicate. They also learned their individual communication strengths and weaknesses.

The Whys, Hows and Whats of the Different Communication Media

E-mail, snail mail, fax, telephone, voice mail or face to face? Which is the appropriate medium to use in a given situation? You're the one who will have to make that decision; however, I am providing you with some points to consider to help you make better decisions and build rapport with others.

Start with the end in mind by asking yourself these questions:
- What is your purpose for communicating with this person?
- What information are you sending?
- What do you need from the other person?
- What do you hope will happen as a result of communicating with this person?

In other words, understand what you're after so you know how to communicate (although sometimes you may just be responding to the speaker or sender of information). I'm not saying that you always need to stop, think and analyze first before speaking or writing. But taking these steps will reduce stress, increase productivity, reduce rework and increase customer satisfaction. They will also build personal and professional relationships, eliminate hurt feelings and diminish needless steps.

A long-time client of mine contacted me one day requesting fees and a time frame for me to develop a one-day refresher course. One of our trainers had taken about a hundred of the company's employees through an eight-part program a year earlier, so the human resources department felt it would be a good idea to have a short refresher class that would build on the topics taught previously. The client made the suggestion, and I agreed, to survey past participants for topic ideas and learning exercises. After the surveys were returned and our client summarized the results, she e-mailed us the information. This medium was appropriate for that type of information, considering we were just in the first phase of the project.

Once you determine your goal in communicating, try to answer the following questions. Are you:

- Trying to build rapport or gain trust?
- Introducing yourself or a product?
- Relating a message?
- Expressing an idea or thought?
- Informing co-workers of important news?
- Providing data?
- Disclosing confidential information?
- Enlightening others to a new idea?

Next, think about your relation to or relationship with the recipient of your communication.

- How long have you known him/her?
- Is he/she a client? (If so, new or long-time?)
- A co-worker?
- A high-level executive?
- A vendor?
- A business associate?
- Mentor?
- Civic figure?

The length and depth of your relationship makes a difference. If you are just starting to get to know someone, more verbal and face-to-face interaction would be extremely helpful. Remember the benefits of Human Moments. If you have known someone for a long time and she knows when you are serious and not serious and can accept your views and opinions, then maybe an e-mail or voice message is adequate.

If you are an employee and your purpose is to let management know you disagree with a policy or a decision they have made, blasting off in an e-mail is not a good choice. Employers have told me over the years that some employees vent via e-mail and that it really comes back to haunt them. Instead, use effective, assertive communication skills and learn how to professionally express yourself on the telephone or face to face. When you are trying to decide which medium to use, also keep the following helpful ideas in mind.

The telephone is a great tool when you need an immediate response or want to hear someone's tone. You should also use the phone to negotiate or to provide confidential information (although with confidential information, you would not leave a voice message).

> Interesting Fact: You can cut the length of phone calls about 40% by creating a min-agenda for each call you make. Simply jot down key words for all points you want to address during a call. Studies show that planned-out business calls last an average of seven minutes, while unplanned calls average 12 minutes.
>
> *How to Organize Your Life and Get Rid of Clutter,* CareerTrack, Inc.

Use e-mail when you need hard copy documentation that you sent information or need a list of requests or steps to be taken. E-mail is good for communicating general information or non-urgent corporate communications such as meeting minutes, news releases, reports and memos.

> In the three seconds it takes to read this sentence, more than a half-million e-mails will land in in-boxes. By 2005, nearly that many will land each second.
>
> *USA Today* 1/6/02

Voice mail should be used to convey information quickly or to reach someone you may not normally have access to. Voice mail communications are more personal than e-mail or fax. It should not be used to introduce yourself to someone, convey confidential or critical information, negotiate or criticize someone.

Cellular telephone guidelines include never discussing sensitive or confidential information. Eavesdropping technology is also advanced, so don't use your cell phone in crowded areas. Also be aware that you may be disturbing others around you. It is never good manners or good business to broadcast your conversations.

If we were to visually map out what we've just discussed, it might look something like this:

Goal/Motive

↓

My Relationship

↓

Media

Goal: to find the root of the problem that is affecting employee performance so I can develop the appropriate speech to meet the client's needs.

Motive: is to educate the client; persuade the client to use me to help them achieve their internal goal; inform the client.

My Relationship: new client.

Media: first, telephone (no voice messages); then might use e-mail; voice mail; telephone communications would still be used throughout the entire project

Below is a chart listing some examples of situations that can occur in the workplace as well as corresponding suggestions for the preferred choice of medium. Of course, you still have to consider the main points mentioned above (motive, relationship, etc.) and other factors such as:

- how much time you have
- the recipient's personality
- previous experience with the person
- the recipient's current situation, sensitivity level

GOAL	PREFERRED MEDIA
Build relationships	Telephone E-mail
Provide support to a peer	E-mail Telephone Face-to-face
Assert one's needs	Telephone Face to face
Work through differences	Face to face Telephone
Confirm a meeting or a product order	E-mail Snail mail Voice mail
Deliver bad news	Face to face Telephone
Manage a dispute	Face to face Telephone

In the end, it's about knowing your goal and your purpose, knowing the recipient and your relationship to that person and knowing his or her communication and personality style. It's also about understanding the pros and cons of each medium and being aware of potential problems. That in itself may help you choose among the different communication media more carefully.

We can't be guaranteed that the people on the other end of the telephone or e-mail will do their parts. The only thing we can do is our very best. Communication is less about us and more about the receivers of our information. If we truly care about internal and external customer service, we will keep these things in mind. We will communicate in ways that others need. And when we go into communication with the intent of giving others what they need, in the way they need it, we often end up having our own needs met in the process.

Joan Burge

Joan Burge is the founder and CEO of Office Dynamics, Ltd. a national leader in the development of sophisticated professional development programs and information for business professionals. Drawing on her 27+ years as a career professional, business owner, entrepreneur, trainer, and professional speaker, Joan shows people that challenges, obstacles, and paths to success are similar for all people. Joan helps people realize that who they are today is not all they are capable of becoming. She helps people improve the quality of their work life and break self-limiting barriers. Her dynamic and energetic style leads people to understand and adopt the proper skills, attitude, and strategies that help them become their professional and personal best. Joan has provided guidance, continuity of purpose, and mentoring to office staff, managers, and CEO's. Her programs have resulted in significant productivity increases to her clients including Caterpillar Inc., The Boeing Company, Humana Inc., Marriott Corporation, LensCrafters, and The Children's Hospital of Philadelphia. Joan has authored 2 books, 12 workbooks, over 100 customized seminars, and regularly contributes to professional and trade publications. Joan is a member of the National Speakers Association, The American Society for Training & Development, The Southern Nevada Human Resource Association, and the Las Vegas Chamber of Commerce.

Joan Burge / Office Dynamics, Ltd.
2766 Evening Rock Street
Las Vegas, NV 89135
(800) STAR-139
Fax: (702) 838-4694
Email: jmbstar@aol.com
www.OfficeDynamicsLTD.com

Chapter 5

Taking Communication Home

Beverly Inman-Ebel

I am sitting in an executive office suite with a Fortune 100 vice president. The topic of discussion in our executive coaching session is the importance of listening to employees. His next remarks divert from the current subject when he exclaims, "My wife complains that I never listen to her, but I do. I don't get it. I listen, offer advice, and then she gets mad at me for not listening." As quickly as he routes our conversation to the topic of spouse relations, he apologizes for bringing up a personal need during a business coaching session.

This scenario is very common. I advise my client that it is appropriate to spend company time and dollars to improve his communication with his wife, because when that relationship is running smoothly, he will perform more effectively at work. Personal relationships affect the quantity and quality of work for both men and women.

In Corporate America, managers of both genders tend to operate in a gender-neutral zone. This charade can last for the eight to ten hours that they are at work, however when he and she go home, they are no longer willing to be anything but themselves. The more they adapt at the office or plant, the less likely they will be flexible in their personal lives.

John Gray has made a fortune convincing America that men are from Mars and women are from Venus. Other researchers and authors, however, such as Deborah Blum (*Sex on the Brain*) and Phyllis Burke

(*Gender Shock: Exploding the Myths of Male and Female*) maintain there are more similarities than differences between men and women. The DISC behavioral profile, which characterizes behavioral traits and tendencies, reports no statistically significant differences between genders. So are men and women really so different?

When we allow ourselves to be men and women, I say we are quite different. We look different, for one thing, and humans have a long history of judging others by their appearance. There are chemical differences, brain differences and structural differences, but perhaps cultural differences are the most significant. Culture determines how these differences are accepted and even dictates which differences each gender should have.

A young woman died suddenly in an automobile accident. She was survived by two sisters and two brothers. One sister cried openly and received much support from family and friends. The other sister was quite stoic, and people were concerned that she was harming herself by holding her emotions inside. Some even thought she was cold and obviously distant from her dead sister. The brother who showed no overt emotion was praised as strong—a pillar to lean on. The emotional brother was encouraged to "move on and help your sisters."

Culture begins to influence us at very early ages. Girls are rewarded for cooperative play, and boys are allowed and even expected to physically fight. I grew up with one older sister. Our fights were mostly cat fights, meaning we'd get our backs up and hiss, but rarely would we do more than scratch each other. When my two sons got out of diapers, the knock down, gut-punching, rock-throwing fights began. I thought I was either a lousy mother or God was paying me back for some earlier sin until I talked with mothers who had two or more sons. They assured me this male bashing was normal.

I could fill these pages with statistical data that would prove to you that men and women are different yet, in some ways, similar. Instead, I will refer you to some heavy reading and point out not just some of the significant, and sometimes funny, differences but also how we can bridge the gap between the sexes.

To accomplish this, I am going to "gendersize" people, which is putting them into two little boxes (figuratively speaking, of course)—one for males and one for females. However, only about seventy percent of us actually fit completely into our own gender's box. In other words, thirty percent of women will not possess all the typical female tendencies, and the same goes for men. As long as we clarify that one "size" does not fit all, we can be comfortable with "gendersizing."

Purpose

The reasons that men and women use communication can be very different. Men communicate in order to report information. If there are no facts to deliver, then there is no need to talk. Women communicate in order to establish rapport.

Two women can carry on a conversation about something they both already know. Instead of sharing information, they are building a relationship. Two men can carry on a conversation about something they both already know, but only if the men have different facts or opinions to share. If they both agree, it is a waste of time to continue. Both genders can fall into a trap here.

Women's trap is that their interest in the details of people's lives can be viewed as gossip, especially when they are talking *against* instead of just talking *about*. Southern women have this problem solved. They do not talk against; rather they talk about, which is followed by, "Bless her heart." For instance, "Mary paid full price for her new car, bless her heart." The implication, of course, is that Mary did not have the sense or ability to negotiate and that she let the dealer take advantage of her. But to say so outright would definitely be gossip!

Men's trap is that they get into a battle of one-upmanship. This happens when a man is convinced that his facts or opinions are superior to the other man's. Some men are sure that saying information louder gives it more credibility. And if volume helps, imagine what speed could do, so men tend to interrupt each other.

If each gender would stay in its own little box, things might not be so bad. Real problems occur, though, when a woman gives details about another person's life to a man and the man interrupts her and yells a short response, which is probably advice that the woman does not appreciate. Remember the different purposes of each gender's communication. Clueless men think women are talking to them in order to get information out of them, and they are dumbstruck when this information or advice is rejected. Clueless women think men want to establish a relationship through communication, so they engage in intimate details and become angry when the man doesn't listen and tries to tell them what to do.

What is the solution? Again, understand the purpose. I tell my female clients to let their spouses know in advance when they want to "talk about." For example, "John, I'm not looking for a specific solution, I just want to talk out loud about some concerns I'm having at work." This can take a lot of pressure off the man, and he may end up being a better listener.

I wish I had known this the first few years of my marriage. Back in the early '80s, I would "talk about" wanting this or that. I did not realize that my husband was busting his butt trying to make all my wishes come true. The pressure starting building until we realized how we were using communication. It wasn't all bad, though. By the time we got it figured out, I had a new house and a pool in the back yard!

I tell my male clients to ask more open questions to engage their women (wives, mothers, daughters) in conversation. Instead of just giving a short report, men can ask a question that begins with "How" or "What" to help build the relationship. For example, "We don't have the money now to go on vacation. What can we do close to home that you would enjoy?" Realize, men, that you may not be wild about her answer, so warn yourself in advance to avoid interrupting her. In marriage, a dog may not be your best friend—it may be a question and the willingness to hear the answer.

Listening Preference

Men tend to place a higher value on the words used, and women tend to place a higher value on how those words are delivered. Take this scenario:

> Husband: Mark and Sue asked me if we wanted to go to the ball game with them on Saturday. Do you want to go?"
>
> Wife: (pauses, exhales audibly, then wrinkles her nose as she says) "Well, okay, if you really want to."

The husband hears the word "okay" and calls the other couple and commits himself and his wife to attending the ball game. The day of the event, the wife is complaining about the heat, how she hates the sport and mentions to her husband how much Sue talks. They will probably end up in a heated argument. The wife may accuse the husband of not listening to her, to which he may respond, "You said you wanted to go!" She will deny this and claim, "You knew I didn't want to go. I always bend over backward for you and your friends. Why don't you take me somewhere I want to go sometime?"

The problem is listening preference. The wife gave many non-verbal clues to indicate that she did not want to go. While she was sending these communications, she noted that her husband did not offer to tell Mark and Sue "no." The wife finally relented, yet felt resentful that she gave in again. The husband was either not looking at her or failed to realize that her hesitancy, facial expression and weak response were intended communications.

What is the solution? It would be very helpful for men to listen with their eyes as well as their ears. Pauses, facial expressions and gestures usually mean something. In my book, *Talk Is NOT Cheap*, I outline the various body language signals and what they can mean. Men, know this: a quick change in your woman's posture or expression means something has changed. It can be helpful to announce your confusion. For instance, "I heard your words; you said 'okay', but I'm not sure how you are feeling. How do you really feel about this?" Not only will you get more information, you'll get credit for being an incredible listener.

Women, select your words more carefully. Make sure your body language matches your words. If the right words won't come quickly enough, buy yourself some time. For example, "I am not ready to commit to plans for this weekend. When do you need to tell Mark and Sue?" If you receive pressure to make a quick decision, you can respond, "If you need an answer right now, the answer is 'no,' because I have not had time to think it through."

A solution for both genders is to schedule a listening date. Plan it like you would any important meeting. Once a week, set aside one hour during a time when there will be few interruptions. For young parents, this means after the children are asleep. Take the phone off the hook or allow your answering machine to retrieve your incoming calls. Each partner comes to this "date" with a list of subjects he and she want to discuss. Let the other person know from the beginning what you want from this discussion. Choices could be bringing up a new subject just for discussion with no decision expected yet, bringing up a previously discussed subject for clarification or calling for a decision. Decide who will go first and follow these guidelines:

- Sit no farther than five feet apart. This closeness helps facilitate listening, increases the length of response and aids in intimacy.
- Allow no interruptions. If you are the listening partner and you're dying to say something, jot it down in a word or two so that you don't have to rehearse it in order to remember it. This allows you to listen more freely.
- Speak in the first person. Say, "I heard" rather than "You said."
- Describe rather than label. Say, "I saw Jim jump up, tighten his jaw and leave the room" instead of, "Jim really got mad at what you said."
- The speaker should invite the spouse to respond by asking for input or their thoughts.
- Before responding to the speaker, make sure you understand the message you just heard. If there is any doubt, restate what you heard your spouse say using your own words—not his or her exact words—and ask for agreement. For example, if the wife talks about wanting to go to the theatre or to a special restaurant instead of a baseball game, the husband might respond with, "So I'm understanding that you want to do some cultured things, right?"
- Keep a curfew. Don't allow the listening date to continue beyond the time you are able to listen with care. Fatigue and listening are mortal enemies.

Response to Stress

Just as a reminder that we are all from the same planet, both men and women experience stress in its various forms. Until recently, it was assumed that both genders handled stress similarly. Women were largely excluded from stress research until 1995, when government grant policies changed. In the July 2000 issue of *Psychological Review*, a UCLA research team reported that while men respond to stress with the "fight-or-flight" response, women are more likely to deal with stress using a "tend-and-befriend" response.

The tending includes protecting and nurturing, and the befriending is sought by seeking social contact and support from others. The male version of fighting is aggressively going after the stress, while the flight is removing oneself from the source of potential threat. Notice that women use a two-step approach and men choose a one-step system. If the source of stress is an angry bear or a terrorist, I think the men have a good plan. The "beat him up or outrun him" approach seems like it would get the job done. Most men are not running into bears or terrorists each day, yet they may feel like fighting at the office before they run home and hide from everyone, even their families.

Kevin is a director of a large IT department. Constantly dealing with self-righteous technical geniuses and frustrated and demanding internal customers, Kevin might welcome a good romp with a grizzly. He comes home and wants to be left alone. It's a jungle out there, and he has been fighting in it all day. He just wants some peace and quiet.

His wife, Shelly, is a sales manager for a carpet manufacturer. The economy, competition and a challenging boss are her sources of stress for the day. She, too, comes home exhausted, only she does not want to hide; rather, she wants to take care of Kevin by doing nice things for him. Then, of course, she wants to talk. Kevin snaps, so Shelly calls one of her female friends, and they spend an hour on the phone. Kevin doesn't want an outsider knowing their troubles, and round two begins.

Sound familiar? President John F. Kennedy once said, "Face your fear and that will be the death of it." Communication and relationships break down when we try to hide our stress from our spouses and then treat our stressed out spouses like we would want to be treated. Women, give your man some time alone when he first comes home. Men, after you have had some solace, reach out to your woman and give her the social contact and support that she is craving, remembering that you don't have to solve her problem—just listen to it.

Language

Last Christmas Eve, my family invited a young Hispanic man and his brother to spend the holiday with us. Sam spoke English better than he understood it, especially at the rate most Americans speak. His brother, who was visiting from Mexico, spoke even less English. All of us were being very attentive to each other, striving to communicate as best we could. We talked slower, watched for facial expressions and chose our words carefully. We ended the evening singing Christmas carols in both languages.

Men and women speak the same language, yet they use it so differently that sometimes I think it would be easier if one were speaking Spanish and the other English. Perhaps then each would expend the effort needed to ensure that communication was occurring. Just how is language used differently between the genders?

Men tend to talk about issues. Women like to talk about life. Let's say that a group of friends from both genders likes football. The men will talk about the percentage of pass completions, third down conversions and running yards. The women might talk about the style or personality of the coach, the evidence or lack of teamwork and notice the emotion of the players.

Men give advice while women give suggestions. The difference between advice and suggestions is the strength of the language. Advice could be, "Call John right now." Notice the commanding tone. The same idea, given as a suggestions could be, "How about calling John now?" Some of the husbands reading this paragraph may remark, "That's not my wife. She gives orders to everyone!" I call that the Mother Syndrome. It comes from years of repeating, "Pick up your clothes. Brush your teeth. Say thank you. Don't hit your sister," etc.

Men do not use as much praise in their language as women do. Women also include more polite words when talking, such as "please" and "thank you." Also, each gender uses different sets of phrases or analogies. Men will refer to "dropping the ball," "having the balls to do something," "hit the target," or "fire one off." These refer to sports and war. When women first appeared in management over the last two decades, they felt it was necessary to add these phrases to their vocabulary base. Women have their own set of phrases that can be foreign to men, such as, "Men!" "Icing on the cake," or "Let's talk about it."

In the early years of my company, we employed all females. Women typically filled secretarial roles, and most of the speech/language pathologists were also female. When we began working with Corporate America instead of children, our staff was balanced between the genders. Within the last two years, the pendulum has swung completely, and now all full-time employees are male. A few weeks ago, I was just a couple of days away from my visit to the hair salon, and I knew that this was starting to affect my mood. I explained to a couple of my male employees that,

"I'm having a bad hairdo day." Their responses were classic. These clueless men half smiled, some made a weak laugh, and all of them had no idea what I really meant. I did what any self-respecting woman would do: I called my girlfriend and vented.

Here are some suggestions for getting along better at home:

- Obtain your spouse's eye contact before you begin speaking. You can accomplish this by saying her/his name or using a light touch.
- When you are listening, stop what you are doing and give your full attention to your spouse. While you may pride yourself on having the ability to multitask, you will not get credit for being a good listener if you are trying to do something else while your spouse is speaking.
- Set aside prearranged time for important discussions. These are dates you really want to keep.
- Demonstrate solidarity in front of the kids when the two of you disagree on discipline or a decision. I know, you have very bright children, but do not allow them to come between you and your mate.
- Ask open questions. This approach—asking questions that begin with "How" or "What"—allows you to be a good listener and will give you valuable information and feelings.
- Get comfortable with pauses. Introverts need time to think about their responses. Don't ask and answer your own questions or you'll soon be talking to yourself.
- Ask one question at a time. Multiple questions make you look controlling and can frustrate your mate. Most people will only answer the last question anyway.
- Do not interrupt. This includes finishing her or his sentence or answering the question before it is fully verbalized.
- Use sincere praise. Tell your spouse exactly what he/she did and how it helped you or someone else. If your spouse is an extrovert, praise him/her in front of other people.
- Speak in the first person, talking about what "I think" or "I feel."
- Correct in private. Nobody else really cares whether you went to Alaska in 1999 or 2000. Correcting in the middle of a story will

just make your spouse mad, your audience uncomfortable and make you look like a control freak.

- Let go of old hurts. Research shows that every time you relive a hurtful event, your brain records all the negative emotion as though it has occurred again. For example, a husband mentions that his wife is gaining a little weight, and for the next 365 days she re-creates this scenario five times per day for a total of 1,825 times!

- Keep the relationship fresh. Every week, find something new to do or discuss. Keep an atmosphere of positive surprises.

There is an old saying that "opposites attract." I agree with this. We find traits in others that we do not have, and we admire those traits. However, I've embellished this quote somewhat: "Opposites attract and then attack." We marry people different than us and then we spend a lifetime trying to change them to be more like us. Men and women are different in some ways. Understand those of the other gender and change your responses to them rather than trying to change *them*.

Questions

Each gender is perplexed about some behaviors that the other projects. Here are some frequently asked questions and answers that may shed some light.

Why are people so quick to call assertive women the "B" word?

Part of this answer is cultural and part is physiological. Let's start with culture. In the United States, approximately eighteen percent of the population is the dominant behavioral style. These people are task focused and extroverted. There is not a significant statistical difference between men and women who possess this behavioral style. So if the genders are split equally, nine percent of women fall into this category, as do nine percent of men. But our society allows men to be more aggressive than women. Men who become verbally abusive may not be praised, but they are not labeled a female dog for all their barking. Come to think of it, I am not sure why the female canine has this derogatory title.

The other reason is physiological. Women typically have thinner vocal cords than men. These cords are the strips of muscle that reside in the larynx, or voice box, that vibrate and create sound. The thinner the cord is, the higher the pitch of the sound. Think of a guitar. The thinnest string creates the highest note. When people get stressed, their muscles tighten, including the vocal cords. Because women have thin cords to begin with, when these muscles become even thinner due to the tightening from stress, the voice sounds very high in pitch. This can sound rather unpleasant to the ear.

Add the woman's high-pitch voice to negative facial expressions and an increase in gestures, and you do not have a pretty picture—thus the negative association. And the longer a woman uses this voice, the more stressed she becomes, so the voice goes even higher. Whenever the voice rises in pitch, it will naturally become louder. (Notice that most singers who hit the high notes tend to belt them out. It takes a very professional and controlled voice to hit the high notes with softer volume.)

By contrast, the lower the voice, the calmer a person sounds. During stress, people are attracted to those who sound calm and reassuring. Men have a distinct advantage here. Because their vocal cords are thicker to begin with, the final result is not nearly as noticeable, even though their voices may also rise in pitch under stress.

Women, when you are feeling stressed, close your eyes for a moment, if you can. This increases relaxation by about twenty percent. Take a deep breath and slowly and quietly exhale. When you begin to speak, purposefully lower your pitch. If you want to know your natural pitch, gently place your fingers on your throat with the middle finger on the hyoid bone, or Adam's apple (Eve has one, too). As you speak you will feel vibration on this middle finger. If you start to feel vibration on your index finger, your pitch is too high. Another test is to answer a closed question by saying "uh-huh" through your mouth without expression. The "huh" will be your natural relaxed pitch. If your conversational pitch is much higher than this, your listener may be thinking about the "B" word.

By the way, men do not escape the ramifications of their physical structure. Because their vocal cords are thicker, it takes more sub glottal air pressure to blow them apart for speech, so many times a man will speak very loudly under stress. Certain words will just jump out to the listener, and if the listener is a female, the man may be accused of yelling. The solution is to slowly exhale before and during speaking to keep the volume from jumping up. Decreasing the rate of speech, or talking slower, will also help.

Why does my husband talk to everyone except me?

Years ago, when our children were young, my husband traveled for business and I did not. I specifically remember one Friday evening when he came home and I asked how his trip had gone. He gave me the one syllable response, "Fine." I am confident that I gave him a monologue about the children, work and current household events. The next evening, we went out to a party that was attended by about eight other people. Someone asked him how his trip went, and he commanded everyone's attention for at least ten minutes with fabulous tales of humor and intrigue. Everyone was laughing and smiling except me. It was humiliating to be learning of his great adventures along with these casual acquaintances.

If I only had known then what I know now. While women talk the most in dyads, men prefer the ears of many. Men talk more in groups than women do, and the bigger the group is, the better the story. If I had known that at the time, I could have kept the boys up and sat the dogs at attention so he would have had an audience.

To be fair to my husband, I certainly could have asked a better question. "How was your trip?" rings very similarly to, "How are you?" We have been conditioned to answer that last question with "Fine," regardless of how we feel. It really is not a question as much as it is a greeting. (Isn't it awkward when a stranger you pass does not know this rule and spends five minutes giving a detailed answer?) A better question would have been, "What did you like about your trip?" or "What unexpected things happened this time?" Women, you can engage your man in a two-way conversation; it just takes a little more planning.

Why do women nag?

This is one question that I get most often from men. Not all women nag, but evidently enough do that women are tagged with this trait. The

Random House Dictionary (I have always found that to be a humorous name for a specific reference source) defines "nag" as "to torment with persistent demands or complaints." Ouch! Torment is a strong word! There has got to be a reason for this.

One reason goes back to gestation. During the 28th week of pregnancy, there is a chromosomal wash over the cortex of the male fetus that causes separation of the connective tissue from the right and left hemisphere. Think of it this way: males have a country road between their brain hemispheres, and women have a super highway. (Women, don't run off and tell your husbands that they are brain damaged. This is a difference, not a problem.) Because of this disconnection, though, men are more focused on what they are doing. They are less likely to be distracted. That is the good news. The down side is that they do not get certain kinds of information from the right side of their brain as quickly—information such as reading body language, voice cues, etc. Because of this, they take words more literally than women do.

Case in point: A woman says, "I'm sick of this kitchen!" The man is at a bit of a disadvantage because there is not enough information for him in this statement. He is not very comfortable with the prospect of asking questions because he fears he will only get more words that are unclear; so he says nothing. The woman feels she has been ignored, and her negative feelings build inside her. The next time she strives to communicate her thought, it comes out, "I don't know how you expect me to cook a decent meal in that kitchen!" Now the man knows he is in trouble. Somehow, something is his fault because he knows, at least, that she is talking about him. There is no way he is going to get into a debate about her cooking, so he not only doesn't respond, he goes out and hides in the garage. By now, the woman is in tears, but she hates crying, so she decides to mask her hurt with anger. And the torment continues.

The solution is twofold: Women need to choose their words more carefully, and men need to ask questions. Instead of saying, "I'm sick of this kitchen!" the woman can choose to be more accurate by saying, "There is not enough counter space to prepare the meals we like to eat." Now this is better, yet it could use one more improvement—a question at the end to invite him to communicate. So she could add, "What can we do about this?" The man now has a chance of answering. Of course, there is no guarantee that the woman will like his answer. Even if the woman is not specific, the man can choose to align with her emotionally and ask a question rather than avoid communicating. For instance, when he hears about his wife being sick of the kitchen, he can respond, "You sound upset (frustrated, angry, annoyed). What will help?" Here again, the man may not like the answer. But he should remember to keep asking questions when a woman is upset because during these times, she talks much better than she listens.

Why doesn't my husband listen to me?

Just like women get accused of nagging, men get credited for having ears made of stone. The males claim that they hear just fine. My mother, sister and I claim that my father has had a selective hearing loss for years. So just what is the problem?

Men prefer quick and to-the-point messages. When women give them excessive details, the men tune out with a plan to tune back in when she gets to the point. The trouble occurs when he gets caught not listening before she gets to her point. Both sides can help. Men, give her eye contact. Wherever the eyes wander, so will the mind. If she goes into detail, strive to find the information and purpose. Ask questions to clarify and keep you on track. Women, timing is everything in communication. Don't start talking to him while he is reading or watching TV. Before you begin, ask, "Is this a good time for you to be able to listen?" As you are talking, insert some questions to keep him involved in the conversation. Many times it is helpful to tell the end of the story and then go back and pick up the details. When he does listen, make sure you let him know that you appreciate his time and attention.

Why are there so many fights over money?

The best reason is probably that there are more bills and wants than there is money. Our society is bombarded with the idea of obtaining everything right now. That aside, there are different approaches to money among the genders. Men tend to see money as power while for women, money represents security and autonomy. Philip Blumstein and Pepper Schwartz (*American Couples*) studied all types of couples and reported that only in lesbian couples did earning more money not make that partner more powerful.

Why do men hold back their emotions while women pour them out?

Both genders feel emotions. Men have been conditioned to control the way they express theirs. In 1971, Balswick and Peck referred to this as "the Cowboy Syndrome," probably after watching some John Wayne movies. Times have changed in the last three-plus decades, yet men are still rewarded for being the silent, strong manly man. Women are attracted to them probably because they seem so secure; then these same women spend the rest of their lives trying to pry them open.

Approximately sixty-eight percent of the people in the United States are warm communicators capable of expressing their emotions. If this trait is important to you, you have the majority of the population to choose from. If you have chosen a cool communicator, it may take time to get that person to realize it is safe to express the emotions he is feeling. If your partner seems to take everything to heart, encourage her to look back only long enough to correct or understand, then move on.

Why do men need to solve all my problems?

This goes back to the purpose of communication. A man may likely think that the reason you are discussing a problem is to get his feedback on how to solve it. Women, if you don't want a solution, tell him before you start. Using that approach, he will not feel as though you have rejected his idea. And men, ask if she wants advice before you give it. That way, you know it will be better received.

Many reasons that we have difficulty communicating at home is due to the fact that we share nearly everything with our spouse (home, children, money) and compromising on a regular basis is challenging. We also tend to be less careful and just say the first thing that comes to our mind. To blame it on being a member of the opposite sex is easy, but usually not complete. Gay and lesbian couples also have disagreements. We'll always have men jokes and women jokes, just like we'll continue to have blonde jokes. It is a very human trait to surround ourselves with people who are like us and to distrust people who are different.

I live in the South, where college football is very popular. Seeing college flags flapping from vehicle windows is quite common. Following September 11, 2001, all the different school flags were replaced with the stars and stripes. It was a time to remember what we have in common instead of focusing on how we are different. Perhaps that is a lesson we should apply at home. A husband and wife are on the same team. Together, fly your flag for all the world to see.

About The Author

Beverly Inman-Ebel

Beverly Inman-Ebel is the CEO of TLC, Talk Listen Communicate, LLC. Beverly and her staff provide personalized corporate seminars and individual coaching to help people become more effective communicators. She has received national coverage in *The Wall Street Journal, Success* magazine, *Glamour, Time* and ABC World News Tonight for her work with voice and communication improvement for business image. She is the author of *Talk Is NOT Cheap!: Saving the High Cost of Misunderstanding at Work and Home* [Bard Press, 1999], and co-author of *Real World Communications Strategies That Work* [Insight Publishing, 2003] and *Success Is A Decision of the Mind* [Insight Publishing, 2003]. Beverly delivers keynote presentations across the nation, specializing in positive attitude, handling change, and communication. She participated in a White House Conference and Reception on brain development and learning with the President and Mrs. Clinton. From 1996-1999, Beverly served on the Tennessee Governor's Task Force for Women Businesses. She was chosen as the 1998 recipient of the Jane Cozby Henderson Woman of Achievement award. She traveled with the U. S. Department of Commerce to South Africa to help establish trade between the two nations. She is currently the National President-elect for the National Association of Women Business Owners.

Beverly Inman-Ebel
TLC, Talk Listen Communicate, LLC
842 South Germantown Road
Chattanooga, TN 37412
(423) 622-TALK (8255)
(888) BECAUSE
tlc@talklisten.com
www.TalkListen.com

Chapter 6

Supercharge Your Communications with Five Steps and Four Styles

John W. Connors & Jon Cooper

Communication is the glue that holds human culture together. Communication allows us to maintain marriages, families, friendships, businesses and virtually every aspect of our lives. Without good communication, things rapidly begin to fall apart.

All of us who want to be more successful in our lives and in our jobs wish that we could do a better job of communicating. And here is the good news: we can! Effective communications can be achieved in five easy steps:

- Engage
- Listen
- Understand
- Take action (or commit to take action)
- Follow up

These steps have been well known for many years. But many people either do not understand what these steps require, or they simply fail to put them into practice on a regular basis. That is where the seeds of non communication or miscommunication are planted.

In the discussion that follows, the information we present will allow you to be easily understood and will help you to understand others better.

Our examples will focus primarily on communications with customers, but the same principles can be applied to personal communications or to any situation in which you want to make sure that effective communication happens. If you make it a habit to faithfully follow the steps we present, they will help you move forward in attaining your personal and professional goals.

The Critical First Step—Engage

The first step in communicating is to engage the customer. As the beginning of the process, this sets the tone for everything that comes after. In many businesses, there is very little time for this step because customers may be hurried or seem rushed. Perhaps to some, engaging the customer may seem like a waste of time because they are anxious to get on with the business at hand. Nevertheless, it is critically important to take time to engage and make contact!

Often this can be done with a simple smile or hello; sometimes this first step can last longer and become more personal. When you engage the customer, it must be a gesture that communicates that you value him or her, and your tone of voice is important. Your gesture and tone should both convey, "I'm happy you are here!" or "I'm happy to be here."

It's such a simple thing, but it sets a positive expectation for the entire process. When you fail to engage customers in a business setting, you set them up to start thinking, even if subconsciously, "Maybe I'll go somewhere else where I am valued."

Some of the biggest complaints customers have are related to their first impressions of a business. Perhaps you have had the experience of walking into a store or restaurant and being totally ignored by the employees.

I've had such negative experiences myself. A bank once hired me to do some service training, and as part of the preparation process, I "shopped" all the branches. It was amazing to see how poorly the employees engaged their customers. They did not make eye contact, they were abrupt, and they did not listen to customers. It was almost as if they were responding mechanically to their jobs.

Customers want to think they are important. To make them feel important, your attitude and behavior must say, "You're the customer, you pay my salary, you make my job possible." The customer-focused organization is one that wants to ensure satisfaction through the benefits of its product/service. Conversely, the organization whose primary focus is to get the product/service to the customer, while leaving him or her to figure out the benefit, is failing to make the most of a critical moment of truth. The differences may be subtle, but the effect is not.

Creating a Great First Impression

How you look is obviously a big part of making a positive first impression. The slogan "You can't judge a book by its cover" may be true, but everybody tries to anyway. Unfortunately, people will make judgments about you based solely on the way you look.

If you don't believe it, let's turn the tables for a moment. Suppose your brand new home appliance is being delivered today. Would you prefer that the delivery person look neat and competent or disheveled and unkempt? Or think about how you would react if your doctor or other service professional had a disheveled and unkempt appearance. What would you think? Wouldn't it distract you? Would it affect your sense of his/her competency?

Personal appearance communicates many things about you, so be sure it's positive. One rule of thumb is to dress in a way that's one step above the company's policy. In other words, learn your company's dress code, or look around at the other employees. Then try to dress like someone your customers would go to for advice.

Let's say, for example, that you are attending a business meeting with a new customer to present a concept that could benefit his business. Showing up in shorts, a T-shirt and sneakers may not exude confidence or professionalism. Conversely, attending the annual company picnic in a tuxedo or formal gown may inhibit your ability to run the bases during the softball game.

Another simple way to make a positive first impression on your customers is to smile. Smiling makes other people feel good, and you may notice that they are often returned!

The Total Quality Management experts have it right—it is easier to make a product right the first time than it is to make it wrong and then fix it. The same is true of the credibility you create with a first impression. It is easier to create a good first impression than to create a bad one and then wage an uphill battle to change it!

The Sweetest Sound in the World

One of the most neglected steps in engaging the customer, whether it is on the telephone or face-to-face, is a formal exchange of names. In some high-pressure transactional service positions, taking the time to exchange names is inappropriate, but many times it is simply overlooked.

The appropriate way to do this is to make strong eye contact, offer a handshake and clearly give your name. Usually the first name will suffice. Then get the other person's name. This very important step is often the open door to instant rapport.

Many of us do not remember other people's names well, and it's a skill worth developing. Dale Carnegie said in his book, *How to Win Friends and Influence People*, a person's name is "the sweetest and most important sound in any language." It is essential that you focus on this process because it will help you move forward with the customer.

In certain situations—if you work at a bank, for example—it might not be appropriate to ask the person's name aloud. In such cases, you might try sneaking a look at the name on his banking transactions or check to see if he's wearing a name tag. If you already know your customer's name, you might use it to establish rapport by asking, "How would you like your cash today, Mr. Talbot?"

Once your name has been offered, use the following formula:

1. **STOP** thinking about yourself and all the other things on your mind and completely focus on hearing the other person's name when it is offered.

2. **REPEAT** the person's name back to him in the first sentence or two. This habit will force you to focus on the person's name and emblazon it onto your mind. In order to reinforce it, you also might want to write it down, particularly if it's a difficult name.

3. **ASSOCIATE** the person's name with something that is very familiar to you. For example, you might want to rhyme the name with something that's easy to remember, or think of someone you know well who has a similar name.

You Gotta Treat 'Em Right

In any sort of communication, we all need to do the same thing: focus on the person with whom we are communicating. Have you ever encountered a service person who was distracted from focusing her full attention on you? It is, without a doubt, an annoying and devaluing experience. The service person who is too unskilled to focus her attention completely on the person she is talking to will have a negative impact. Everything from the phone ringing to computer malfunctions to other customers and co-workers are sources of distraction that can take away the service person's focus. Employees need to tune the world out and act as if their customers were the center of their attention.

Here are a few simple guidelines for customer etiquette that can go a long way to ensuring your success as a service person. It amazes me how often service people fail to observe these time-proven principles.

When a customer enters your place of business, be aware of how long he is present before you acknowledge him. A good rule of thumb is a minute to a minute-and-a-half. Unless you are in a heavily transaction-oriented position, you don't want to be too aggressive. The customer may have various products to look at and may want a few moments to do so. But you don't want to ignore him either. An effective solution: Instead of asking, "May I help you?" (which normally elicits a negative response), try saying, "Good morning! I'll be with you in a moment."

Another terrific greeting is, "How can I help you?" It shows the customer that you want to help and gets the customer thinking about how, exactly, you can help them. Any other positive question that gets the customer talking can be effective, too.

Here are some key things to avoid:

Negative comments. Comments about how bored you are or what a lousy company you work for should be kept out of the service transaction. Such remarks also show that you are not paying full attention to your customer, which will negatively affect your service.

Interruptions. Sometimes they're unavoidable. However, you should make it a personal policy to never turn your back on a customer, no matter what the distraction. If you must step away from the transaction, kindly make eye contact and politely say something along the lines of, "Would you please excuse me? This will only take a second." It is a great idea to apologize when you return as well. A large dose of politeness will go a long way toward keeping your customer happy.

Recommendations that are off track. Pay strict attention to what the customer asks of you. If you don't have the desired service or product, refer him to someone or somewhere that does. This saves him time, and you will be remembered for your gracious attitude.

Treat 'Em Right Graduate School

Want to put your communication and service skills into overdrive? Here are some more useful tips:

Be considerate of the customer's personal space. Each of us has an invisible zone of personal space surrounding us, and we get uncomfortable when other people "violate" that space. The size of people's personal spaces varies from person to person, so it is a good idea to observe The Golden Rule on this one. Notice your customer's personal space, and pay attention to whether he is moving away from you or closer to you. The same principle applies to the volume of your conversation. Speak clearly if the area is crowded, but give your customer time to think. Remember, you want to be of service but not so aggressive that you make him feel uncomfortable.

Show up on time for appointments and be prepared (if you provide on-the-road service). Customers appreciate people who are considerate and on time. If you can't be on time for an appointment or a callback, let the customer know. Also, prepare yourself in advance with the information your customer will need. Don't just make up anything. If you don't know something, tell your customer that you will take the time to find the person who does know.

Be nice to all the people around you. Kindness is contagious, so be kind and friendly to your customers and fellow employees alike. When it comes to dealing with co-workers, it's important to be nice not just to the people above you but also to the people who support what you do. By the same token, when dealing with another business, be sure to treat all its employees with the same courtesy and respect that you would reserve for the company president.

Keep your word. If you tell your customer you are going to do something, then by all means do it. If you can't fulfill an obligation, let the customer know it, then figure out what will satisfy him.

Step Two—Listen (But Prime the Pump by Asking Questions)

A wise person once remarked, "There's a darn good reason why we have two ears and just one mouth. That's so you can spend more time listening than talking."

Now that you have dressed properly, put on a smile, exchanged introductions and used all the proper etiquette, it's time to move to the next step, which is finding out what the customer wants or needs. This is primarily a listening step, but you will need to ask questions first. The opening question should be, "Would it be alright to ask you a few questions?" or "I'll need to get some more information from you." With that information, you can then determine how to help the customer.

The process of uncovering customer needs will also help you to do a number of other important things that aid the service process:

- qualifying the customer
- building credibility
- establishing rapport
- finding key issues
- verifying that you understand correctly

Finally, asking questions helps you interact with customers in a way that develops:

- Trust—so that people feel comfortable with you.
- Empathy—so they understand that you care about their needs.

Recently, my wife and I decided to put down a new ceramic floor in the foyer of our home. We decided to visit Best Tile to see what we could find. The salesperson was very professional. She began by asking us questions about the flow of traffic through the foyer, how many rooms were located off it, total square footage, colors of paint and wallpaper and more. Based on the answers, she began to display selected styles, colors and textures of floor coverings.

This was one of those classic cases in which sales and service were intermixed. She wasn't just selling us something; she was also helping us to decide what we needed. It made the experience very enjoyable and gave us a high degree of confidence that we were making the right choice because she took the time to uncover our needs.

To "prime the pump" and get the customer talking, you'll need a set of preplanned questions. And yes, you should memorize them first.

Closed-End Questions

Some of the questions need to be clear and concise, answerable with specific responses. These are called closed-end questions, and when a customer is in a hurry, they allow you to cut to the chase. Such questions usually begin with words like Do, Can, Will, etc. and often have to be answered with a "yes" or "no."

Some examples of closed-end questions include:

- Are you ready to buy now?
- Will this help you with what you are looking for?
- Do you need this now?
- Will you be taking this with you, or do you want it delivered?
- Can you take delivery on Saturday?

Open-Ended Questions

Some questions need to be open-ended to encourage the customer to talk. These questions force an individual to elaborate on a response and usually begin with the words What, Where, When, Why, How and Who.

Here are some examples of open-ended questions that you can memorize:

- Why are you interested in this product?
- What problems do you want to solve?
- How did you find out about our company/store?
- What was your past buying experience with us like?
- What is your price range?
- What is your time frame?
- What are you going to be using this product for?

A Black Belt in Listening

As you have seen, the best way to get someone talking is to ask questions. But the primary focus is to get information, so you want the customer to do at least eighty percent of the talking. That means you'll have to do eighty percent of the listening.

All of us, at one time or another, have "drifted off" while someone was talking to us. The person is busy telling us something that he feels is important, and we are, mentally at least, somewhere else, lost in our own thoughts.

Have you ever wondered why that happens? There is actually a good reason. The average person can understand up to 600 spoken words per minute. Most people, however, only speak about 160 words per minute. That 440-word differential between what you can understand and what is being said creates the opportunity for the mind to be distracted by its own internal workings.

One moment, you're listening; the next, a thought pops up about your plans for the evening. The next thing you know, you're paying more attention to the chatter from your mind than to the words from the speaker.

But good listening has several benefits. First it forces people to focus attentively on others. Second, it avoids misunderstandings. Third, it tends to open people up, to get them to say more. Fortunately for anyone who wants to be a success both in the service business and in life, listening is a skill that can be learned. And the expertise with which you do it can be improved.

Here are some principles of listening that will serve you well:

1. Tune the world out and the person in.

2. Clear your mind of all thoughts except what the person is saying.

3. Be conscious of the person's nonverbal communication and body language.

4. Maintain strong eye contact.

5. Demonstrate encouraging body language.

6. Avoid interrupting.

7. Periodically summarize what the person is saying.

8. If necessary, write down notes.

9. Remain friendly at all times.

10. Practice on your family and friends.

World-class listening requires patience. Tell yourself to "kick back" (mentally, not physically) and hear the other person out. You may be distracted by environmental noise and activity; if that happens, try moving to a quieter spot where you can concentrate fully on what is being said. You might also be distracted by your own brain formulating what you want to say next (so much so, in fact, that you fail to hear completely what the other person has said). When that happens, it can be useful to simply jot a word or two on a piece of paper as a reminder of what you want to say, then return to listening with full attention.

Step Three—Understand (And Make Sure You Do)

After you have listened, make sure you understand what the customer has said to you by repeating it back to him. "Mr. Jones, let me make sure that I've got this straight. You want me to close your passbook savings account, deposit half the money in a money market account and the other half in a five-year CD. Is that correct?" Then make sure that Mr. Jones confirms you are on track.

The Silent Language of Communication

When we communicate, words are only part of the story. In fact, experts estimate that as much as ninety-three percent of communication is nonverbal—expressed through the tone of voice, eye movement, posture, hand gestures and facial expressions.

Almost everyone has had the experience of hearing a store clerk saying something like, "Have a nice day." That certainly is a friendly thing to say, and not a bad way to end the transaction. But what if the clerk delivered the remark in a completely monotone voice and was turned away from you? What did that communicate? Answer: "I'm completely bored with my job, and I don't care about you or your business."

If you want your nonverbal communication to be as positive as the words you say, try doing the following:

- Face the customer
- Make eye contact
- Adopt a relaxed posture
- Maintain a pleasant tone in your voice
- Smile
- Be sincerely interested in communicating with your customer

Anyone who has been in business for any length of time can tell you that there are moments when it is tough, and sometimes it can be difficult to maintain a positive attitude. But what if someone were to tell you, "During the next thirty days, a man or woman will come to you for service, and based on the quality of that service and your attitude, you may be offered a promotion or an exciting new job." That would change your outlook, wouldn't it?

Step Four: Take Action (Or At Least Commit to Take Action)

Once you fully understand what the customer needs or wants, it's time to take action. You've asked you questions and listened, and you and the customer have interacted and agreed on a course of action. Now is the time for you to commit to doing something (even if it means saying you can't do anything to help) to execute a definable, measurable action. Sometimes the action occurs face to face, and sometimes it happens over the phone, through e-mail or by fax. Sometimes the move to action happens immediately, or perhaps not for weeks. No matter what the circumstances, such moments of action occur hundreds of millions of times each day in the business world:

- I'll get you the burger with no pickle.
- I'll send you the loan papers.
- I'll put the new tires on your car and have it ready by 3 p.m.
- I'll order the parts for your lawn tractor and call you when they have arrived.

Once you have made a commitment, make sure that you keep it. Take ownership and responsibility for the process. Keeping commitments builds trust with customers, and with trust comes a preference for doing business with you. In addition, keeping commitments makes people want to refer their friends and business associates to you because you are someone who can be counted on to get the job done.

We all know, however, that things can and do go wrong. When that happens, sometimes commitments cannot be kept. As soon as you have the first indication that there might be a problem, inform the customer. "Mr. Jones, I'm sorry, but we're having trouble locating tires in the correct size for you car. I will call you by two o'clock if we need to special order them. I don't want you waiting while we try to locate tires."

Most people will be very understanding if you inform them very early that there is a potential problem and that you are working to correct it. A major exception to this rule would be if you had known for two weeks that you needed to order Mr. Jones's tires but waited until the day of the appointment to try to find them.

Step Five: Follow Up for Solid Gold Satisfaction

The area where many businesses drop the ball is in customer follow-up. A formal follow-up program drives home the point with customers that you value their business and care about their satisfaction. Also, if you feel that your credibility or trust has been damaged with a customer, the follow-up can begin to repair the relationship. It can also help you spot problems, if any, in how service is being provided.

The follow-up can be a letter, a fax, an e-mail or a phone call (or, in rare cases, a personal visit), but it should be done within a five-day period.

Whoever does the follow-up should be armed with the information about the customer's case, so that he can personalize the call. "Mr. Smith, I'm calling for Elliott Motors. Last week we put new brakes on your Buick, and I just wanted to follow up to make sure everything is performing satisfactorily." Then you can roll into the other questions that you might want to ask, such as, "Were the service personnel courteous?" or "Was your service completed at the promised time?"

It is also helpful if the follow-up call reiterates any promise that was made. "I see that we are ordering parts for your exhaust system, and we will be sure to give you a call as soon as they come in." This will strengthen the relationship with your customers and solidify the bond between you.

On other hand, it can be very annoying to receive a follow-up call from someone who is clearly following a canned script and has no clue about who you are or what interaction you may have had with the company. It sends the message, "We care about service, but we don't care about you personally."

The bottom line is that if you are going to make the effort to follow up with your customers, do it right so they know that you care.

Understanding Different Communication Styles

For those who wish to take their communications to the next level of power and effectiveness and for those who have been frustrated by communications that have apparently gone unheeded, I'll share with you an often-ignored secret.

To maximize the effectiveness of communications, the behavior style of the people you are trying to communicate with must be considered. Why? Because, depending upon their style, people want to be communicated with in specific ways. If you understand this and communicate in a way that is appropriate to the style, you speed up communications and make it more efficient. In some situations, if you don't recognize the style and act accordingly, you can hopelessly bog down the entire process. And in the worst case scenario, you can actually anger people and alienate them by communicating in a style that doesn't fit their needs.

There are four different behavior styles:

1. Persuader

2. Supporter

3. Controller

4. Analyzer

Each behavior style has its own characteristics and its own communications needs and preferences. Most people are not just one style. They are usually a combination of two (and sometimes more) personality types, with one playing the dominant role. In addition, the predominant behavior style may change depending upon the situation.

Recognizing the various behavior styles requires that you tune in to the verbal and non-verbal signals that the person is giving you. Once you understand and respond to the style that is being presented to you by an individual, you can customize your communications for far greater effectiveness.

Let's take a look at the different behavior styles and see what makes them tick.

The Persuader Behavior Style

Persuaders have a high degree of assertiveness and view the world in a positive light. They are generally upbeat, enthusiastic, have high energy and prefer to work with others. Persuaders are very attentive to how they are perceived. Words that describe this behavior style are:

*   Outgoing
*   Enthusiastic
*   Persuasive
*   Humorous
*   Lively

Key Persuader Behaviors:

*   Uses rapid hand and arm gestures
*   Speaks quickly with lots of animation and inflection
*   Has a wide range of facial expressions

- Uses language that is persuasive

You'll notice that Persuaders are friendly and outgoing. They like to engage in dialogue, to interact with people.

Key points for dealing with Persuaders:
- You have to let them talk, because they'll tell you what they want. If you cut them off, they'll perceive it as rude.
- You must have a smile on your face.
- You have to be upbeat.
- You have to focus a lot of attention on them, not so much on the product itself.

The challenge with Persuaders is to get them to the point, but you can do that by focusing on the individual person and using that to drive the discussion of the product.

Note that the Persuader will still want to interact with you and talk even after the sale has been completed. You need to end the interaction in a friendly way that encourages the Persuader to come back so that you can serve him or her again.

People you may recognize with the Persuader Behavior Style:
- Bette Midler
- Arnold Schwarzenegger
- Oprah Winfrey
- Robin Williams

The Supporter Behavior Style

A person with Supporter behavior has a low degree of assertiveness and a high degree of emotional expression. People with this style are responsive and friendly but are not necessarily forceful or direct. They are very interested in and good at building and nurturing relationships. They are attentive listeners.

Statistics reveal that forty-two percent of the population falls into this category. So when in doubt, it doesn't hurt to approach a customer as if he or she were a Supporter. You have a reasonable chance of being right, and you probably won't annoy the other behavior styles. You can adjust your style as you read the signals more accurately. Words that describe this style include:
- Cooperative

- Friendly
- Patient
- Relaxed.

Key Supporter Behaviors:
- Has a friendly facial expression
- Makes frequent eye contact
- Uses non-aggressive, non-dramatic gestures
- Speaks slowly and in soft tones
- Use language that is supportive and encouraging

Since Supporters are not risk takers, they are likely to focus on issues such as quality, warranty, the ability to get service and so forth.

Key points for dealing with Supporters:
- You have to be encouraging; being aggressive is a big turn-off for them.
- You have to treat them well; they are very loyal if you do so.
- You have to have tremendous patience; they are very detail oriented.

People you may recognize that exhibit or exhibited the Supporter Behavior Style:
- Mother Theresa
- Tom Brokaw
- Gandhi
- Michael J. Fox

The Controller Behavior Style

These people have a high degree of assertiveness and a low degree of emotional expression. They know where they want to go and how they are going to get there. They are good at managing tasks and are results oriented. Controllers like competition (especially when they win.) Words that describe this style include:
- Decisive
- Independent
- Efficient
- Intense
- Deliberating

- Achieving

Key Controller Behaviors:
- Makes direct eye contact
- Moves quickly and with purpose
- Speaks forcefully and at a fast pace
- Uses direct, bottom-line language
- Has symbols of achievement displayed in his or her office

Controllers are extremely assertive. They want everything done yesterday and are very results-oriented.

Key points for dealing with Controllers:
- You have to be direct.
- You need to maintain eye contact.
- You have to get to the point.
- You have to be fast paced.

People you may recognize with the Controller Behavior Style:
- Ross Perot
- Jack Welsh
- Fidel Castro
- Barbara Walters

The Analyzer Behavior Style
Analyzers have a low degree of assertiveness and a low degree of emotional expression. They focus on facts more than feelings. They evaluate situations objectively and gather lots of data before making a decision. They prefer an organized work environment where they know exactly what is expected of them. Words that describe this style include:
- Serious
- Well organized
- Systematic
- Logical
- Factual
- Reserved

Key Analyzer Behaviors:
- Shows little facial expression
- Has controlled body language
- Has little vocal inflection and may tend toward monotone
- Uses language that is precise and focuses on specific details

Key points for dealing with Analyzers:
- You have to be fact specific.
- You have to get to the point, using as few words as possible to express it.
- You have to realize that Analyzers may know more about the product than you do; don't try to snow them.
- You may have to show results by demonstrating the product.
- You have to realize that Analyzers are not gregarious and are not taken in by charm.

A Mixture of Styles

As I mentioned earlier, it's important to realize that most people are not just one style. They are usually a combination of two or more personality types with one emerging as more dominant than the others. The most common style combinations are:
- Controller/ Persuader
- Persuader/ Supporter
- Supporter/ Analyzer

In addition, the predominant behavior style may change, depending upon the situation. For example, when a Controller/Persuader is looking at a product that is within his or her field of expertise—computers, for example—the Controller style will be most visible. But if someone with this same style combination is in "unknown waters"—baby furniture, perhaps—the Persuader behavior may be more evident. What's important is to understand and respond to the behavior style that is being presented to you at that moment.

Remember, by analyzing your customers' behavior styles, you can determine the best way to present your product or service to them and sell them the way they want to be sold. If you respond appropriately, you provide service faster, more efficiently and more pleasantly.

Sender and Receiver

When it comes to dealing with the different behavior styles, it is a good idea to understand what style you are and to realize that, based on your style, you may be on the uncomfortable receiving end of some communications.

For example, let's say you are an Analyzer. You like detail, and you like to think things through. Now let's suppose that your boss is a Controller. One day, he tears into your office and delivers some rapid-fire information—ba-da-bing, ba-da-boom—and he's all set to race off to the next crisis. You, on the other hand, would like more information.

A really smart boss would realize in the first place that you are an Analyzer and deal with you accordingly. In your case, however, the overwhelming odds are that you will not be able to change the behavior of this Controller boss. You can, however, adapt in a way that makes sense. Before your boss disappears, you could ask, "Where can I get more information if I need it?"

The bottom line: remember that you have a style, too, when you are dealing with others, and do your best to adjust accordingly.

When and Where to Communicate

All too often, people do everything right when it comes to communications—except for choosing the right time and place.

The best principle to apply is the Golden Rule: treat others as you would like to be treated. So if you enter a colleague's office and see her deeply involved in some complex problem, ask if it is a good time for an interruption. If your manager spends the first two hours of every Monday getting squared away for the upcoming week, it would be a good idea to save non-urgent communications until later.

If you want to ask an associate to carefully consider something, perhaps the best time to present the request would be on a Friday afternoon, so that he or she can think about it over the weekend.

If you have bad news, criticism or embarrassing information to communicate, do it in private. If, however, you are in the enviable position of delivering high praise to someone you work with, feel free to do so in public!

In communications, as in so much of life, a little bit of consideration can go a long way. Therefore, remember the six "P"s: Proper Prior Planning Prevents Poor Performance.

Game, Set, and Match

When communications don't go well, it's often because one or more of the basics are being ignored. It's a good idea to give yourself an "instant checkup" to make sure you observing them:

- Engage
- Listen
- Understand
- Take action
- Follow up

Finally, make a note to yourself on your appointment calendar to periodically review the different behavior styles and the best ways of responding to them. You'll find it will pay handsome rewards when it comes to the power and effectiveness of your communications.

John W. Connors

 John is a principle of Partners & Associates a firm that is committed to helping organizations develop strong relationships through customized sales, sales coaching and client service programs that truly "value" the client. John's outstanding presentation and facilitation skills, along with highly interactive sessions has inspired thousands of sales and client service professionals in a wide variety of industries including banking, retail, chemical, energy services and telecommunications companies. John is also the author of two other very exiting books called *Everybody Sells* and *Client Excellence*.

John W. Connors
1 Devonshire Ln.
Ballston Lake, NY 12019
(518) 399-5872
Fax: (518) 399-0972
E-mail: partners@nycap.rr.com

Jon J. Cooper

Jon began his career as an auditor for KPMG after graduating from Fordham University in 1974. After working there for 2 years, he decided to become a banker and has remained in that field for 26 years. Initially, Jon worked for a small community bank which was later acquired by Fleet Bank. While at Fleet, Jon became a Senior Vice-President and worked for the company for over 15 years. During his tenure at Fleet, he had as his main responsibility the management of Fleet's Consumer banking franchise for the Western New York Area. As such, he had direct responsibility for the sales production of over 90 branch offices. Learning to motivate people, developing winning sales techniques, and most importantly effective communication strategies, were key in making his region one of the top producing in the Fleet franchise. Since 1997, Jon has been the President & CEO of the Wyoming County Bank and a Senior Vice President of Financial Institutions, a publicly traded 2 billion dollar inctitution. Undor Jon'o lcadcrohip, thc bonk hao morc than doubled in size growing from 280 million to the present 630 million. In addition, net income has more than doubled, all being accomplished through internal growth in existing markets. With a passion for client excellence Jon has built an effective team through effective communication and leadership strategies.

Jon J. Cooper
3244 Dick Road
Warsaw , New York 14569
Office: (585) 786-4301
Home: (585) 786-3519
Mobile: (585) 739-3172
Fax: (585) 786-2024

Chapter 7

Discovering & Developing Your Own Communication Style

Donna Baylor

Have you ever listened to the words of the 1960s hit, "(I Can't Get No) Satisfaction" by The Rolling Stones? Do you suppose they were referring to communication? Getting "no satisfaction" from communication is something we all can relate to at one time or another. Sometimes our efforts to communicate are successful—and sometimes they're not.

Some people, no matter how you communicate with them, just don't seem to get it. It's as though they are from another planet and don't understand your language![1] Statistics show that eighty-two percent of all business problems can be traced directly to poor communication. And considering that people tend to take better care of their businesses than they do their personal lives, the actual percentage could be as high as ninety or one hundred percent! Take a look at your interaction with others—not just the ones who are easy to communicate and interact with but the ones who are not. Be brutally honest with yourself. How's it going?

Helen Keller wrote, "Life is either a daring adventure or nothing at all." Communicating is, indeed, a "daring adventure." Possessing powerful communication skills involves respecting yourself and the people with

---

[1] I'm not referring to Mars/Venus differences here.

whom you interact. It means watching the tone of your voice and your body language as well as choosing words that convey an easily understood message.

Throughout this chapter you will learn that it is the responsibility of the person doing the communicating to make sure that the message is understood. That is what it means to have a powerful communication style, whether the medium is written or verbal. Your style also includes listening and understanding what the other person means, not just what you think he means. Powerful communication calls for suspending judgment and asking clarifying questions.

The benefits of developing a powerful communication style include less friction, less stress and less confusion. Less time will be wasted because both parties to the communication will know what is expected of them. That increases the chances that effective communication will take place and that both sides will get it right the first time.

As you go through the chapters of this book, you are essentially sitting down with some very dynamic communicators who are sharing not just information but their personal experiences; you can even consider us your mentors. While I'm sure you'll come across some concepts that you've heard about or read before, look for subtle differences this time around. It may be that you're ready for (or more open to) this information now. It may be that the ideas are worded differently than you've heard before. Or it might simply be that at this point in your life, you've had an experience that has given you a reference point you didn't have before. Whatever your reasons, the point is that you get it now and the connection has been made. So I encourage you to look for information you're ready to *use*.

To get the maximum benefit from this chapter, you must become a participant in the process. There is an Oriental proverb that says: "Tell me, I hear. Show me, I learn. Involve me, I understand." I encourage you to keep several pencils and a notebook available as you read so you can record any memorable thoughts, ideas or "Ah-ha!" moments that you may have. And I promise—you will have some.

Talking To Yourself Again?

Before you can develop your communication style, you first have to assess the "materials" you already have on hand; that is, what you are currently doing that works and doesn't work. This may take some commitment, but it will be well worth the effort. You should also realize that discovering your communication style is like reading a map. A road map can show several ways to get from where you are to where you want to be; however, it is important to know where you *actually* are—not just where you *think* you are or where you *hope* you are.

Let's begin by focusing on the most important communication you will ever have in your entire life—the conscious and subconscious conversations you have with yourself. Did you know that each minute, an average of 15,000 words are going through your head and that each thought is either positive or negative? If that's the case, which thoughts do you think benefit you more? The positive ones, of course! But unfortunately, our world is such a negative place (as are our minds, in many cases). You and I have been bombarded with negative messages from the outside world throughout our entire lives. And the sad truth is that we cannot afford to think them, much less say them out loud!

When I first became a hypnotist in 1986, I learned that anything we think or say about ourselves is taken into the brain as programming. Much like a computer, the brain accepts the information put into it without judging the content or differentiating between real or imagined. It subconsciously accepts the input and goes about transforming thought into reality. Therefore, when setting any type of goals, the secret is for us to talk to ourselves as though those goals are already accomplished. Our subconscious "genie," then, starts to make them come true.

When I was a child, my mom didn't believe me when I said there was a monster under my bed. She would look for it and never see it, of course, so she didn't understand how I could be afraid of something I couldn't see.

But I wasn't operating under my mom's belief system; I was operating under mine. And I believed the monster was there. I didn't have to see it physically; I saw it in my imagination—in my mind. The physical reaction I experienced—pounding heartbeat, shortness of breath, shaking in terror and afraid to stick my feet out from under the covers—was as real as real could be. To me, it was truth.

How the brain operates doesn't change when you become an adult. Our monsters may be different, but if you believe they're there (stopping you from accomplishing what you want to accomplish), your dominant thoughts will become your reality.

Your brain doesn't look at each item and say, "That idea is outmoded," or "I am too old for this thought" or "I don't accepting that belief." If you say, "I'm no good at remembering names," what do you think that little operator's manual in your head will say when you try to remember a name? It will say something like, "Sorry! But it says here on all these pages of programming you've given me that I can't remember names."

Your inner dialogue will make or break you. Do any of these sound familiar?

"I am so stupid."
"I'm so clumsy!"
"I could never do that."
"How dumb can I be?"
"I'm too _____ to be able to do that."

Negative self-talk is the most damaging thing to which you can subject yourself. It destroys healthy self-esteem, which is the building block of all success. The dictionary defines the verb "esteem" as: "To value highly, to have great respect for, to hold in high regard." To have healthy self-esteem is to value and respect yourself and to hold yourself in high regard.

The good news is that you have a choice when it comes to what you tell yourself! To communicate successfully with others, start by communicating effectively and positively with yourself. The Bible says, "Ask and you shall receive." So stop asking for things that limit you, and you will reach more goals and communicate with positive results.

Jack Canfield, co-author of *Chicken Soup For The Soul*TM, teaches that only one adult out of three has high self-esteem. One major way to build and maintain self-esteem is through positive self-talk. Be aware of what you say to yourself. Stop whenever you catch yourself saying negative things, even if you're in the middle of a word. If the message is negative, then replace it with a positive phrase.

The more you are aware of what you say and the more you restate the negative in a positive way, the more likely you are to repeat the behavior. Soon it will become a habit. It takes twenty-one consecutive days and consistent use to break an old habit or make a new one. It takes *consistency*.

Remember, though, that if you break a bad habit and don't replace it with something positive, your brain will sense a void that, sooner or later, will be filled by the old, bad habit. The mind hates voids, so be sure to change your routine and fill that space by replacing the unproductive habit with a new one that will be more useful for you.

As parents, it sometimes seems we repeat ourselves again and again before our children pay attention to us. There's a reason for this. According to statistics, the brain must hear something six times before it acknowledges or accepts the message. This means that you only have to say or think a negative thought a few times before your personal genie says, "Your wish is my command!" Remember, your mind doesn't differentiate between what's real or what's imagined; it just accepts your dominant thoughts. So why not be in charge of the dominant thoughts you send to your brain?

Forming and repeating positive affirmations and self-talk is an important part of success. Use your imagination in a positive way.[2] Make your mind a partner in your success. If you do slip and say something negative about yourself, immediately rephrase it in a positive way. For example, rephrase, "I'm stupid" as "I learned how *not* to do that. Now I'll look for another way to do it better." Or "I am so clumsy" becomes, "I am a graceful person." (Grace is not a gender issue, guys. Don't be afraid of being graceful. Look at Fred Astaire, Patrick Swayze, Tiger Woods, Arnold Palmer and Wayne Gretsky.)

I happen to be a big fan of *Star Trek: The Next Generation*. I love it when Captain Picard tell his first officer, "Make it so!" There's no indecision, no wishy-washiness. Picard is focused on the outcome, period! Likewise, you should state your intentions not only in the positive but in the present: "I do," "I am," "I have." Our minds don't have a sense of time. Everything happens in the now—you breathe now, you think now, your heart beats now.

Examples:

"I treat everyone, including myself, with respect."
"I am a successful communicator."
"I love to communicate clearly."
"I communicate in positive ways."
"I am a positive person."
"I am successful."

---

[2] Mind is a function of your brain. Imagination is a function of your mind.

While this idea is in front of you, take a minute and write three positive affirmations about yourself. Affirmations are powerful and personal, so write your own, using mine only if they would truly apply to you as well.

How We Communicate

Now that you've built a foundation for communicating with yourself in positive ways, let's take a look at communicating with other people.

We all want to know, WIIFM? (What's in it for me?) Communication is about getting something. It could be a job, a raise, good grades, information, a sale, love, affection, a smile, a hug or even a fish! If you aren't getting what you want, then you aren't doing something right.

You actually started communicating before you were born. In the womb, you communicated with body language. A well-placed elbow in your mother's ribs let her know you weren't happy with the position she was in. You learned quickly that your body language was either rewarded with attention and a reaction (mom repositions herself) or it was not.

Once you entered the world, you became vocal in your communication. A cry in the middle of the day or night usually got you something. You learned quickly that your vocal actions were either rewarded with attention and a reaction (feeding, changing, holding) or they were not.

As you grew, a new way to communicate was added—language. You learned to use the words that you heard people around you use. You learned quickly that those words were either rewarded with attention and reaction (you got acknowledgement or what you wanted) or they were not.

These three ways that you learned to communicate are still with you today. They determine your communication patterns as well as how you receive all of your communications.

Body language accounts for about fifty-five percent of how we say something. It is so powerful, it comes across in all of our communications, whether by telephone, the Internet or the written word. Body language is almost eight times more powerful than words alone. Even animals are sensitive to our body language.

Vocals account for thirty-eight percent of the message others pick up from you. The tone and the pitch of your voice are more than five times powerful than the words you say. This adds credibility to the old saying, "It's not what you say but how you say it."

Words account for only seven percent of the message others receive from you, but it's important that we choose them carefully nonetheless. The average American communicates only on a 9th grade level. By making it easy for people understand your meaning, you get more of what you want and foster better relationships at the same time.

When a communications gap exists, you can help close it by owning up to the fact that the way in which you communicate may be part of the problem. Let's take a closer look at the way you communicate and the words you use in the process.

Which do you prefer?

- Auditory phrases: "I hear what you're saying."
- Visual phrases: "I see what you mean."
- Kinetic phrases: "I understand how you feel."

These preferences can give others clues about your communication style as well as give you clues about others' styles. There is no right or wrong preference, however. You communicate your values to others every time you interact. Recognizing and using other people's preferences reduces differences and makes communication easier. You can validate others by showing you are listening, which lets them know that they are worthwhile.

Attitude Problems

How you feel about the world, your job, the people you interact with and yourself becomes your attitude. My definition of attitude is, "An outward projection of an inward perception." This is important because *how* you see things inwardly determines the choices you make outwardly and, consequently, how you behave.

Look at the attitudes you project by your actions:

- Passive actions say, "I have no rights. You have them all."
- Aggressive actions say, "You have no rights. I have them all."
- Assertive actions say, "You have rights, I have rights, and they are equally important; however your rights end where my nose begins."
- Passive-aggressive actions say, "Don't get mad, get even."

It is easy to see the differences between passive and aggressive behaviors or passive and assertive behaviors. It is more difficult, however, to understand the differences between assertive and aggressive behaviors. I believe that is because our mental filtering systems determine how we were conditioned to see those differences. All of us have these filtering systems that put words, meaning and actions together in a way that makes sense to us.

Remember that your attitude is reflected through body language, vocals and words and subsequently processed through the receiver's filtering system. For example, the following are my perceptions of body language, vocals and words, as seen through my own personal filtering system:

Passive body language: slumps shoulders, avoids direct eye contact, shuffles feet, avoids people, wimpy hand shake or no handshake at all, timid, tearful or sad

- Passive tone: soft, tentative, silent, inappropriately gentle
- Passive words: can't, yes, no, none
- Aggressive body language: points fingers, invades personal space head first, clenches hand, tightens muscles, frowns, snarls, furrows brow
- Aggressive tone of voice: loud, angry, demanding, intimidating
- Aggressive words: you, no, can't, mine, me, blame, fault
- Assertive body language: upright, at ease, smiles, comfortable
- Assertive tone: firm, clear, even, professional, self-confident
- Assertive words: solutions, you, us, we, I, win-win.

Assertiveness respects the needs of all individuals and remains balanced.

Is Anybody Listening?

Just as speaking is a major part of one's communication style, so is listening. When someone speaks to you, how well do you listen? Do you simply wait for the other person to stop talking so you can start? Are you an "empathetic" listener or an "autobiographical" listener?

Empathetic people listen with the express intent of finding out what the other person is talking about. They want to understand the other's point of view and feelings—not necessarily to agree with it.

Autobiographical people listen for a common word that they can turn around and relate to themselves. They seem to take over conversations.

Look at the following scenario:

After taking a two-week vacation, you go back to the office with your Mickey Mouse ears, a nice tan and a big smile. A co-worker says, "Hey, I haven't seen you in weeks! Where have you been?" You smile, point to the black ears on you head and say, "I've been on vacation!" She says, "Vacation?! Sounds great! Where did you go? Tell me about what you did. Did you have fun? What did you enjoy most?"

This is an empathetic listener. She asks mostly open-ended questions to get more information and to find out *your* view of your vacation.

Now let's say you walk into another department, where someone says, "Hey, where have you been?" You say, "I've been on vacation!" They reply, "Vacation!? I can't tell you the last time I was on vacation." You continue, saying, "Yeah, took the family. We really enjoyed ourselves." Now the co-worker replies, "You took your family? What kind of vacation is that? I hate taking my family—everyone arguing about where they want to go and whining about..."

This is an example of an autobiographical listener. This person heard the word "vacation," and you were pushed out of the conversation.

I believe there is also a third type of listening that combines the two styles—empathic listeners who periodically refer to their own experiences to reduce differences. This often builds rapport by relating similar experiences. For example:

> "Vacation? Where'd you go? Florida? Hey, I've been there. You look like you had a great time. I stayed with my sister; where'd you stay? That sounds great. One of the things I liked was the..."

You get the point. Empathic and combination listeners are open listeners, and others welcome a conversation with them because it is a give-and-take situation. Autobiographical listeners make most people uncomfortable. Others try to avoid them, or they take them only in small doses.

So which type are you? Be honest! To become a better listener, ask more questions and really listen to the answers. Like my grandfather always used to say, "God gives you two ears and one mouth for a reason—so that you listen twice as much as you talk." Listening is a great way to learn about the people in your life—at work, at home and socially. It is also a great way to tell the other person you value him or her. The people you like to be around are the ones who validate you and make you feel worthwhile by listening to what you say. Therefore, others will want you around when you make them feel worthwhile by listening to them.

Say What?

As I mentioned earlier, everything we do, see and think goes through a mental filtering system. But each person's system is different. Anyone who has ever done much traveling, knows that. In our country alone, words and phrases mean different things in different places. Make it part of your style to ask questions to make sure that your words and the other person's words have the same meaning. Often we can fine tune our understanding by questioning things we think we understand.

For example, I'm from Michigan, and when you want a soft drink back home, you ask for a "pop." Several years ago, I visited a friend in Austin, Texas. At dinner one evening, the waiter asked me what I wanted to drink. I said, "I'd like a pop," expecting him to ask what kind. Instead, he said in a rather chilly voice, "You mean a soda." I replied, "No, I'd like a pop," Again came his chilly, "You mean, a soda." I was getting upset at the tone of his voice and his attitude. You see, in Michigan a "soda" is ice cream, carbonated water and flavored syrup. "No," I stressed. "I want a pop. I want a Coke™." Before I could say any more, my friend patted my hand and said, "Donna, down here, they call it a soda."

That was a big lesson to me, and let it be a lesson to you, also. Make sure your words mean the same to the people with whom you are speaking as they do to you.

What's Your Style?

Before you can develop your communication style, you need to first figure out what type of communicator you are. The bottom line is that each of us has a different style, which means that we have preferred ways of processing information and conveying messages to other people. Some people require more information while others need only a brief overview (with the ability to get more details as they need them). Some need just the highlights; some need firm direction; others need no direction at all. It all boils down to the old saying, "different strokes for different folks."

Do you know your communication style? If not, I encourage you to learn what it is. Many different programs and books will help you discover which style, or type, you are, including the DiSC profile, the Meyer-Briggs Type Indicator and Tony Alessandra's Relationship Strategies.[3] You could read *The Birth Order Book*, by Kevin Lehman or Ron Willingham's book, *Hey, I'm The Customer*, which talks about how each communication style prefers to give and receive customer service. Each of these resources, as well as many others I haven't mentioned, will give you some insights into the type of communicator you are and how you interact with others.

Let's look at how communication styles work. Picture yourself interacting with someone you like—your best friend, spouse or co-worker—in a stressful situation. How are you speaking to this person? Are you clear and concise, asking for feedback with open-ended questions?[4] Think about your tone of voice. Is it harsh, soft, high-pitched, forceful, threatening, loving, considerate or silent? What about your words? Are they over the head of the person you are speaking with? Or are they kind, cruel, slang, easily understood? Are you speaking too fast, too slow, or are you matching the speed of your words to the speed of the other person? (People speak at the same rate they listen, which means that fast talkers are also fast listeners and that slow talkers are slow listeners. This is important to keep in mind when you want to get your ideas across.)

For example, I like to communicate face-to-face and spend time chitchatting before I get to work. And I don't like to work alone. I meet others easily, and as a result, I know a lot of people. I hate details (giving and getting), like to figure things out myself and am great at motivating others and getting them involved in whatever I'm excited about. I hate rules and think of them as a starting point for change. I can come up with lots of ways to do something in a new way. I am a true believer in working smarter not harder. My desk is messy, but I know where things are. Hey, it works for me!

Some of you can relate to what I just described while some of you are frowning because I just described your worst nightmare. If that's true, you are probably very organized. "A place for everything and everything in its

---

[3] For recommended books, tapes and classes, see the resources listed at the end of this chapter.

[4] Open-ended questions cannot be answered with a single word, a grunt or a nod. They require a response of more than one word and usually begin with Who, What, When, Where, Why or How.

place," may be your motto. You love details and rules because they give your life and/or job structure and foundation. You might prefer your information in writing, with very little, if any, personal or emotional input to cloud the issues. You might be task-focused; you have a job to do, and getting it done (and done right) means a great deal to you, even if it means taking a little longer to do it. Your desk is organized, and you can quickly access memos that are older than dirt; you keep them because you never know when you might need to refer to them later.

So let's examine how you prefer to communicate with others. In this example, we'll deal with people who irritate you (because we don't really need to worry about those with whom you deal well). Specifically what about these people irritates you? Take a step back and look at it objectively. At first, it may be frustrating to even think of leaving your comfort zone, but it's well worth the effort.

Use the following exercise to help you understand your communication style:

On a piece of paper, draw two lines. The first line should be horizontal, about two inches from the top of the page. Write your name above that line. The second line should run vertically, starting just under the horizontal line and dividing the page into two sections. This is a basic "T" chart. (By the way, did you wait for me to finish the instructions before you drew the lines, or did you jump to a conclusion and then read the directions to see if you guessed right? In either case, your choice says something about you!)[5]

List your strengths on the left side of the chart and your weaknesses on the right. Be honest. And don't ask others for their opinions as this is based on your view of yourself. List a minimum of three items on each side.

Example:

STRENGTHS	WEAKNESSES
Great at getting projects up and running	Not good at following through

---

[5] Every action is a mirror that reflects your style for other people to see.

Strengths and weakness can often be similar. Do you see any similarities in yours? I learned from one of my earliest mentors,[6] that a person's greatest strengths, taken to the extreme, can also become his or her greatest weaknesses.

For example:

- "Fiercely loyal" may translate to, "Stays in jobs and relationships longer than necessary"
- "Follows all the rules and regulations" may translate to, "Can't think or act outside the box"
- "Takes charge and gets things done" may translate to, "Bossy and insensitive; a bully"
- "Gets along with everyone" may translate to, "Unable to make a decision; a 'yes' person, a doormat, a victim"
- "Risk taker; makes quick decisions" may translate to, "Unpredictable"

Now make another "T" chart on a separate piece of paper and think about how people speak to and interact with you. First, think about the communication qualities you don't like—the things that tick you off, make you dig in your heels or make the hair stand up on the back of your neck—in other words, the things that don't work for you. List these on the left side of your "T" chart. Be honest. There's no one here but you and me, and I'm not going to tell (although you should).[7]

Example: "I dig in my heels, clench my fists and grit my teeth when people..."

- Talk to me in a condescending tone
- Don't give me all the information
- Get overly emotional
- Tell me their problems
- Aren't friendly
- Are overly demanding
- Don't socialize before telling me to do something

---

[6] Shirley Schmidt, national marketing and sales director, Entertainment Publications
[7] More about that later.

On the right side of the chart, list the things that do work for you and make you excited and/or eager to do something for someone. In other words, list the ways that you like to be treated.

Example: "I am so easy to get along with when people..."

- Treat me with respect
- Listen to me
- Ask for my opinion or thoughts
- Give me enough details
- Give me a brief overview of the project
- Give me deadlines
- Ask me about my personal life

This information should provide you with a reality check. Once you see these things written down, you should be able to acknowledge that there are different ways to communicate with and motivate you. It's a step toward understanding your personal style. And that's okay because you are not generic; you are unique. It is okay to be who you are. In fact, if you are willing to accept the consequences of *not* adapting, that's okay, too.

But realizing that each person you communicate with is unique and that he or she is also okay allows you to focus on adapting to each other instead of trying to change one another. So let's put the shoe on the other foot. Think about a situation in which you communicated something to someone and the result was less than successful. Write it down if that helps you examine the situation objectively. Be thorough, and include what you said as well as how you said it. Note your tone of voice and body language. Were you clear, or did you expect the other person (or people) to fill in the blanks when you didn't give them all the information they needed to accomplish what you wanted? How do you know? If it wasn't that, why do you think your communication was unsuccessful?

When you develop the ability to adapt to another person's style of communication, you'll find that all the pieces of the puzzle will come together. Take another look at the "T" chart where you noted the communication methods that work and don't work for you. Most people communicate the same way they prefer to receive information. "Doing unto others," of course, is the Golden Rule. But to communicate successfully, try the Platinum Rule: "Do unto others as *they want* to be done unto." In other words, give them information in the manner *they* need or want it. (And when you keep in mind the concept of WIIFM—

What's in it for me?—it is then easier for you to give the other person what he/she wants while also asking for what you want. This goes right along with my philosophy of working smarter not harder.)

While it is the responsibility of the person doing the communicating to make sure the message is understood, few people follow that rule. Or maybe most people know the rule but just don't care. Some people actually gain a sense of control by making others guess (and fail) about the meaning of their message. You've probably met or even worked for people like that. They make it difficult to communicate and work with them. Remember that it is okay to ask clarifying questions to help you understand what they mean.

Just as it is best to convey information the way others prefer, you can also enhance communications by letting others know how you like to receive information. How do you let others know the best ways to communicate with you? When you argue, pout, hold a grudge, dig in your heels, swear, argue, ignore or give them the silent treatment, does that usually work? What if you smile, ask questions, nod and encourage them by responding positively? How can anyone communicate effectively with you if you don't send out signals or give examples of what works?

Communicate Proactively To Resolve Conflict

Being proactive means foreseeing possible problems, then communicating and acting in a preventive way. When people are proactive in their communications, they are able to respond in appropriate ways—thinking about and choosing their words before speaking. On the other hand, when communication is reactive, our emotions are usually in control. Being reactive means waiting for problems or misunderstandings and only responding to them when they occur. Often, the results of reactive communication lead to confusion and/or conflict.

Resolving conflict in an assertive manner requires problem-solving skills. To quote Dr. Stephen Covey, "Seek first to understand then to be understood" truly applies here. During a conflict, establish the facts and feelings of the situation and find areas of agreement. Discover what the other person's feelings and needs are and how those needs compare with your own. By adopting the proactive approach to conflict and communication, the likelihood of a win-win outcome is increased.

Another part of handling conflict is effectively communicating your feelings and needs. What happens when you speak to someone about your unmet needs? No one likes to be reminded of areas in which they are weak or how they didn't succeed, so your effectiveness in handling this is determined by your approach. Think of it as sharing your needs so that this and future communications between you can go smoother. Success is even more likely when the other person is open to this sharing and the two of you have a successful track record of communication based on mutual trust and respect.

To initiate the proactive approach to any communication—whether at work or at home—find out what the other person needs. What does he or she want to gain from the situation? How strong are his/her feelings about the situation? Then, think about your answers to those same questions. Ask yourself, "What is it I want to accomplish? Is my ego involved? Do I want to show my muscles, or do I want to get something done or get a problem solved?" In other words, think about what your intentions are and the results you want. You can now share your intentions with the other person, provided that the intentions are conducive to a win-win outcome.

Seldom are situations a hundred percent black or white, good or bad, right or wrong. Ask yourself (and the other person) if there are solutions between the extremes that you may not have thought of yet. Discuss them. Look for solutions where both people can save face. Cooperation has long-term benefits. When each side wins (at least in part) both develop a track record that does wonders for future teamwork.

Open dialogue is a requisite of this approach, as are good negotiating skills and the ability and willingness to recognize the other person's basic rights while not neglecting your own. Think of the situation as a problem-solving exercise rather than an interpersonal conflict, and think of the other person as your partner not your opponent.

I believe that personality/style differences are the source of most conflicts. We just don't understand someone who is so different from us—different values, ideas, methods and objectives. But it may be that the two of you have common ends in mind but are just getting there by different means. Don't let your ego get involved. Just because you know you're right and someone disagrees with you, it doesn't mean they're wrong. It often means others just perceive situations and think differently—uniquely. That's the way it is—and the way it is should be.

If all this sounds difficult, refer back to the section on positive self-talk. Use your imagination and visualize yourself doing it. Focus on every detail of constructive behavior, effective communication and positive interaction. The more complete the vision, the sooner the change. Then "just do it." Nike made a fortune with that phrase, so they must know something!

Some final thoughts on conflict resolution:

- Criticism is *not* proactive and will lead to conflict. Feedback and requests are more productive. Criticism does two things: It makes one person feel big and the other feel small. Usually, people do their best at any given time based on their knowledge, skills and frame of mind. Meeting people where they are rather than where you want them to be, will go a long way toward your getting what you want from your communication.
- A person's frame of mind is flexible and changeable. Someone may not act or communicate the exact same way when he is feeling down and distracted as he does when all is right with the world. Expect this from others, and understand it.
- Give people positive feedback. Tell the other person that what she did was helpful and thank her for trying, even if the outcome wasn't ideal. Ask her what you both could have done differently to make the situation work, or tell her how you would rather have had her do/say something different. People don't know when they don't know something.

Effective Written Communication

Writing is another important part of effective communication. If you are good at it, I applaud you. It doesn't happen to be my strong suit. If it isn't yours either, take a class to become better, or find a mentor. Diana Sheets, an associate of mine, is my mentor. Writing is her strength, and she has given me tips for remembering punctuation and usage rules. I call Diana (who has written a writing training program) when a client of mine requests grammar and business writing classes. My recommendation for you: Find someone who can help you with the mechanics and the content of writing. People make judgments about our intelligence, education level and competence based on how we write. That's how important written communication is.

In written communication, use the same verbal communication rules we discussed earlier in the chapter. Make your message clear. Use an active voice. Give your reader the five "W"s: Who, What, When, Where, and Why. Be sure to discover the other person's personality style before you tell him how to do something, however; you don't want to micromanage him unless he needs to be micromanaged.

Our communication styles are reflections of how we feel about ourselves. Learning to communicate effectively involves knowing yourself, your true motivations, your place of integrity and what you want. Communication is the beginning, and like any skill, it takes practice to be effective.[8]

We are who we are and where we are not because of circumstances but because of the choices we have made regarding those circumstances. The results of our choices are part of our track record. Each of us has an individual track record as well as a track record with each person in our life. And that is the bottom line of effective communication. Take time and think through the consequences of your choices before you act or speak on them. Effective communication is a choice. Making it your choice is the biggest step to developing a successful communication style.

Reference Materials

Personality And Styles
- DiSC Personal Profile System, Carlson Learning
- *The Art of Speed Reading People*, Tieger & Barron-Tieger
- *Hey, I'm The Customer*, Ron Willingham
- *Know Your Personality*, H. J. Eysenck, Glenn Wilson
- *Organizing From The Inside Out*, Julie Morgenstern
- *People Styles at Work*, Robert Bolton and Dorothy Grover Bolton
- *Relationship Strategies* (audio tapes), Tony Alessandra
- *Discovering Your Personality Type*, Don Richard Riso
- *Type Talk*, Otto Kroeger & Janet N. Thuesen
- *Communicating At Work*, Tony Alessandra and Phil Hunsaker
- *Who Do You Think You Are?* Keith Harary and Eileen Donahue

Workings Of The Mind
- *The Power Of Your Subconscious Mind*, Joseph Murphy

---

[8] Each situation is different. Do you want to sell something, end an argument or prove you're right?

- *Living Deliberately*, Harry Palmer
- *Managing Your Mind*, Gillian Butler and Tony Hope
- *Imaging Success*, Kurt Schneider
- *What To Say When You Talk To Yourself*, Shad Helmstetter
- *The Owner's Manual For The Brain*, Pierce J. Howard
- *Before You Think Another Thought*, Bruce Doyle, III
- *You Already Know What To Do*, Sharon Franquemont
- *How To Build High Self-Esteem*, Jack Canfield
- *Your Mind, The Magician*, Allen Rosenthal
- *Self Matters*, Phillip McGraw

Success
- *The Four Agreements*, Don Miguel Ruiz
- *1,000 Things You Never Learned In Business School*, William N. Yeomans
- *Succeed And Grow Rich Through Persuasion*, Napoleon Hill
- *How To Win Friends and Influence People*, Dale Carnegie
- *Beauty Fades, Dumb Is Forever*, Judge Judy Sheindlin
- *The Everything Coaching & Mentoring Book*, Nicholas Nigro
- *The Psychology Of Winning* (audio tapes), Denis Waitley
- *7 Habits Of Highly Effective People* (audio tapes), Stephen R. Covey

Communication
- *Speaking Up*, Mark Ruskin
- *Negotiating For Dummies*, Donaldson and Donaldson
- *Getting Past No*, William Ury
- *The Gentle Art Of Verbal Self-Defense*, Suzette Haden Elgin
- *Get Anyone To Do Anything*, David Lieberman
- *The Art Of Managing People*, Tony Alessandra and Phil Hunsaker
- *Secrets Of Power Persuasion*, Roger Dawson
- *High Impact Communication* (audio tapes), Bert Decker

I'd like to thank all of the authors and speakers listed above for being my personal mentors. To anyone else I may have forgotten to mention, I thank you from my heart.

Donna Baylor

Donna Baylor believes "*Impossible" is only an opinion!* And it isn't an opinion she subscribes to. Donna shares this idea and concept with each and every person she comes is contact with. She believes in personal growth and has a passion for helping people help themselves.

A hypnosis instructor, she teaches the importance of positive self-talk, "The greatest communication you'll ever have is with yourself! What you say about your actions and interactions comes from how well you understand yourself, and how you communicate with others."

Donna is a business consultant and corporate trainer. Ms Baylor is a member of ASTD and NSA. She was included the in 1999-2000 Edition of Lexington's Who's Who of Business Leaders and Professionals.

Donna Baylor
President, TRANSITIONS Seminars, Inc.
PO Box 427
New Boston, MI 48164
(888) 474-9528
Fax: (734) 753-5081
Email: donnabaylor@transitionseminars.com
www.transitionseminars.com

Chapter 8

How To Present Like A Pro
At Your Next Business Meeting

Tad Kallini

Introduction

"Good morning. Today I'd like to share with you our fourth quarter operating results. As you will see, we had a very good quarter. This first slide shows our revenues compared to one year ago. There are several reasons for this..."

And so begins another "presentation" of business data to a group of executives who would much rather receive a briefing via e-mail than sit through yet another of those pesky–dare I say *boring*–business reviews. Thirty minutes into the presentation, the marketing director, who loves to doodle, has created some art work that could fetch a pretty penny at auction. Forty-five minutes in, we've seen more the back of the presenter's head than the front. An hour later, the finance guy, who has been wondering for the last sixty minutes how he's going to finish the budget for next week's review, has emptied his bottle of Tums and is searching the room for anything with sugar.

There are two kinds of people in the business world: those who have experienced this, and those who will. Some of the most brilliant business strategists have lost their competitive edge by delivering presentations that should have stayed on paper. In my first eighteen years of formal education, presentation skills (or what was then called Speech) was an elective course. It really didn't rate up there with English, history, math or the sciences. During my MBA program, we did have to present in almost every course—a good start, but there was no course we could take that would actually allow us to become better speakers. After all, if you can talk, you can speak, right? Not!

The topic of communications always surfaces as one of the biggest challenges to any organization—even "communications" companies. The reason is simple: communication is more than delivering information; it is delivering the right information to the right people at the right time in a manner consistent with how they best receive and understand information. When we write, we are communicating verbally (i.e., using words)—the toughest form of communication (particularly for me, according to my editor!). When we speak on the phone, we add the vocal (i.e., tonality) to the verbal, which certainly helps with mutual understanding. And when we speak face-to-face, one-on-one, we add the visual to the vocal and the verbal, making this the most effective of all forms of communication. But somewhere along the line, when we take that next bold step and speak to a group of people, the effectiveness often drops off—just as the audience nods off.

Communicating effectively to a group of people is both a skill and an art form that can be learned. I've played golf since I was ten years old. I've played a lot over the years, not with the competitiveness and dedication of a Tiger Woods, but primarily for fun. But I didn't break 100 until I took a lesson and learned how to do a few things differently from the way I had been doing them. Perhaps it's that way with your presentation skills. Perhaps you want to "break 100" on your presentation skills score. If so, let's get started.

In this chapter, we'll focus on the extemporaneous presentation—one which requires some preparation but isn't fully written out or memorized. We'll also look at other factors that can make or break the presentation that are often overlooked. These include the presentation room, your own inner fears about presenting, the unspoken word (i.e., body language) and the impact of simplicity.

The Extemporaneous Presentation

The word "extemporaneous" is often confused with "impromptu." While the first definition for extemporaneous in my dictionary suggests they mean the same thing, further reading results in a better understanding of the difference between the two. The great majority of business professionals often speak extemporaneously. They have (or someone else has) prepared at least an outline of what is to be presented. Perhaps they have handouts or other visual aids to support the points they are making. And they have thought about the key points to be delivered. It's not memorized and it's rarely rehearsed, but some planning has occurred.

Impromptu suggests that the topic to be spoken about has just been raised and that no previous thought has gone into a discussion on that topic; it's totally unplanned and unrehearsed. Perhaps you've seen an extemporaneous presentation that appeared to be impromptu? Unless you're heavily into improvisation, I'd suggest you avoid these at all costs. Or take Mark Twain's advice: "It takes me three weeks to prepare an impromptu speech."

Eight Best Questions to Ask Yourself

Best Question #1
Why am I making this presentation?

This falls under the category of what I call a "BFO." Don't know what a BFO is? It stands for "Blinding Flash of the Obvious." (And you thought it would be dirty!) Knowing the "why" does seem rather obvious, but it's more than that. Your answers to this question need to address two areas: the specific reason for the presentation (objective) and what you want your audience to take away from it (outcome).

"If you're in sales, raise your hand!" I frequently ask this question of my audiences, and when I don't get a roomful of hands in the air, I ask it again. The response is always the same. After a few seconds, people get it and start raising their hands. We're all in sales. And we're all selling—every day and in every way. The way you look, act, dress and speak are all designed to sell something—*you*! Keep this in focus when you're structuring your presentation. Chances are, one of your "whys" is to get the audience to think, say, feel or do something differently. You have to sell them, and one of the keys to selling anything is to help them understand the great WIIFM (What's in it for me?).

Perhaps you're a trainer or a facilitator. Those types of sessions are usually designed to teach the audience how to do something. If this is the case, it's important to build into your presentation some time for them to practice using the knowledge you've given them so they can begin to turn it into a skill. And your odds of successfully converting that knowledge to skill after the session is directly proportional to the commitment of the managers of those people to reinforcing the behavior you've demonstrated. Perhaps those managers should also attend the presentation or at least an executive overview of the content and what you expect them to do after the session is over.

Perhaps your objective is to simply get the audience fired up! Motivated! Inspired! Go! Fight! Win! This is probably the toughest of all presentations. To get something beyond a few hours of feeling good requires more than just the ability to communicate effectively. You've got to grab 'em by the heart first and then the mind and really discover their WIIFM. But your presentation could serve as a starting point.

Or you might just simply want to pass along information. Those informational presentations can become real snoozers if you let them. Before you get into one of those, make sure that the information you want to pass along is not something that could just as easily be read. If there's a need for understanding and retention of that information, you'll need to build in some exercises designed to ensure that happens: tests, contests, reviews, follow up, etc.

Once you've figured out your "why," you can also determine what you want your audience to take away from the presentation. It's critical to know this up front, so you can gear your presentation to the take-aways. Experience tells me that no matter how superb you are on the platform, the audience will remember the last thing you say. So build those take-aways into the closing.

And regardless of the "why"—sell, train, motivate or educate—keep in mind that every presentation should be designed to entertain. Make it interesting and make it fun. More on that later.

Best Question #2
How Should I Begin and End My Presentation?

I can't honestly say that this question is any more or less important than the other seven. They're all important. But I will say that it takes a long time to come back from a bad first impression. People will tend to decide whether they like you or not within the first thirty to forty-five seconds of your presentation. I'm not suggesting you can't come back from a bad opening, but why make it so tough on yourself? Start strong! And end strong! People may not remember anything you say except the very last thing. Let's look at some techniques for opening the presentation.

Open With a Question

Questions get the audience thinking about something. Good questions get them thinking about the topic at hand. Great questions get them excited and interested in you and in the topic you are about to present. I've delivered a number of programs on presentation skills, and my favorite opening goes something like this:

"Anyone here get nervous before a presentation? I can relate to that. I've been presenting professionally since 1991. I've delivered more than 600 programs across forty-five states and four foreign countries. I've spoken to audiences as large as 35,000 and as small as three. And you know what? I still get nervous!"

Let's look at some of the benefits of these introductory remarks:

1. The opening question gets to the heart of the reason why most of the audience is there. The surface reason (I want to be a better presenter) is overshadowed by the *real* reason (How do I get rid of the nerves?).

2. "I can relate to that." I'm working to develop a bond with them. People like people who are like themselves. If I get nervous, too, then we're the same.

3. "I've been presenting professionally..." I'm working to establish my credentials and my credibility (Why am I in front of the room?).

4. "I still get nervous." The typical audience reaction to this might be, "Oh, man, if he still gets nervous after all that experience, maybe he has some secrets to getting through this nervous thing!" I'm not saying to them, "Let me tell you what to do." It's more like, "Let me share with you what works for me—maybe it will

work for you." I'm selling, not telling! I want to make it a safe environment for everyone—me included.

State the Agenda

One of my responsibilities as an officer with the United States Army was training. I went through a course for trainers, the gist of which was very simple: "Tell them what you're going to do, do it, then tell them what you did." The principle still works, and the key is "Tell them what you're going to do." Lay out the agenda, and if appropriate and possible, find out what they want to take away. You might not be able to deliver on those surprise requests (if you can't, tell them up front), but if you know your topic well enough, you may be able to adjust the presentation to meet those needs. And then hail the conquering hero!

Begin with Half a Story

Another approach to the introduction is to tell half a story, stop, and then tell them you'll finish it at the end. And the story must relate to the topic. Of course, you will need to practice the story and build some suspense, but if you're willing to risk it, you will be pleased with the results. The strategy is to gain their interest, encourage them to stay with you (mentally and physically) until the end, then end the suspense and tie the story to the take-aways. Here's an example of a story designed to challenge people to use the knowledge they've received in the presentation:

"The year—1869. The place—Niagara Falls. The great Blundin is about to cross Niagara Falls on a tightrope, and the only thing separating him from certain death is a long, thin strand of wire. He mounts the tightrope and slowly proceeds to walk across the falls. Step by step, closer and closer to the middle of the falls. Suddenly, a gust of wind comes up, and he struggles to regain his balance (long pause). He regains his balance and continues to walk toward the Canadian side. Suddenly, he stops, and he smiles (long pause)... and I'll pick up this story a bit later today."

If you are interested, chances are your audience is as well. In fact, I have had people tell me that they had planned to leave before the end of the program but canceled the meeting so they could hear the end of the story. And here's how it ends:

"Suddenly, he stops, and he smiles. Because he has an idea. He continues across the tightrope and dismounts on the Canadian side to the thunderous applause of the assembled crowd. And he speaks. 'Ladies and gentlemen, I thank you for your applause. Without your support, I could not have accomplished this feat. Without confidence in my own abilities, I *would* not have attempted this feat. And now that I have proven to you and to myself that I can do it, I'd like to ask one of you to climb onto my shoulders and accompany me back to the American side of the falls. Who will join me?' For a full minute, no one speaks. No one moves. Finally, Blundin's manager steps out of the crowd and says, 'I've seen you do it once; there's no reason to believe that you cannot do it again. Let's go!' He climbs on Blundin's shoulders, and together they cross the falls again—back to the American side. What's the point? Simply this: I want you to be like Blundin's manager. I want you to be different. Most people who attend this program will go back to work tomorrow and within three days will have forgotten most of what they heard today. And that's a shame because knowledge is absolutely useless unless you *do* something with it. Make a decision *now* to pick three techniques from today's program and put them to use immediately."

Using Humor

I'm frequently asked, "Is it okay to begin a program with a joke?" I usually respond, "Yes, if you're like Jerry Seinfeld and get paid for telling jokes." Most of us just aren't that good in the humor department. Even if you are, the diversity of the audience might make it a bit risky. And if the joke bombs, you've really lost your audience. Go ahead if you're really good, but the smart money is on waiting. Once you're into the presentation and have begun to develop rapport with the group, bring on the humor.

Warning: Test your humor before you use it. What you or I might find amusing may not be to others. Practice it with family and friends in non threatening situations. And by humor, I don't mean just jokes. There are a variety of ways to tickle the funny bone of your audience. Do some research, and find your own techniques.

Closing the Presentation

It's important to determine how you want to end the presentation before you put it together. The ending pretty much determines the content that will lead you to that ending. Regardless of which tip(s) you use, end strong!

- Close with a summary of what you have just discussed and ask for any final questions.
- Close with a quote that ties it all together for the audience.
- Close with a challenge to the audience to think, say, feel or do something.
- Tell them how much you appreciate their having spent the time with you.
- Finish the story you started in your opening.
- Ask members of the audience to share which part of your speech they felt to be the most important to them.

Best Question #3
What Do I Want to Say?

When I began developing and delivering presentations, I faced the fear that I would not be able to fill up the time available. I had this recurring nightmare that the program was supposed to end at 4:30 p.m., and I'd be standing in front of the room at 2:00 p.m. with nothing left to say. The reality is that more often than I care to remember, I have found myself with thirty minutes left in the program—and seventy-five minutes' worth of content—wondering how I was going to finish on time! Circle this next quote:

"Content expands to fill available space—and more!"

Here's a helpful process to determine what the body of the presentation should include:

Step #1: Brainstorm your ideas. Brainstorm with others or by yourself, but do take the time to write down the key points you want to make. To make this happen, I highly recommend the technique of "mindmapping" as well as the book, *Mindmapping: Your Personal Guide to Exploring Creativity and Problem-Solving,* by Joyce Wycoff.

Step #2: Limit yourself to three key points. How many bears in the house that Goldilocks found? Three! How many Stooges? Three! Name them! Curly, Larry and Moe. How many dwarfs in the Snow White story? Seven! Name them! Sleepy, Sleazy, Slimey, Sloppy... We can't remember seven! But we can remember things in groups of three!

Step #3: Test each topic (and any subtopics) against the following questions:
- Is this relevant to the objective of the presentation?
- Does it meet the needs of the audience members?
- Is it absolutely necessary to include it today?

Step #4: Build an outline from your list of topics, and fill it in with content. Determine the order that makes the most sense, and add the content as appropriate. I follow this exact process when preparing for a keynote presentation. Once I've added content to the outline, I actually write the script, word for word, for what I want to present. That process continues until I have taken this script back down to an outline, which I keep handy during the program (my safety net, which I'll refer to again later in the chapter).

Best Question #4
How Do I Make It Entertaining?

Woe be unto the presenter that doesn't add something every six to eight minutes to keep the audience engaged.

Question: How long is the attention span of a teenager?

Answer: We haven't developed equipment sophisticated enough to measure something that small!

And the attention span of the average business audience is not much longer. I look at the opportunity to present my ideas to others as a privilege, and I won't abuse that privilege by beating my audience to death with boredom! Part of my role as a presenter is to make it entertaining, and I have to do it throughout the presentation. Start early and fade— you'll lose them by the end. Start late and build—there won't be anyone mentally there to build for!

So how to keep them engaged? Here's a summary of a variety of techniques and categories of what I'll call entertainment:

Quotes

Someone once told me, "You can't be a prophet in your own land." But people love to hear what someone else has said. The Mark Twain quote I used earlier in this chapter is an example. It's old, but it fits. And it gets people interested.

Visual Aids

"A picture is worth a thousand words." If that were the case, I'd have simply inserted six pictures into this chapter and gone out to dinner! Visual aids are designed to enhance the presentation; they are not designed to *be* the presentation. But I've seen too many presentations during which even the speaker focused on the visual aid (like the PowerPoint presentation slide) and forgot that there was a group of people in the room. Whether it's the good old chart pad or a snazzy electronic presentation with lots of color and animation, stick to the following basic principles:

- No more than three or four colors per slide
- No more than six lines per slide
- Use words and phrases, not complete sentences
- Make the characters big enough to be seen from the back of the room

More on visual aids later.

Puzzles

Picture puzzles, mind games, etc. can be used to get your point across and make it fun for the audience at the same time.

Games

Also called "experiential exercises," games can help the audience learn the topic by actually doing something relating to it. Remember, just because it's your presentation doesn't mean that you have to do all the work!

Silence

In the U.S. business culture, silence usually means that no one has anything to say. *That* gets attention. We are very accustomed to hearing noise from the front of the room, and when we hear silence, it grabs us. A pause of four or five seconds will wake people up, and just about the time they begin to wonder if you've lost it, your next words will be heard loud and clear.

Stories

We mentioned stories in the beginning of the chapter (Best Question #2). They work just as well in the body of the presentation—a *whole* story, that is; not just a half. Some tips on stories:

- Use your own. Your stories are easier to remember, and they are usually original enough to keep the audience engaged. If you use someone else's story, though, be sure to give credit to the original storyteller. That's what professionals do.
- Make sure they connect with the content and that they enhance or reemphasize a point you've made or are about to make.
- Keep them short. Three to four minutes is about the max for a good story; a little longer if you are a good storyteller.
- Track the stories you use. Keep a record of when and with whom you used a particular story. It can be embarrassing when you're fifteen seconds into your story and an audience member shouts, "Aw, you told us that one three weeks ago!"

Facts and Statistics

Did you know that your audience will stay engaged fifty-seven percent longer if you use facts and statistics? Well, if you didn't, that's okay because I just made that up. But I do know that people love statistics, figures and interesting facts that relate to your topic. As you do your research, look for the interesting facts and figures that apply to that topic. Use them sparingly, bringing them in to enhance the key points you want to make.

Voice Inflection/Volume

I'm sure you remember that certain teacher who used to raise her voice to get her students to do something. But do you remember how effective it was when Mom began talking really slowly and really softly? When she yelled, she was angry, but when she talked softly, you knew you needed to listen and do exactly what she asked—"or else!" You and I still play some of those tapes that were programmed into our psyche during our early years. And when the person in the front of the room begins to talk slowly, it's like a subconscious signal to pay attention and listen very closely to what's being said.

Remember, keep it lively and keep it entertaining. It's your responsibility to do so. I tell many of my audiences that I've delivered more than 600 presentations in the last six years, and I have never fallen asleep in any one of them. And neither has anyone in my audience.

Best Question #5
Is the use of visual aids all that important to this presentation?

Generally speaking, the answer is "yes." It's important to understand when to use them, when not to use them and what they are. Let's begin with the last one first.

What are visual aids?

Visual aids are anything used during the presentation that the audience sees. This includes posters, charts, PowerPoint presentations, handouts, equipment, live demonstrations, role plays or anything else that might fit into to the category of "something we can see." One of the most important visual aids is you. *You* are the presentation—the rest of the visual aids are designed to enhance the presentation and make you, the presenter, look better. More on *you* later.

When should I use them?

Remembering that they tend to spice up a presentation and keep the audience engaged, you want to use no more than one every two to three minutes. If you're conveying a lot of numbers, and you don't need the audience to remember them specifically, use a graph of some sort to get your point across. It's much more effective because the visual aspect of the aid enhances the audience's ability to understand what you're saying. Visual aids also enhance your credibility and your professional image.

When should I avoid them?

* If you're using statistics, facts or figures, make sure they are current. Statistics of how cellular phones were selling five years

ago might not be at all useful unless used in conjunction with more recent figures.

- Make sure the size of the visual aid fits the audience. A chart pad for an audience of 300 doesn't work. I once came across a very interesting tag that used to hang from a dress in a department store. I wanted to use the tag in a presentation but didn't imagine that someone sitting even fifty feet away could see it, so I scanned the tag into my computer and made a slide of it. The tag is now almost six feet tall!

- If you don't know how to use projection equipment, either get someone else to operate it or don't use it. We've all seen the person who drops the overhead on the projector and snickered when the transparency appears upside down and backward on the screen. Even PowerPoint presentations using an LCD projector lose their effectiveness when the operator is fumbling with the laptop or the remote, moving too may slides at a time, etc. If you use it, practice with it first!

Best Question #6
What about the audience?

As a member of the National Speakers Association and the National Speakers Association/Washington, D.C. Area, I'm frequently asked by new members and emerging speakers, "What is the single most important thing you could tell me that you wish you knew when you began speaking?" My answer is always the same: Focus on the audience. The success of a presentation is not based on how well you do but on how well the audience responds to what you do. To ensure they respond well, you have to know a little bit about that audience and gear the presentation to the people in the room.

This is perhaps a radical example—not one you run across every day—but it does serve to make a point. I was hired to deliver a time management program to the entire twenty-person staff of a local engineering company. I talked to the meeting planner in advance, asked tons of questions about why they wanted the program, who was going to be there, etc. and felt pretty knowledgeable about this audience. About thirty minutes into the program, I sensed they were not with me. I stopped and said, "I get the sense that time management is not the real issue here. Is there something else we should be talking about?" The president of the company replied, "We're dealing with some other issues that we really need to resolve. Perhaps you could facilitate a discussion about that?" With no knowledge of engineering or their issues (which had not surfaced during the earlier interviews) and minimal facilitation experience, I of course responded with, "Absolutely—let's forget about time management and work on what's important. Tell me, what are the big issues?" As I began to leave seven hours later, figuring that I'd blown it, the president stopped me and replied, "You did great—thank you so much!" It really didn't matter how I performed. What mattered was what they got out of it.

On the other hand, you may know about your audience all too well. If so, just spend a few minutes thinking about the different personalities and work to connect with each of them. And if it's a new audience, consider the following:

- What is the gender breakdown of the audience? Historically, most men tend to be visual learners (learning based on what they see) while most women tend to be auditory learners (learning based on what they hear). So a predominantly male audience will need more visuals while a predominantly female audience won't need them quite as much.
- Are they "students," "vacationers" or "prisoners?" This is something I can usually determine in the opening moments of my presentation. How? I simply ask. Here's how:

"Most of the groups I work with are made of three subgroups. The first subgroup are the students. These folks were here early, seated on time with pen in hand, ready to take some knowledge back to the workplace and apply it. I love the students. The second subgroup are the vacationers. These are the people who look at the next few hours as a vacation—don't have to talk on the phone, don't have to deal with customers, don't have to deal with the boss! And I love the vacationers because they're relaxed, and because they're relaxed, they're open to new ideas! And then there is the third subgroup—the prisoners! You don't want to be here, right? You were "sent" here, right? Well, the good news for the prisoners is this: you will be paroled at 4:00 o'clock today, so hang in there."

In doing this, I've made a connection with everyone in the room. Of course, I won't know who is in which group until we get a little further into the session.

- Which generations do I have in the room? The stories and the terminology you use must match the people in the room. Citing examples from *All in the Family*, a 1970s sitcom, won't fly with your young twenty-somethings. And talking bits, bytes and cyber seconds at the senior citizens home might not fit with some of the residents. Young audience—more casual, more laid back, certain words and phrases that fly. Older audience—more formal, traditional, understand Archie Bunker references.

- What is their position within the organization? First, position is an indicator of age—not always but more often than not. Second, position will tend to indicate the level of knowledge about the topic (and the need to go into more or less detail). Third, I've found that the higher the position, the more they want the information quickly and the less they are concerned with the entertainment value (these are the bottom-liners).

The reality is that you will often have a mix of all types. Do your best to identify each and to incorporate language and stories that will appeal to as many as possible.

Best Question #7
How can I effectively present information
without memorizing it?

There is an old Japanese proverb that applies here:
"The short way is the long way.
The long way is the short way."

There is a variety of ways to deliver the content of your presentation to the audience. It's important to remember, however, that there is no substitute for knowing your content and, if needed, rehearsing the delivery of that content. You may save time now by not spending time with that presentation, but in the long run, you'll save time—and embarrassment—by being well prepared.

There is no agreement among the professionals regarding the use of notes. I believe it depends on your confidence level and your knowledge of the material, but I encourage the use of notes if there is the slightest doubt about either. I use them, even for presentations I have delivered multiple times. I choose to have them handy for a variety of reasons, but the bottom line is that they are my safety net. Even if I don't use them, the comfort of having them within arm's reach makes for a better presentation.

If you are the president of the United States, or perhaps the president of your company, you may be fortunate enough to have the use of a teleprompter. It's a nifty little gadget that projects the text of your presentation on see-through glass, so you can actually read the text or notes and appear as if you are not using notes. Most of us won't get to that point, but it deserves a mention because even that technology requires rehearsal in order for you to appear as if you are not using it.

I used to use 3 x 5 index cards for my notes. As I aged, the size of the cards grew to 4 x 6, then to 5 x 7. When computers came along, I found that the art of making notes became much easier. I just keep increasing the size of the font to meet my visual needs. But there's more to this than just having notes. Let's look at how to put them together and how to use them.

Developing Your Notes

If you've started with an outline of your presentation (well, of course you did, right?), you may already have your notes prepared. But there are few more things you can do to make them work for you.

- Using an LCD projector: The laptop you will probably use can serve as your notes. If you stick with the rule of no more than six lines per slide, you should be able to read from the laptop screen from a good distance.
- Font Size: If you're going to be holding you notes, the font size should be big enough so you can read them when they are held at waist level. If they will be on a lectern or table, the size should enable you to read them when laid flat on that furniture.
- Words/Phrases: More than an outline, your notes should be nothing more than words and very short phrases, designed to remind you of the next point. Once you've learned several points

that go together chronologically, you only need one word or phrase that will lead you to that string.

- Color Coding: I've found it helpful to color code certain types of information. You'll want to develop your own code, but here's what works for me:
    - Blue = topics and subtopics
    - Red = story
    - Green = exercises
    - Purple = quotes (I want to ensure that these are delivered word-for-word, so they are written out as they were originally said.)
    - Black = everything else

Using Your Notes

- Laptops & LCD Presentations: Position the laptop so it is between you and the audience, angled (about forty-five degrees) to the side of the laptop on which you will be standing most of the time. When you advance to the next slide or to the next bullet point on the current slide, use a remote (if available) and glance at the slide without lowering your head.

    Do not look at the screen that is behind you!

    I know I shouldn't tell you what not to do, but simply suggesting that you read the laptop screen just isn't enough, based on what I've seen over the years. Two weeks ago, I watched a presentation during which the speaker stood with his back to the audience and read each slide word for word. I don't have to tell you how painful that was for me—and for the audience. It was his first presentation, but it should not have been; even the first one should be rehearsed to the point where reading is not necessary. Looking back at the screen results in lost eye contact. You still lose eye contact even when you use your notes effectively, but it's for a much shorter period of time (and as far as the folks in the back of the room can tell, not at all!).

- Other Notes/Outlines: If you tend to move around a bit, carry the notes with you, and keep them below waist level at all times. This means you only get to gesture with one hand, but that may be a good thing. When you lay them down, position them so you can glance down at them with your eyes only—i.e., do not lower your head to read them. This will take some practice until you find a comfortable position and an appropriate font size. I know several professionals who create two or three pages of notes, lay them on the floor or platform and either glance down to read them or pause, as if thinking about something, and pick up the next thought from those notes. Even when you know they're doing it, it does appear as if most of the program is done without notes.

If you're using notes from a three-ring binder, open the binder rings at the beginning of the program, and, if you have to move away from the table holding the notes, take only the page or pages that you will need. Leave the binder where it is.

As with everything else in this chapter, the more you practice using notes, the more proficient you will become and the more professional and prepared you will look!

Best Question #8
Should I rehearse?

Yes.

I really wanted to leave it at that, but the editor wants a little more. So here's a little more. Simply stated, the more you rehearse, the better you will present. Rehearse in the room in which you will be presenting, if possible. If not, re-create the room layout as closely as possible. Rehearse what you will say, how you will say it and the gestures you will use. Rehearse with your visual aids until you are comfortable using them. And if you really want to take it to the next level, audio or video tape your rehearsals. The best feedback you will ever get is the feedback you give yourself as you watch yourself on video tape. You may want to rehearse your body language after viewing that video!

The Importance of Body Language

I've seen a set of percentages that defines the relative importance of body language, tonality and words to the communication process. While the actual percentages are not that important, the relative weight is extremely important and needs to be considered when preparing to deliver the presentation.

Words

John Fitzgerald Kennedy is considered by many to be one of the greatest speakers in the last fifty years. It is said that he asked his speech writers to write as if he were delivering to a group of sixth graders. While on the surface that sounds a little insulting, it's important to note that the average reading level (not intelligence level) in the United States is at about a sixth or seventh grade level. The point is that Kennedy (or his speech writers) wrote his speeches so that the majority of people could understand them. What a concept! Keep it simple and they will love it— and they will understand it!

Tonality

The inflection, volume, pitch, pace and tone of your voice will have an impact on the message as well. Using the same words with a different tonality will result in a totally different meaning. The message: make sure you sound like you mean what you say.

Body Language/Appearance

By far, body language and appearance have the greatest impact on the effectiveness of your presentation. Things like smiling, making eye contact and having an open posture tell the audience that you're glad to be there with them. Too much movement can be distracting. Too little movement makes you appear stiff and unfriendly. Hand gestures can be used to make a point but detract from the presentation if they are constantly used.

The single best advice I can offer is to look like you belong in front of the room. I suggest your style of dress should match the general style of the audience and that you dress one level above the best dressed audience member. If they are casual (picnic wear, shorts, T-shirts), the presenter should be business casual. If they are in business casual attire (slacks, sport shirts, dresses, shinable shoes), the presenter should take it to the business level (shirts/blouses, ties, suits, sport coats). For a business-dressed audience, tuxedos and evening gowns (just kidding!).

Summary:

The successful presentation begins with your answers to the following eight questions:

1. Why am I making this presentation?

2. How should I begin and end my presentation?

3. What do I want to say?

4. How do I make it entertaining?

5. Is the use of visual aids all that important to this presentation?

6. What about the audience?

7. How can I effectively present information without memorizing it?

8. Should I rehearse?

In closing, I am reminded of some advice I received when I first got into the business of professional speaking. As a trainer, and later as a seminar leader and facilitator, I had in the back of my mind a series of nagging fears. What if I mess up? What if I deliver an absolutely horrible program? What if there's a subject matter expert in the audience who knows a lot more about the topic than I do? One day, a colleague of mine suggested the following, which I pass along to anyone who is willing to listen:

"The worst you'll ever do
is the best they'll ever see!"

Simply stated, most of the people in that audience would much rather have you up there than be there themselves. And the fact is that we tend to be overly critical of ourselves. You don't have to know all the answers to present, but if you answer the eight best questions outlined in this chapter correctly, chances are you will be uncommonly good!

Tad Kallini

Tad Kallini, MBA, CSP (Certified Speaking Professional) is a speaker, facilitator, author, and President of Growth Systems Unlimited, an organization dedicated to developing the frontline leadership of today and tomorrow. He has delivered over 600 workshops and keynotes across 45 states, England, Scotland, Australia, New Zealand, and Greece, and inspired thousands to achieve better results by helping them embrace who they are, what they do, where they want to go and who they want to be. He has authored a number of programs focused on communication, stress management, and coaching, to include *Creating the Motivational Environment*, *Understanding Business Communication*, and *Dealing with the Stress of Change*. His first book, *I Know You Know It, But Do You Do It?*, was published in December 2002. In both his written works and his programs, Tad relies on a 20-year career with two Fortune 500 companies, and an incredible story-telling ability, to bring the key message to life for the reader and the listener. He has also earned the designation of Certified Speaking Professional, the highest earned designation of the National Speakers Association, and a designation held by only 450 speakers worldwide.

Tad Kallini, MBA, CSP
Growth Systems Unlimited
Columbia, MD, 21044
(410) 992-0432
Fax: (410) 992-7474
Email: unstuck@tadkallini.com
www.TadKallini.com

Chapter 9

Straight Talk—When What You Say
Makes a Difference

Donna Fisher

Talk, talk, talk. Have you noticed how much talking goes on in our world? You can talk to yourself, your pet, your loved ones, the TV, the computer, your car, the stars and drivers on the freeway who don't even know you exist.

Everybody has something to say, and they often say it with certainty and conviction. Yet how much of it is really necessary, productive and contributing? Between television, radio and now cell phones, people are pretty much talking everywhere, all the time.

But what are we really saying with all this talking? And are we really communicating, or is everybody too busy talking for much real communication to happen?

Real Communication

When you talk to the stars or to your computer, you aren't talking to get a response. You're talking to vocalize a thought or feeling. Although talking does not require a response, real communication involves both a sender and a receiver of a message. With real communication you convey a message through your speaking, and the message is received in such a way that you make a connection.

How does real communication make a difference? The truth is that all communication makes a difference. When you gossip, you make a difference in the way others relate to and perceive a certain person or situation. In this case, you make a detrimental difference. Gossip, however, is not real communication in that it's not authentic, actual or serving.

Detrimental Difference
- Gossip
- Harsh words and tone of voice
- Destructive intent

Beneficial Difference
- Praise and acknowledgement
- Pleasing words and tone of voice
- Positive intent

Real communication gives you power—the power to bring a tear of joy or sorrow to someone's eye. You have a great responsibility with your speaking. Do not take it lightly.

The root of the word "communication" is "commune," which means coming together, sharing with each other and holding something in common. The Latin word *communicare* means "to make common, to converse intimately or to exchange thoughts and feelings." All of this emphasizes the nature of communication as a means of coming together, creating a union, creating a bond, joining as one. Through communication, we are able to understand one another, and this understanding creates a connection.

Communication is basic to who we are as humans. It is the way we convey information, express ourselves, connect with others and gather information on which to base important life decisions. Most problems can be traced back to some miscommunication or misunderstanding. We have this great tool for connecting and creating, but it gets misused in ways that create havoc in relationships, businesses, countries and even the world.

Everything you say and don't say, do and don't do communicates something. This goes for your facial expressions, body language, tone of voice and the words you choose. You are always communicating something whether you mean to or not. It's time to be responsible for your communication, to make wise choices and to have your communication make a beneficial difference in your relationships, your business, your country and our world.

Real communication contributes to your productivity, happiness, health and well-being. It is about conveying a message and connecting. And when you are connecting with the world around you, you experience more power, creativity, self esteem and spiritual, mental and emotional well-being. Real communication is not just a good idea. It is the ideal way to enhance all areas of your life.

Real Communication is Straight Talk

Straight talk is saying what needs to be said, saying what is real and authentic, being honest with yourself and others. Straight talk does not mean blasting, blaming, ridiculing or vocalizing all the judgmental thoughts that go through your head. (Some things aren't worth vocalizing because they're useless, petty and/or insignificant.) Rather, straight talk is a style of assertive communication because it's both authentic and respectful. It conveys respect and dignity for both you (the speaker) and the person to whom you are speaking. Even difficult communications can be delivered with respect and dignity. Straight talk is meaning what you say and saying what you mean.

When I was the director of the Center for Attitudinal Healing, I had the opportunity every day to witness the power of communication to heal, soothe, uplift and energize. At the center, we provided emotional support for children and families dealing with life-threatening illnesses. When people came face to face with life and death, they began to say everything that they hadn't said throughout their lives. They began to communicate things they previously felt like they couldn't say. As a result, they started reconnecting with their own hearts and souls as well as with the other people in their lives. They gained a greater sense of self, freedom and energy. There's no need for you to wait until faced with dramatic circumstances. You can start today with a commitment to powerful, straight communication that makes a difference!

You gain tremendous power through your ability to communicate effectively. With straight talk, you can communicate about problems, criticism and suggestions without having others get defensive. Straight talk helps to establish a level of trust and commitment so that people are able to stay with the conversation until each person is complete. Straight talk happens when honesty is conveyed in a way that people are respected.

The Power of Straight Talk

Just one word, one comment has the power to transform your life! One word or statement may be all that someone needs to complete a project, pursue her dream, take responsibility for her life or stop a destructive behavior. The words you speak have the power to transform the lives of others when you speak words of encouragement, vision, opportunity and commitment.

Your ability to choose words and the way that you speak those words gives you power, and with that power comes responsibility. We're talking about the power to make a difference and the responsibility to make a difference in a positive way for yourself and others. It is your right and responsibility to use the power of words to make a difference.

Elements of Straight Talk

- Rapport-Building Communication
- Intentional Communications
- Conscious/Mindful Communication
- Complete Communication
- Insightful Communication
- Grateful Communication
- Requesting Communication
- Word Power Communication
- Creative Communication

Rapport-Building Communication

Rapport is that feeling you get when a conversation goes well and you connect with someone. Oftentimes, this develops through small talk—conversation geared toward building rapport and discovering commonalities. It is much more than social chitchat. It is the first stepping stone to connecting with someone.

The purpose of communication is to connect, and connecting happens through the sharing of common interests and experiences, personal stories, similar dreams and challenges, etc. And it is through small talk that you can discover those similar interests, experiences, dreams and challenges. The flow of small talk is one of exploration. You explore a wide range of topics to find something that "clicks," which can be a common like or even a common dislike.

Tips for building rapport and turning conversations into interesting connections and opportunities:

- Be interested.
- Be pleasant and responsive.
- Explore topics until you find a common interest.
- Be curious.
- Don't prejudge.
- Identify several topics and questions that you can comfortably use to generate interesting conversation.
- Listen.

Don't ever underestimate the power of small talk or the power of connecting. As Dr. Edward M. Hallowell relates in his book, *Connect*, "For most people the two most powerful experiences in life are achieving and connecting. Almost everything that counts is directed toward one of these two goals. The peaks of life for most people are falling in love (connecting) and reaching a hard-won goal (achieving)."

Communication creates connection, and connection is what we thrive on. As Dr. Hallowell says, "Moments of connection boost our spirits." And in the same sense, "Disconnection can be devastating. Nothing hurts more. This is why the ancients feared banishment worse than death. Indeed, we have scientific evidence now that social isolation leads to death."

Problem: People treat social conversation and small talk as insignificant and thus leave the other person feeling insignificant. Because we live in a fast-paced, results-oriented culture, people sometimes get impatient with casual conversation. People don't reveal enough about themselves to establish a real connection. People get bored with shallow conversations in which no connection is happening.

Solution: Be responsible for doing your part to make a conversation interesting. Don't leave that up to the other person. Participate in such a way as to make the conversation enjoyable. One of the ways to get into a conversation is to be curious.

> When people complain about a conversation
> being boring, my response is, "You're part of the
> conversation—do something about it." Try coming
> up with three questions that you feel comfortable
> asking people that can lead to conversation and
> connection.

The question that I tend to ask people (that seems natural for me) is, "So, how long have you ____?" Examples: How long have you been playing the drums? How long have you worked for XYZ Company? How long have you lived in New York? How long have you wanted to start your own business? How long have you been a member of the Business Exchange Group? It's a question that's easy to ask and easy for people to respond to, yet it can be just enough to get an interesting conversation started.

Another question that works well is, "How did you ____?" Examples: How did you get into the music business? How did you decide to become a Peace Corps volunteer? How did you happen to move from Charlotte to Houston? How did you go from engineering to printing? How did you find out about the Arlington Breakfast Club?

One more for you to consider is, "What do you like most about ____?" Examples: What do you like most about being a speaker? What do you like most about living in Chicago? What do you like most about working for XYZ Company? What do you like most about being a musician? What do you like most about being a member of the Wednesday Group?

Just as important as the question you're asking is the way you ask it and your immediate response once you ask. Your body language and tone of voice must be friendly. And as you ask, you must already be in listening mode. You asked, so make sure you follow through with a genuine interest in the person's answer.

Another way to prepare ahead of time to generate interesting conversation is to identify three topics in which you are interested and would enjoy talking about. These topics can relate to business, hobbies, sports, vacations, movies, books, etc. I enjoy hearing about great movies and books through talking with people. I also love to hear about great places to travel, music performances, dance events and interesting conferences. Even with topics that I may not have a lot of information on or interest in, I can oftentimes generate a curiosity regarding what someone else finds interesting.

Intentional Communication

Intentional communication obviously carries with it some purpose or intent. It's not just an automatic comment, although it can be spontaneous. You can at any moment choose to say something with the intent that your comment make a difference.

What if every time you started to say something, your mind automatically took one second to answer the question, "What do I want to accomplish with this communication? Do I want to inspire, gather more information, get people thinking, create an upset, show how smart I am or simply generate more conversation?"

Example: My friend, Katherine Ashby, is an image consultant and feng shui consultant. Katherine has worked with me for years to update my wardrobe and my image and to arrange my home and office for maximum energy flow. From the beginning, I noticed that Katherine has this wonderful ability to tell people that their clothes are all wrong or their houses are a mess, without coming across as mean, critical or aggressive. I believe part of Katherine's ability lies in the strength of her intent. She is so clear about being there, to be of service to people and to help people move to the next level with their image and their environment, that words that could seem confrontational when spoken by others come across as helpful when spoken by Katherine.

Her intent comes through as the context in which the words are spoken. The words therefore end up fitting inside the intent, and Katherine's commitment to be of service shows up foremost.

Elements of Intentional Communication
- You know what you want to create as a result of your communication, i.e. a feeling, a result, a certain action.
- You identify the elements that will support your desired result in being accomplished.
- You identify the most powerful way to communicate the result you wish to accomplish.

Example: Someone on your staff is not working up to par, and you are both disappointed and frustrated. You may decide to have a conversation with him about this and expect that he will probably respond with upset. On the other hand, you can choose to have your intention be that the conversation go smoothly, clearly and that both of you communicate professionally in a manner that leads to a satisfying resolution. Now think about it! When you have that intention, will you approach that person a little differently and possible say things a little differently than if you just communicate to express your upset?

You have the power to communicate in a way that heals or harms, and oftentimes, the difference lies in having the maturity to choose an intention that heals.

Intentional Communication
- What's the purpose of your communication?
- What's your message?
- What do you intend to have happen as a result of your communication?
- What do you intend that people feel or experience as a result of it?

According to Webster, the word "intend" means "to have in mind a purpose or goal." When you communicate, do you have a positive intent in mind? When others communicate with you, are you able to choose a positive intent rather than judge them? There is so much blaming, victimizing and judging in conversations. People communicate how bad things are as if that's something to be proud of. Or they communicate how difficult things are as if they have nothing to do with their own experience of life. People focus on the faults of others in order to not be responsible for their own contributions to the world. What if we turned all the blaming conversations into communication with some positive intent?

> Problem: Getting upset and letting emotions get in the way

> Solution: Stay true to the message you want to communicate, and set the emotions aside to deal with later on your own.

When you're upset, can you say what you want without going off the deep end emotionally? Ask yourself, "What do I want as a result of this conversation? What are the words, tone of voice and body language that will be most conducive to creating the result that I want? Is my (insert emotion here) more important than the result I want from this conversation?" Stay true to your message rather than getting sidetracked by your emotions.

Problem: Judgment taints the communication

Solution: Be perceptive and speak positive intent

Give people the benefit of the doubt and assume a positive intent behind their mistakes or problem behaviors. We tend to judge others by their actions while we judge ourselves by our intent. You gain great power by shifting your focus to the positive behind the actions of others. By identifying the positive intent, the other person is released from blame and attack and moves into unconditional acceptance. The choice is yours—look for the negatives or look for the positives. You can take whichever stance you choose. But the more powerful stance is to look for the positive intent and thus create cooperation with others.

Example: Ed found himself consistently upset with other drivers on the freeway. His upset was causing problems with the people in his carpool as well as his spouse and children. He was challenged to make up a feasible reason for why each driver needed to be driving the way he or she was. "He must be rushing to the hospital to be with his wife during the birth of their first baby." "She must be late for a very important meeting." "They must be very happy about getting to the airport to welcome their son home from his assignment overseas." Those pretend scenarios are just as possible as the other things we make up in our heads. We might as well give people the benefit of the doubt; it makes us feel better. The focus changes the whole perspective—"I can be at odds with people, or I can be supportive."

In fact, giving the benefit of the doubt is a powerful key to bringing out the best in people when they're at their worst. Assume a positive intent behind their problem behavior, and then deal with them accordingly. If you're not sure about someone's positive intent, make something up. Practice asking yourself what the positive intent is behind another person's actions and behaviors. What else could he or she mean?

What positive purpose might this person be trying to accomplish? You can express what you want (your intent) in the form of Positive Anticipation.

Speaking Positive Anticipation
- "That's not like you. You're capable of…"
- "One of the things I like about you is…"
- "My experience with you shows that you can handle…"
- "I admire your attention to detail, which is one of the reasons I'm asking you to…"
- "I figure you must have a really good reason for nor responding because you have a great reputation for getting back with people promptly."
- "You have presented five reports this year that have been on time and well done. I noticed that the report you handed in last week was late. Is there anything I can do to help you maintain your excellent performance record?"

For positive anticipation to work, it must be sincere, specific and reasonable.

Problem: Fear of confrontation

Solution: Be inquisitive and state the facts

During communication workshops, it is very common for people to come to me for advice on problems they're having with other people. They typically do a great job of explaining the problems, but then they ask, "What do I say to this person?" Often, my response is, "Tell her what you just told me." They'll say, "I can't tell them that! You want me to tell them that?!" And I always point out that if they don't, they can't expect to clarify or resolve the problem. Of course, we use the workshop to talk about the best way to handle the situation in terms of the words they use, their tone of voice and the time and place that they choose.

Straight communication means getting all the facts straight (clear and accurate). If you and I are dealing with misleading and/or inaccurate facts, how can we make wise decisions on how to deal with the situation? Yet this is what people tend to do. And then we wonder why situations don't get resolved!

Why do we tend to think that we can't be straight in our communications? Do we think what we have to say is hurtful or not nice? No matter what there is to say, we can find a way to say it straight and do so with respect and dignity.

Conscious/Mindful Communication

So often, communication is simply a knee jerk reaction. Maybe you can recall a time that you said something and then immediately wished that you could take it back, erase it.

And then there are those times when you planned to say "ABC" and then "XYZ" came out of your mouth. And then maybe there are times when you've said something and then realized you said it just to fit in, to be accepted and/or to appear knowledgeable.

It happens all the time. Someone says something without thinking and either:

- Someone's feelings are hurt
- A friendship or relationship is ruined
- A prospect or client is lost
- A fight, argument or conflict escalates
- A prospective customer is "turned off"

This kind of thing happens when you are being lazy and automatic. Staying aware and being conscious of what you are saying and how it may affect people requires maturity and commitment. With even just a little bit of thought, some of the most disastrous upsets can be avoided.

It's like one of those toys that has a string to pull or a button to push to make it speak. It obviously doesn't have a mind of its own. In fact, it usually only has a handful of words or phrases that it can say. What are the words and phrases that you tend to say automatically, over and over, like a programmed toy? When you operate this way, you appear to be in a real conversation, yet there is nothing real about it. Everything being said is preprogrammed.

By identifying your "automatics," you naturally become more mindful and conscious about your speaking. Just as a little preparation can go a long way, a little thought can go a long way toward your communication being productive rather than reactive.

Slow your responses down. Practice giving yourself ten seconds of thought before you jump in to respond or say what you have to say. It takes only one moment to choose to communicate powerfully, yet the results of a powerful statement can last a lifetime. You gain great power when you practice choosing rather than reacting.

Problem: Knee jerk reactions

Solution: Thoughtful responses

Knee jerk reactions lead to ineffective, unauthentic conversations in which nothing useful gets accomplished. These reactions occur when someone says or does something and you respond automatically.

Thoughtful responses are ones to which some thought or consideration has been given—thought to what you are saying, the possible effects of what you choose to say and what you want to accomplish with what you say. Communication is a powerful tool and is worth giving some thought to.

Rather than react with a knee jerk response, expand your choices. The more options you have, the more power you have. Anytime you feel backed into a corner, you begin to feel powerless and fearful and respond accordingly. If, however, you have lots of options, you have choices and you have power.

Problem: Treating communication in a happenstance, lackadaisical manner.

Solution: Remember that everything you say is representative of who you are

When you are a public figure or celebrity, you have to be careful about what you say because the press and/or public may pick up on something that could harm your reputation, fame, fortune and future opportunities. We've seen this especially with politicians who slip up and say something when they think they're not "on the air" and then later have to explain how they didn't really mean it. Make sure you can always stand by what you say.

Complete Communication

Complete communication entails saying everything that there is to say in a situation.

Recall how you feel when you complete a project. There is a feeling of freedom and space and new opportunity. The same thing happens with communication. When you don't leave things hanging and you complete your conversations so that nothing's left out, you have that same experience of being whole and complete, with nothing left out. Completion is a state of mind that allows you to move forward.

Can you recall all the times you've communicated something to someone, knowing at the time that you weren't saying everything you needed to say? "Did I say what I wanted to say? Did I communicate in a way with which I am pleased? Did I honor myself and others with my communication?"

Problem: Partial communication

Solution: Complete communication

Sometimes you know that you have only said part of what needs to be said and that that's what you're choosing to do at that moment. In this situation, you are actually withholding information. At other times, partial communication is not intentional, and you actually don't even know that you haven't been complete with your communication. It's not the same as lying and withholding information. In this case, not everything gets said because you assume it's already understood or known by others. However, with partial communication, other people "fill in the blanks" and typically they fill in the blanks with words, thoughts, meanings and feelings that are different from what you meant to convey.

Communication is too important to allow for inconsistencies and misunderstandings. Misunderstandings lead to upsets, mistakes, conflicts, divorces, loss of jobs, loss of sales, etc.

Complete communication doesn't necessarily mean to tell people *everything*. It means to include everything that relates to the message you are conveying. Here are a few examples:

Partial: "I'm busy right now."

Complete: "I'm busy working on the monthly
financials that are due by 4:00 p.m. today. I would
like to schedule time to talk about your results
once this is complete."

Partial: "I will call you later."

Complete: "I will call you later so that we can finish
this discussion. I will be at a conference all day
tomorrow. So, it will be sometime Thursday."

Partial: "I can't talk with you right now."

Complete: "I can't give you my full attention right
now because I've got this 2:00 conference call on
my mind. Would 3:15 work for you? That way I
can be more focused and attentive."

Insightful Communication

What do you tend to believe most—what you see, what you hear or
what you perceive? The way our minds work, we believe what we perceive,
regardless of what we see or hear. That's why some people say that
perception is reality. The way you perceive your world is the reality that
you live with and relate to.

Perception is what you decide about a person or situation based on
the information that you choose to pay attention to. What you perceive
can be (and often is) totally different from the perception of others, yet if
you say it is so, then that becomes your experience. You see or hear
something, you have thoughts about what you see or hear, your perception
leads to certain actions and behaviors, and those actions and behaviors
support the original perception.

Problem: Hallucination perceptions

Solution: Insightful inquiry

As I mentioned above, when people communicate with us only
partially, we naturally tend to "fill in the blanks." We add our own
thoughts and ideas to what is said and then operate as if that's real.

Sounds a little like hallucination, right? Perceiving something that's not real and operating as if it is real. However, the thoughts in your head are not "real." They are just thoughts in your head.

When you notice you are filling in the blanks, stop yourself and check with the other person to verify, clarify and identify for sure what is being said. You have the right to have complete and accurate information in your life on which to base your decisions. Yet most people are walking around in life with partial, incomplete and inaccurate information, operating as if their information is completely authentic and accurate.

The way you inquire about a perception is to state what happened (actually, what you noticed happening), state your perception regarding what you noticed and ask for verification and clarification. Your job is to inquire sufficiently to get complete and accurate information.

Insightful Inquiry:
- Self awareness: Notice your perception
- Make a statement as to what you noticed and/or heard
- Acknowledge what you perceive that to mean
- Inquire about the accuracy of your perception

Example: Several years ago, I was on the phone with a friend, who was telling me about his unhappiness with his job and his difficulty in finding another one. I had heard similar comments from him before, so I came back with some pretty strong words about how to turn his situation around. As soon as I hung up the phone, I became concerned about whether I had come across too strongly. Maybe he just needed a friend to listen with compassion. Did he want my advice? Did I cross the line with my comments? As soon as I noticed my concerns, I knew that I would have to clear this up and ask if my thoughts (perceptions) were correct or not.

Since I knew that I would see him later that day, I decided to wait and ask him in person instead of calling him back. When I did see him that afternoon, I said, "After we talked on the phone earlier, I was concerned that I might have come across too strongly and sounded like I was on 'my soapbox.'" He immediately said, "Oh, no. No problem. I appreciate everything that you had to say. Whether it's something that I'll do or not, I'm not sure yet. But the conversation was fine, and your response was appropriate."

Thank goodness I checked it out. Because I had noticed that as soon as I saw him I imagined that he seemed a little more distant than usual. I convinced myself that I probably had indeed said too much. By inquiring, however, I learned that those thoughts were part of my "hallucination." If I hadn't inquired, that one little misperception on my part could have had a ripple effect on future misunderstandings. A masterful communicator knows to inquire and verify a message.

When you're faced with uncertainty:

- Ask for the meaning of words, phrase or statements.
- Ask for restatement: "Tell me again."
- Ask for a recap or review: "If you were to recap everything we just talked about...".
- Ask for confirmation: "Does that mean...?"
- Ask for clarification: "Just to make sure I'm clear about this..."

Insightful inquiry provides you with the ability to have complete and accurate information on which to base your thoughts, actions and decisions. You have the right to ask for clarification and have clear and complete communication.

Grateful Communication

Acknowledgement is the act of giving positive, sincere feedback and reinforcement to people. It is food for the soul and spirit. It is much more than a compliment; it is an expression of something you value and appreciate. In an ideal world, everyone would be giving and receiving positive feedback on a daily basis. In your world, you can do your part to accomplish that by making sure you acknowledge people on a daily basis. Acknowledgement is a simple communication tool that makes a big difference.

In *The Magic of Conflict*, Tom Crum references a study done in Iowa by a group of graduate students who "followed a normal two-year-old throughout a day." The child was "told what not to do 432 times, as opposed to 32 positive acknowledgements." According to the study, the national average of parent-to-child criticism is twelve to one; that is, twelve criticisms for every one compliment. "And we wonder why our children so often have low self esteem," says Crum as he emphasizes the importance of getting positive strokes at any age. In her book, *Dare to Connect*, Dr. Susan

Jeffers emphasizes that the purpose of grateful communication "is not to make (people) like you, but rather to enrich their lives in some way."

> Problem: Assuming people know that we appreciate them and being lazy in expressing appreciation to people
>
> Solution: Give acknowledgement on a daily basis. Have it become a natural and consistent part of your conversations. Sprinkle in the word "thanks" throughout your day. Be specific, and let people know exactly what they are doing that you appreciate.

Examples:
- "Thank you for being my friend."
- "I appreciate your support in making this a successful event."
- "I acknowledge you for your persistence in getting this problem resolved."
- "I am grateful to you for consistently being on time with your reports. That makes my job so much easier."

Tips for communicating acknowledgements powerfully

Be specific. Let people know exactly what you appreciate about them.

- "I appreciate that you always get back to me when you say you will."

Acknowledge people both for what they accomplish and the qualities and strengths they have that made their accomplishment possible.

- "You did a great job updating our procedures manual. I acknowledge you for your persistence in gathering all the information in such a timely manner."

Acknowledge people as promptly as possible.

- "I saw the way you just handled that upset customer. You exhibited excellent listening and communication skills."

Acknowledge people whenever you feel grateful (even if it's years later).

- "When I was driving to XYZ Company yesterday, I recalled our first sales call and how much I learned from you when I was just getting started. I am so grateful for the success I've experienced and how you helped me get started on the right track."

Make eye contact and connect with them. Don't let the acknowledgement be a "comment in passing."

Use the word "you!"

- Say, "You did a great job organizing that manual" rather than simply, "Great job" or "Great manual."

Requesting Communication

My premise in life is that everything you want and need is available and right around you. It is yours for the asking. Anything can be accessed through your network of support by asking the right questions. However, most people are hesitant to ask; they hint about what they want or they beat around the bush or they don't ask because they're afraid of being rejected. Note the distinction in this example:

Providing information only:
"Here's a report I need for you to review."

Making a specific request:
"Do you have ten minutes to review this report with me?"

Problem: Complaining and hinting

Solution: Make requests

Asking can be simple and powerful. What most people do instead of asking for something is complain. Complaining ends up being very frustrating, draining, ineffective and disempowering. Turn your complaints into requests and watch what happens. Become a requester rather than a complainer.

Behind every complaint there is (1) a commitment to something that is not getting fulfilled and (2) a request in hiding. Notice when you have a complaint. Clarify what the complaint is about. Figure out what you need to request to turn that complaint into a motivator for positive action. Give up complaining now and forever more. Instead of just telling people what not to do, make sure you request what you want them to do as a replacement for their current behavior.

Every time there's something that you're upset about, there is also something that you want. However, most of the time people continually talk about what they're upset about rather than about what they want or intend to create in the future.

Criteria for Asking
- Be clear about what you want and need.
- Be concise with your request.
- Give people a chance to respond.
- Thank people for giving you what you ask for.
- Be assertive (make a clear request without being demanding).
- Be specific so that people know exactly what's being asked of them.

Complaint:	Positive Request:
"Don't interrupt."	"Let me finish what I have to say, and then you can share your ideas."
"Don't give me that look."	"Tell me what is making you frown that way."
"Don't be late."	"I must have that report by 3:00 p.m. this Wednesday."

> Problem: Others are not "straight" with their
> communication
>
> Solution: Ask for clarifying information from
> someone who isn't being forthright.

Communication that's not straight leads to a pattern of misunderstandings because you don't ever really know for sure if the message is received as intended or not. Things are left unsure and questionable, stressful and lacking certainty. Don't assume. You deserve to have complete and accurate information.

Word Power Communication

Just as one ingredient can completely change the flavor of a dish, one word can change the meaning of a sentence or the way people respond to you. When someone says, "I like you, but . . ." the whole phrase "I like you" gets negated by the word "but". When someone says, "I like you and . . ." then it is easier to hear and accept what is said both before and after the word "and". This is just one example of numerous cases where one word can completely change the perceived meaning of a sentence.

Some words are empowering while other words automatically disempower. You have the power to make a difference with your speaking by choosing words and phrases that give people a chance to respond in a respectful and supportive manner.

> Problem: Using words and phrases that tend to
> generate awkward, uncomfortable and even
> resentful interactions.
>
> Solution: Choose your words wisely. Speak so that
> others have a chance to relate and respond in a
> respectful manner.

Making wise word choices can also apply to simple words and phrases we use every day. Consider these word substitutions that can generate more positive responses:

- Substitute the word "and" for "but."

- Say what you "can do" rather than what you "can't do."
- Say "no" and "I don't know" positively.
- Don't use "no" as the first word of the sentence.

Notice in the following examples how changing a few words shifts the communication. In each example, think about how the change is more likely to elicit a different response.

A) "We insist that you immediately begin to use this new procedure in your department."

B) "This new procedure is to be implemented in your department starting on the first of January to ensure that you have..."

A) "No, we don't have that in stock."

B) "Although we don't have that particular brand in stock, we do carry a similar drum set made by HPCustom, and we have several on the showroom floor that you can see and play."

A) "You'll have to wait until after you've been here six months for a discount card."

B) "Once you've been here six months, you'll receive a discount card good for..."

A) "Your request cannot be reviewed until the committee meets again."

B) "Your request will be reviewed once the committee meets again so that we can get a consensus and agreement from everyone involved."

A) "You will have to start using a new security badge to maintain access to certain areas of the manufacturing facilities."

B) "You will start using a new security badge next month in order to provide you with a safer environment in our meeting facilities."

A) "I like your ideas for the new advertising campaign, but I'm not sure now is the best time to present the proposal."

B) "I like your ideas for the new advertising campaign, and I want to make sure we pick the best time to present the proposal to get their support."

Words can either draw people in, turn them off or leave them cold. Words and phrases that give power include: thanks, I will, I promise, I am (with a positive attribute as a declaration), I appreciate, choose, accept, you (in a grateful communication). Words that drain power include: try, always, never, but, should, if only, you (in accusatory tone).

Defense-Free Communication

It's easy to think that other people are always at fault when a conversation becomes difficult and argumentative. Yet, there are things that you can do that make it less likely that people will respond in a defensive manner. Two key elements of defense-free communication are tone of voice and keywords. To generate a conversation or inquiry rather than an upset or argument make sure your tone of voice is neutral. A neutral tone of voice indicates that you are inquiring rather than judging or blaming. Some keywords that tend to put people on the defensive include: why, should, YOU and if only. Notice in the examples below how different words make a difference in eliciting a different response.

> Problem: Speaking in a way that puts others on the defensive, which usually leads to arguments and butting heads
>
> Solution: Communicate with personal responsibility and positive intention.

Examples:
- Creates defensiveness: "You're not much of a detail person, are you?"
- Doesn't create defensive: If you're interested, I have some ideas that might be helpful to you regarding ways to handle a project with so many details. A lot of it I learned when I headed up the XYZ project several years ago.

Keys to defense-free communication
- Use "I" statements.
- Take responsibility.
- Inquire.
- "Why" questions lead to defensiveness. Instead, ask "What?"
- Creates defensiveness: "Why are you late?"

- Doesn't create defensiveness: "What happened? We were expecting to have you join us at Noon.

Tell people they're doing something wrong, and they tend to get defensive. Minimize defensiveness by informing and inquiring.

Creative Communication

What you say is what you get. We've all heard that phrase before, but when it comes to communication, it takes on a whole new meaning. It means that you are the one who has the power to intentionally create what you want in life. Rather than giving your power away to your thoughts, beliefs and words, you can use your power to create with your words. Words create images, feelings, impressions and experiences. They carry energy and have the power to influence your experience of self, your ability to accomplish what you want in life and your ability to connect with others; therefore, the stories you speak about yourself and your life create your own experiences of the world. You are giving fuel to your mind.

When John F. Kennedy said that we would put a man on the moon by the end of the '60s, was he predicting, declaring, hoping or creating a new idea for people? He spoke something into existence! He was willing to create with his speaking a new realm of possibility. And of course, he had the power and ability to influence the actions that would fulfill the vision that he was creating with his words. Everything starts as a thought, which is then put into words, which is then put into action.

When you speak about your own dreams and goals, you create a vision for yourself. If you continue to say something over and over, you begin to not only think it but believe it! Your words become a self-fulfilling prophecy. You will listen to yourself and take on whatever quality it is that you continue to speak.

Be aware, however, that this can work negatively as well. If you keep saying to yourself, "I'm too young (old, small, big, poor, clumsy, etc.) to (take up drumming, apply for that job, take that kind of vacation, etc.), then what do you think is going to happen? You will honor what you say, and your words become the truth. In this case, which came first—what you were saying or what you believed?

Remember that when there is a positive vision, people flourish. Unfortunately, too much of our communication is based on the past, and positive vision must be forward-seeing. So give up speaking from the past use the power of your words to create an incredible future, not just for yourself but for the people whose lives you touch every day.

Self Assessment

Personal Review:

- Name the last three times you really spoke from your heart to someone.
- Name the last three times you said something without thinking that caused either hurt feelings, upset, misunderstandings or conflict.
- Who are the people that you tend to have knee jerk reactions to?
- In what situations and regarding what topics do you tend to have knee jerk reactions?
- How often do you give generously to others with praise and acknowledgment? Daily? Weekly? Occasionally? Seldom?
- Recall a time when you made something up that turned out not to be so (misperception). Recall a time when you really connected with someone, and identify what it was about that conversation that helped to generate that connection.
- Recall a time when you cleared a communication misunderstanding.
- Recall a time when your not saying everything there was to say led to problems.
- Identify some of the words you use that may be difficult for others to understand.

Respond to the following statements in the way that most accurately describes your behavior pattern—Occasionally, Sometimes, Frequently or Most of the time:

- I communicate to contribute rather than to get attention.
- I consciously communicate with people to connect rather than to create distance.
- I consciously choose words that best represent the situation.
- I attempt to point people in the right direction when communicating about upsets, mistakes or misunderstandings.
- I ask for what I want and need rather than hint at it.

- I am able to notice my tendency to react in a knee jerk fashion to someone and take a minute to choose my response more wisely.
- I am able to generate interesting social conversation.
- I choose my words wisely so as to make a beneficial difference when speaking.
- My focus is to communicate with respect and dignity—for myself and others.
- I have the ability to override my emotions with a higher purpose when necessary.
- I am willing to give people the benefit of the doubt as I gather information to verify my perception.
- I know how to inquire of rather than confront people.
- I am able to turn my complaints into requests that produce positive actions.
- I use words to create images and experiences that support what I want to create in my life.

REVIEW

Common Communication Problems
Knee jerk reactions
Partial communication
"Hallucination" perceptions
Treating social conversations as insignificant
Fear of confrontation
Treating communication in a happenstance, lackadaisical manner
Letting emotions get in the way
Not getting straight communication from others
Assuming
Laziness
Complaining and hinting
Using words that others do not relate to or understand
Speaking in a way that puts others on the defensive

Communication Solutions
Be curious, interested and willing to make interesting conversation.
State the facts.
Remember that everything you say is representative of you.

Remember that everything you do communicates.
Stay true to the message you want to communicate.
Communicate directly and with respect and compassion.
Ask for clarifying information.
Give thought to your responses.
Use complete communication.
Make insightful inquiries.
Acknowledge people on a daily basis.
Make clear requests.
Choose your words wisely.
Communicate personal responsibility.

When you master the art of communication, you will experience more ease, less stress and a greater sense of well-being and connection.

Communication makes a difference in the following ways
Encourages cooperation
Increases trust
Reduces stress
Resolves conflicts
Creates understanding
Increases efficiency
Produces results

Communication is about connecting. And as Dr. Edward M. Hallowell says in his book, *Connect*, "Strong connections make life feel satisfying and secure. But many of us have started to neglect the life of connection, giving most of our time to achievement and daily success. This is a dangerous trend. It is time to make connecting a top priority again, because our health and our happiness depend upon it."

It's time for all of us to take responsibility for our communication and the effects that what we say have on ourselves and others. In his book, *Raising an Emotionally Intelligent Child*, John Gottman reveals how researchers have found that "emotional awareness and your ability to experience and communicate feelings will determine your success and happiness in all walks of life." Heartfelt communication carries with it passion and compassion, the balance of mind and heart, full of power and full of wisdom.

Communication influences your life in major ways every day. It can be the number one reason why you don't have what you want in life, or it can be the number one reason why you are happy, fulfilled and successful. It's a challenging skill that can be hugely rewarding. And your future will be greatly influenced by what you say, how you say it and who you say it to.

Donna Fisher

Donna Fisher, Certified Speaking Professional is a marketing consultant, author and nationally known authority on the importance of *people skills*, *networking*, and *the personal touch* in today's busy, topsy-turvy world. She is the president of both Donna Fisher Presents, a provider of keynotes and trainings for corporate meetings, conferences and conventions, and HiHat Inc., a manufacturing and retail business for drums and percussion instruments. Her four books, Power Networking, People Power, Power NetWeaving and Professional Networking for Dummies have been translated in 4 languages, recommended by Time Magazine and used as reference books in corporations and universities. She is a regular guest on Wisdom Radio and has been quoted and featured in numerous national magazines and newspapers. Donna's mission is to be a catalyst for people to communicate and relate with respect and dignity and connect with people to make a difference. She provides programs and products for companies who want to bring out the best in their people and people who want to soar to success. Her Certified Speaking Professional (CSP) designation is an honor held by less than ten percent of professional speakers.

Donna Fisher, CSP
6524 San Felipe #138
Houston, TX 77057
713-789-2484
Email: donna@donnafisher.com
www.donnafisher.com, www.drummingupbusiness.net
www.onlinebusinessnetworking.com

Chapter 10

Communicating With Humor

Cynthia Hernandez Kolski

"You lose the power to laugh, you lose the power to think straight."
E.K.Hornbeck, *Inherit the Wind*

Imagine, if you will, a warm, sunny, late December day in Chicago. My family had agreed to help me move a dear friend two days after Christmas. I had told our friend that we would be out to finish packing by 11:00 that morning. But it was now almost noon, and we were just getting on the expressway. We were running late, we were low on gas, my children had wanted to sleep in, and my daughter, Christina, was on her cell phone, trying to locate her father to find out where he was going to meet us. It was obviously a tense moment. Everyone was very quiet, afraid to say anything, when my son, Joe, said in one of his many voices, "Do you remember the time we were running late going to help Uncle Mike pack, and we couldn't find dad, and we ran out of gas, and we forgot to bring empty boxes with us, and we..." At that point, we were all laughing, and things didn't seem so stressful any more.

This is a perfect example of how using humor to communicate can put things in their proper perspective. With his animated voice and exaggerated stories, Joe reminded us not to take things so seriously and to laugh at ourselves. When conversations seem intense, adding humor can diffuse the moment; however, humor itself is nothing to joke about. "Business executives and political leaders have embraced humor because humor works," says Robert Orben, former director of the White House speech writing department. "Humor has gone from being an admirable part of a leader's character to a mandatory one."

In the 1970s, Norman Cousins—editor, writer and professor of medical humanities at the UCLA School of Medicine—started investigating the impact that humor has on the human psyche. In his book, *Head First: The Biology of Hope and the Healing Power of the Human Spirit*, Cousins asserts that positive emotional states enhance physical and psychological healing. He writes that sustained laughter makes us feel better physically by stimulating the release of endorphins, a pain-killing substance naturally produced in our bodies.

Other studies have proven the positive impact of humor and the benefits it has on well-being. Dr. William Fry, Jr., of the Stanford Medical School psychiatry department, says that laughter plays an invaluable part in strengthening the heart muscle. According to Fry, just twenty seconds of laughter is equivalent to three minutes of cardiovascular work.

As a pediatric nurse, I saw how laughter could ease children's pain, so I quickly learned the art of making children laugh. Directing their attention to something funny helped us accomplish what we needed to do. If we dressed up as clowns or wore colorful clothes, the children's physical exams went much faster and easier for everyone.

I'm sure you have witnessed the power of laughter in your own life; you just know that a sick loved one is on the road to recovery when he or she starts laughing and developing an appetite. I have heard many a member of my own family say, "He must be feeling better—he's laughing!"

Humor has become such an important subject that classes are taught, organizations are formed and conferences are held, all with the a common purpose—promoting the art of making people laugh. Many professionals base their careers on communicating with humor. Newsletters, cassettes, videos and books on the subject are in big demand. Of course, countless television programs are built around humor (the term "sitcom" does stand for situation *comedy*, after all). Communicating with humor can even save

---

"The absolute truth is the thing that makes people laugh." -- Carl Reiner

relationships—or end them. The challenge is to know when and how to add humor to communication.

The art of communication can be a challenge. The fact that you bought and are reading this book on effective communication skills attests to that. It does not matter if your communication is with someone you know very well or a total stranger—sometimes, your message seems to fall on deaf ears. You find yourself wanting to grab the person and say, "Watch my lips as they move. Words will come out!" You may find yourself asking, "Is it me? Am I speaking a foreign language? Is that why people are not understanding my message?" Getting your message across is very important or you wouldn't continue to be so persistent, would you? Being able to express ideas and thoughts through words, gestures, facial expressions and body movements is a major goal for all of us.

How many times have you been in a discussion with someone and found yourself tongue-tied? Have you ever been in a conversation and couldn't think of anything to say? Then immediately after walking away you said to yourself, "Why didn't I say ___?" or "I should have said ___" Do you ever wonder *why* getting a message across can seem so difficult when you have been talking since you were a young child?

I believe you are truly communicating with someone when the other person can echo back what you have said to your satisfaction and you can echo what they have said to their satisfaction. Now that doesn't seem too hard or complicated. But when was the last time you were truly understood in a conversation? Communicating effectively is a skill that anyone can learn with practice, practice and more practice. Likewise, adding humor to your communication is also a learned skill. It requires tapping into the right side of your brain—the creative side—to expand your imagination.

Throughout this book, you will find techniques and strategies for communicating effectively with people. Practice again and again the methods that relate to you or even the ones you don't feel comfortable with. Those are probably the ones you need to practice the most because they pose the biggest challenge. Only through practice will you will see improvement in your communication skills. It will take some work and some time in order to be successful, so don't be too hard on yourself if

---

"Comedy is simply a funny way of being serious." -- Peter Ustinov

you don't see an immediate change. Remember, you have to hear something eight times to remember it and twenty-one times for it to become a habit.

Please remember that this is not a psychology book and that I am not a therapist. None of the information in this chapter is meant to offend or insult anyone. This is a "How-To" book, and the information we are giving comes from many years of personal and shared experiences. I believe in that old adage, "Walk your talk." So know that every example, method, tool and technique mentioned in this chapter has been used, practiced and proven successful or it would not appear here for your benefit and future use.

As a professional motivational speaker, trainer and personal coach, I look for opportunities to add humor to my seminars and workshops. It keeps the audience awake and entertained and gives them a way to see and hear new things, from new perspectives.

In this chapter, we will explore the benefits of adding humor to your communication. We'll also discuss successful techniques for using humor to spice up conversation. Finally, I will give you a list of resources to read, listen to or watch, to assist you in discovering the strategies that work best for you.

Whether your message is technical, political or social, using humor helps you get the point across without insulting the listener. You can add humor to your communication in many different ways—through words, gestures, body or sign language, stories, props or even comic strips.

Don't misunderstand me: I'm not talking about becoming a comedian or telling jokes. I'm talking about enhancing your message with humor to make it more understandable and to emphasize your point. We'll also discuss when not to use humor, which is sometimes more important than knowing when you should use it.

Let's look at some of the benefits of using humor to optimize your communication:

"There are things of deadly earnest that can only be mentioned under the cover of a joke."
-- J.J. Procter

Humor relaxes you and the person with whom you are communicating.

When people first meet, there can sometimes be a certain amount of tension between them. It can be due to their unfamiliarity with each other or perhaps their environment. Sometimes it's simply apprehension about the unknown.

When people show up for my seminars for the first time, they can be a little wary, even though they are the ones who have chosen to be there. To put them at ease when they are checking in, I inject a little humor by asking them to fill out name tags. I say, "Please write your first name—or whatever you want to be called today!" This always gets people talking and laughing. As people enter the room, I can still hear them buzzing about what I just asked them to do; most of them emphasize the "whatever you want to be called today" part. I have found that this simple technique sets up my audience to be relaxed and open to learning and having fun.

Humor connects you to others.

When communicating to people, you want to say things that will bring you together in thought and idea. Using humor to make that connection is an effective tool because it helps others feel less threatened and pressured.

I often work with gang members who are sent to me through the criminal justice system. These young men have a choice—my classes or jail. I can say with little doubt that some of my students are not happy about attending my classes. They see me as just another part of the system, and my being female and a Latina carries very little weight, if any.

At the beginning of my classes, I am constantly being tested. I once had a student who sat slumped down in his chair, arms crossed, looking down at the floor. As I began speaking, he yelled loud enough for everyone to hear: "So I have to f~ing sit here for two f~ing hours?" "Yes," I said, to which he replied, "So if I have to go to the f~ing bathroom, are you going to f~ing go for me?" "No, but I'll give you a cup," I said, handing him an empty Styrofoam cup. The rest of the students laughed, and even this young man smiled. With a little humor, I was able to pass the test given to the "outsider" and show the room I could take care of myself and carry my own. This levity brought us a little closer together and

---

"One never needs their humor as much as when they argue with a fool." -- Chinese Proverb

made them a little more open to hearing my thoughts and ideas, even ones that were from a different perspective than theirs.

Humor assists in clarifying your message.
Remember first dates? New jobs? Those times when you were hoping to impress someone? When you are nervous, it's usually harder to find just the right way of saying what you want to say. Your emotions are running high, and you want to make sure you say the right thing at the right time. It is also at such times that you may not be thinking clearly. This is when humor can help.

Humor helps soften negative messages.
If the message you're communicating is difficult for others to hear, adding humor seems to get their attention and make the message more acceptable. Watch the program *Will & Grace*. They demonstrate how to use humor to relay a negative message successfully. Or reruns of the *ROSEANNE* Show. She adds humor when she is disciplining her children.

Humor relieves tension.
Clear communication can be difficult if there is tension in the room. Whether the listeners are defensive, hostile or uncomfortable, going for the funny bone can break the tension and discomfort. This, in turn, lowers any defensiveness or hostility that may have previously existed.

The television series $M*A*S*H$ expertly did just that. Laughter helped the soldiers keep their sanity and focus under the daily pressures of war. Another example is the program, *Everybody Loves Raymond*. The title character is a sports writer with a wife and three children, who lives across the street from his mother, father and brother. Raymond is constantly using one-liners to add comic relief and relieve the tension when he's around his family.

"You grow up on the day you have your first real laugh at yourself." -- Ethel Barrymore

Humor helps make a dull subject more interesting.

Statistics say that when speaking to people, you need to do something different at least every fifteen minutes in order to keep their interest. I'm not sure what kind of commentary this is on the attention span of the typical American, but adding something funny that's related to your topic or making your point from a humorous perspective does work.

Humor helps us keep things in proper perspective.

There is a scene in the movie *The Day Reagan Was Shot*, in which Secretary of State Alexander Haig is furious because he feels he is being undermined. He is so disturbed that he is ready to turn in his resignation. Looking out his office window, his back to his aide, he says, "Pat says that I am more irritable and short-tempered since the triple bypass. What do you think?" "Well," says his aide, "Before the surgery, you weren't exactly a pussycat either." Haig quickly turns around, looking very somber. After a few suspenseful moments, he smiles, breaks into a laugh and says, "You keep me in line, Buddy. You keep me on the straight and narrow." Both men smile and laugh. Even in the White House, humor is used to keep things in their proper perspective, no matter how serious they may seem. So when things aren't looking up, try asking yourself, "How important is this, really? How important will this be tomorrow?"

Humor gets people's attention.

Whether you are speaking for a short time or all day, keeping someone's attention can be a hard thing to do. The bigger the audience, the harder it is, since most people are not accustomed to giving anyone their full attention. Bringing in elements of humor gets people's attention and can generate laughter in a room, which is always a plus!

Many years ago, I was speaking before a small group of university administrators. The audience got out of hand, arguing and talking with each other at the same time. Even raising my voice to get their attention failed. Since I was standing in front of everyone, I walked over to the side.

"Among those whom I like or admire, I can find no common denominator, but among those whom I love, I can: all of them make me laugh." -- A. H. Auden

"The laughter costs too much which is purchased by the sacrifice of decency." -- John Quinton

Making sure my back was to my audience, I started talking to the wall. Softly mumbling, I could hear the audience gradually settle down. I then heard someone point out to everyone that I was talking to the wall. Hearing this, I started to talk louder: " I don't know what to do. I don't know where I failed and lost control of this meeting. What? You say they're looking at me?" I slowly turned my head, then quickly looked back at the wall. "You're right. What do I do now?" By this time, the whole audience was with me, and I had no problems keeping their attention the rest of the day. I will admit that what I have just described to you is a little unconventional, but it took no more than a few minutes, it gave me back the control of the audience (which is what I needed to succeed for the day), and the audience had a good laugh. I assure you, this group has never forgotten my name. In fact, they have invited me back again and again.

Martin Short, Harpo Marx, Charlie Chaplin, Jim Carrey, Carol Burnett, John Ritter, Red Skelton, Jerry Lewis, Kathy Griffin, Steve Martin and my all time favorite, Lucille Ball: These are just a few of the many celebrities who have taught us all how to laugh—not just at them but at ourselves. Tripping over our feet, getting our words tangled up and spilling food or drinks on ourselves are just a few of the situations where we can save face by pointing out our errors before others have the opportunity to do it for us.

Did you know it takes more muscles in your face to frown than it does to smile? So make people laugh! Laughter is contagious, it clears the mind, and it puts people at ease. When you can make people laugh, you are accepted, and others begin to feel more comfortable. They seem to lighten up, even if for a little while.

Communicating with humor is a learned skill. Saying something in a funny way does not necessarily make it funny. Or simply dropping something funny into your conversation may not always work either. What makes something humorous is its presentation and appropriateness (which we will talk more about later). These are two of the keys, I believe, to using humor in a way that communicates your message clearly and puts you in a good light.

"I can usually judge a fellow by what he laughs at." -- Wilson Mizner

How you say something alerts people to your attitude, and attitude brings a great deal to your conversation. The following joke about a newlywed couple illustrates this point:

While on their honeymoon, a new husband takes off his pants, hands them to his bride and asks her to put them on. She tries them on and says, "Honey, I can't wear these pants. They are way too big for me." The husband quickly responds, "You remember that. I am the man, and I wear the pants in this family." A few moments later, the new wife goes up to her husband, hands him her panties and asks him to put them on. He tries to squeeze into them but is only able to get them up to his knees. Struggling with the undergarment, he exclaims, "There is no way I'm going to get into your panties!" Without missing a beat, his new wife says, "That's right, and you never will until you change your attitude!"

Both the husband and the wife understood each other's message. Each made his or her point. But the husband left the humor out of his message, whereas his wife added it so as not to offend her groom. Our attitude tells people whether we intend to be funny or offensive. It plays a big part in making our humor succeed or fail.

Incidentally, if you are interested in learning more about attitude, please read, *Love Is Letting Go of Fear* by Gerald G. Jampolsky. It is a very fast-reading and basic book, which I highly recommend.

Now that we have discussed the right times to insert humor into your conversation, let's talk a little about when not to tickle someone's funny bone. You do not want to use humor:

To embarrass, humiliate, attack or make fun of someone. Many people use this supposed "tongue-in-cheek" humor all the time.

To hide from your true feelings. People will sometimes bring humor into their conversation in order to avoid sharing their true feelings or being honest with you.

As a defense mechanism. When we feel threatened, we may use humor to protect ourselves. It is a human and automatic reaction.

To avoid a subject. Ever been in a conversation about a sensitive topic, when someone randomly chimed in with something along the lines of, "Say, how 'bout them Cubs?" Using humor to draw attention away from an important issue is disrespectful to those with whom you're communicating.

"Against the assault of laughter nothing can stand." -- Mark Twain

I also would add that you take a risk when you use humor:

With someone who has been drinking too much.

Case in point: hecklers. Alcohol hinders them from seeing the benefits of humor. Don't give your energy to someone whose goal is to put others down.

That contains sexist language.

Neither men nor women appreciate the negative portrayal of their gender.

At airports.

Even before September 11, 2001, we knew that a security checkpoint at an airport or government building was *never* an appropriate place to inject even the slightest form of humor.

Once, I was subjected to a short investigation while traveling through an airport. And believe me, I'm here to say that airport security personnel don't play around! It all started when I was on my way to San Francisco, where I was scheduled to conduct a stress workshop. I had brought along a bunch of stress balls (the kind you squeeze to relieve tension), but they didn't fit into my luggage, so I threw them into a carry-on bag. As I was going through the security checkpoint at the airport, two officers took me by the arms and said, "Quietly come with us, please."

As they led me to a small room, I asked with a big smile and a sing-song voice if I had been the millionth customer and won a ticket to Hawaii. With straight faces, they started asking me for my identification, where I was going, why I was going there, who could identify me and what I could tell them about the hand grenade. My mouth fell open, and I told them I had no idea what they were talking about. I learned later that one of the stress balls was in the shape, size and color of a hand grenade. Needless to say, airport security does not like jokes or think very many things are funny!

With law enforcement officers.

"Law enforcement officers are trained to be on guard for everything and everybody. Expect the unexpected," says Officer Patricia Lloyd of the

---

"If you find yourself going through hell, keep going." -- Sir Winston Churchill

Chicago 25th Police District. "We first assess each situation and evaluate the person or people involved." That is why when you are pulled over for a traffic violation, it is not the time to joke or play with the police officer who has pulled you over. On duty, law enforcement officers take their positions very seriously, off duty, is another story.

Ethnic or cultural humor.

I am Mexican-American and my husband, Philip, is of Polish descent. I even coined the term "Policans" to refer to our two children, Joe and Christina, since they are half Mexican and half Polish. In this case, I felt that we could poke a little fun at ourselves. But it's a different matter when such humor comes from an outsider. I'll illustrate with a true story:

Years ago, one of my husband's co-workers came into his office to share this joke with him: "What do you call the offspring of a Polack and a Mexican?" We were new in town at the time, so this man had not had an opportunity to meet me or our son (I was still pregnant with our daughter). Philip's supervisor, however, who was also in the room, had met us. He gently nudged this gentleman, saying, "I wouldn't go there if I were you."

The man did not listen. He thought the joke was funnier than funny and was sure that my husband would love it as well. He repeated, "What do you call the offspring of a Polack and a Mexican?" Without looking at the man, Philip said, "I don't know—what do you call the offspring of a Polack and a Mexican?" "Ricky Retardo!" the man blurted out. He started laughing hysterically, although no one else in the room was. Finally, my husband looked up and softly said, "My wife is Mexican."

Perhaps you've had a moment like this, when you wished the earth would open up and swallow you whole. Or maybe you've been on the receiving end of an ethnic slam. In either case, ethnic humor is a *big* no-no. If you think this kind of humor is going to be positive, you're mistaken. If you're looking to add humor with an ethic tone or cultural flavor, you had better be absolutely sure you know what is acceptable and what is not. Otherwise, it will turn around and bite you in the butt.

Remember, using humor in any of the situations we've just discussed could backfire. Humor should be used to enhance communication, not

"Man is the only animal that laughs and weeps; for he is the only animal that is stuck with the difference between what things are and what they might have been." -- William Hazlitt

sabotage the message. Having said that, you are probably asking yourself, "How do I know when and when not to add humor?"

Let's take a look at the etiquette of humor—a few unwritten, easy-to-remember rules for judging when and when not to use it. Ask yourself these questions:

- Is what you're about to say appropriate for the situation?
- Is it relevant to the point you want to make?
- What do you know about your audience?
- Are you comfortable? This is the most important question to ask yourself. You need to be comfortable if you are going to be playful with people. If you are nervous about saying something, the other party will pick up on that, and you may fail to send the correct message.

We are all just regular people, looking to make this world of ours a better place in which to live. I believe using humor in our everyday conversations is one way of making that happen. Using humor is power.

When you are interacting with people and have the ability to make them laugh, you are bonding with your audience, and they are building their confidence in you. And who wouldn't want that?

Don't confuse the simple act of talking with communication, however. Anyone can repeat something that is funny or has humor in it. But it takes a person with a learned skill to transform the communication into an appropriate and acceptable message without losing or taking away from the meaning.

Part of the skill is being comfortable with the child within you; in other words, being able to be silly or to laugh at yourself. Practice getting comfortable with your silly side, if you aren't already. Play with some kids you know; go to the mall and make funny faces in one of those photo booths; watch the Three Stooges, Martin Short, Saturday morning cartoons, Carol Burnett or Tim Conway on television; listen to the comedy of Bill Cosby, Bob Newhart, Chris Rock or anyone you can relate to, and add their style of humor into your communication. And when I say watch, listen to or read, I mean do it again and again. Sometimes I will listen to someone's technique ten or twenty times, write it out in my own

---

"People who laugh actually live longer than those who don't laugh. Few persons realize that health actually varies according to the amount of laughter." -- Dr. James Walsh

words and practice it thirty to fifty times before I will use it in a presentation. It is essential that you know your material so well you could do it in your sleep or say it backwards.

Communication is divided into two parts: verbal (words) and nonverbal (tone and body language). When adding humor to communication, it is important to have your words be in line with your tone and body language (gestures, facial expressions, etc.).

Here are some ways you can maximize both verbal and nonverbal communication to enhance your message:

Words

Sometimes, I make up words to help me communicate in a humorous way. "Yaka-maka-taka" is just such a word. When I am lost for words, feeling stuck in a situation or feeling like using profanity, I make up words or speak Pig Latin to express my frustration. Using the Spanish slang word "caca" instead of the English "s" word brings laughter to the room and is accepted instead of being seen as insulting.

Tone

Speaking at different volumes and pitches or even singing utilizes varying intonations to emphasize your message.

Body Language

According to the experts, seventy-seven percent of communication is based on body language. People pay more attention to what they see than what they hear. Simple things like crossing your eyes, making faces, exaggerating the movement of your arms or legs or changing your stance will cause people to laugh.

Here are some recommended exercises for using words, tone and body language to enhance your communication. These exercises work great in workshops and seminars. You may find them helpful with your staff or team members.

The "Oh" Exercise

Write the word "Oh" on a flipchart or overhead so your whole audience can see it. Ask your audience to stand and say the word aloud

---

"He deserves Paradise who makes his companions laugh." -- The Koran

(making sure that you don't say it yourself). Now ask them to say the word with different emotions, i.e. as if they were happy, sad, angry, in love, etc.

The "O.K." Exercise

Start by making the "O.K." sign with your thumb and index finger and ask your audience to do the same. Place your "O.K." sign on your chin as you are asking your audience to do likewise. Remove your "O.K." sign from your chin, again asking your audience to do the same. Now here's the tricky part: Quickly ask your audience to put their "O.K." sign on their cheeks while you, however, place yours back on your chin. Watch how many people put their "O.K." sign' back on their chins instead of their cheeks, as you had asked them to do. People will do what they see before they do what they hear.

The "I Like You" Exercise

Have your audience frown or make a mean face. Now ask them to turn to the nearest person and say, "I like you!" It is impossible to do!

The "Get Your Applause" Exercise (a personal favorite)

Have your audience stand, then sit. Do this a few times, asking them to clap as loudly as they can, or even to yell, if they wish. Do this for a few minutes, then ask them to sit down again. When it is quiet, tell them, "Getting a standing ovation from you has made my day, and I want to thank you for that!"

Here are a few more techniques for incorporating humor into your message:

Quotes

I use quotes frequently in my presentations. You can find them by the thousands in books as well as on the Internet. You'll find one quote web site on the resource page at the end of this chapter. You've probably also noticed that there's a quote at the bottom of each page in this chapter.

"Time spent laughing is time spent with the gods." -- Japanese Proverb

Jokes

I'm not a big joke teller, but when I do, I usually change it to a story and use someone's name from the audience to make it more personal. That seems to work, and the audience usually figures out that it is a joke. Even the chief probation officer in Washington, D.C., laughed when I used him in a story. If you have children in your audience, jokes work very well too. Here are a few pretty safe ones:

What do you get when you cross a snowman with a vampire?
Frostbite.

What kind of coffee was served on the Titanic?
Sanka.

How do you catch a unique rabbit?
Unique up on it.

How do you catch a tame rabbit?
Tame way—unique up on it.

Limericks

Limericks work very well as warm-ups to exercises or at the beginning of a communication workshop or discussion. I use a limerick that relates to the topic or to my audience. Again, you can find them in books and on the Internet. Here are a few I use:

There once was a man from Great Britain
Who interrupted two girls at their knittin'.
Said he with a sigh,
"That park bench, well I
Just painted it right where you're sittin'."

An epicure dining at Crewe
Found a very large bug in his stew.
Said the waiter, "Don't shout

"I always knew I would look back at the times I'd cried and laugh, but I never knew that I'd look back at the times I'd laughed and cry." -- Shaun Prowdzik

And wave it about,
Or the rest will be wanting one too."

Props

Magic wands, koosh balls, bubbles, laminated cartoons, exaggerated objects and pencils with humorous sayings on them are all excellent visual aids that can flavor your message with humor.

Funny but true medical stories

One day I had to be the bearer of bad news when I told a wife that her husband had died of a massive myocardial infarct (a heart attack). Not more than five minutes later, I heard her reporting to the rest of the family that he had died of a "massive internal fart."

A young MD doing his residency in obstetrics was quite embarrassed when performing female pelvic exams. To cover his embarrassment, he had unconsciously developed the habit of whistling softly. One middle-aged lady upon whom he was performing an exam suddenly burst out laughing, which embarrassed him further. He looked up from his work and sheepishly said, "I'm sorry. Was I tickling you?" She replied, "No doctor, but the song you were whistling was 'I wish I were an Oscar Meyer Wiener.'"

Now it's time for a sidebar discussion about your audience. It is important to know as much as you can about them—size, gender, age, occupations, etc. Do they know each other, or are they strangers? What's the purpose of the meeting? Are there any sensitive issues that should be avoided? Is this a mandatory meeting, or did they volunteer to come? Having my local contact person fill out a preprogram questionnaire that tells me about my audience helps me understand who I am speaking to.

It is also important to relate to your audience when using humor in your communication. If there is no connection, the humor will fall flat. A few ways to connect with your audience include:

Meet and greet them before you speak. As I said earlier, I always ask my audience to wear name tags.

- Walk through the audience as you speak. You would be amazed at the funny material you'll discover.

"Let there be more joy and laughter in your living." -- Eileen Caddy

- Use your audience by incorporating their names, business or other relatable topic into your speech.

A few Ifs:
- If your speaking time is short, then you will want to use short stories or one-liners.
- If your time is longer, the stories or quotes can be longer.
- If your audience is mostly male, your humor will be different than if it were mostly female.
- If your audience consists of senior citizens, use jokes and stories. They love them.
- If you don't get an opportunity to know your audience, always have some general humor in your bag of tricks.

Since we are talking about audiences, I would like to share with you a technique I use all the time. It always makes people laugh. Whether I'm presenting, standing in a crowded elevator or just talking with friends, this technique is a sure-fire way to get a conversation started on a good note.

When I make a move to touch someone (male or female), I always say, "This is not a sexual come-on or pass. I am touching you just as part of the exercise," or "I am touching you because I like your energy," or "I am touching you to demonstrate something. Are you willing to be a volunteer?" By this point, everyone in the room is laughing, and the participant usually has a cute remark to add.

Remember, the only safe and acceptable places to touch anyone in public are the shoulder, the forearm or the hand, and only if you ask permission first. This technique should only be used if you are very comfortable and secure, because if the participant turns things around on you, you must be able to maintain control of the situation.

There are so many topics and styles of humorous communication that we have not even touched on—political humor, dry humor, self-effacing humor, etc.—which means we'll just have to write a sequel to this book! But before closing, I would like to address one other situation in which humor can be a great benefit to your message. That is when you are speaking to very sick people.

" Warning! Humor may be hazardous to your illness." – Allie Katz

As a volunteer who sits with the terminally ill, I know that sometimes humor is the saving grace for both the patients and their families. Humor can take the discomfort out of the room and put people at ease. When my mother was diagnosed with Alzheimer's Disease, humor helped my family deal with the seriousness of the situation. I have assisted many friends who had cancer, and humor has saved many a day and helped play a big part in either the cure or the emotional uplifting of each patient.

My niece, Susan, was recently diagnosed with stomach cancer, and she uses a positive attitude and humor to help her spirits remain high. It was Christmas Eve and just about time for Santa to make a visit. The Kolski women were asking the men who would like to take the job. There wasn't much cooperation, so I said, "Let Susan pick who's going to be Santa." And they asked, "Why Susan?" "Because I have cancer and no one would turn me down!" Susan said. Susan has the stamina that will care her to good health and she has earned my admiration as well as many others! Using humor during a very trying time such as this relieves tension and helps keep in focus the goal of getting well.

When using humor in your communication, remember to relax, enjoy and have fun. I hope these exercises, techniques and examples I have shared are beneficial to you. Please e-mail me and let me know how they have worked for you. I would very much like to hear how things are going.

Resources

My personal resources can be just about anything—books, videos, tapes, clip art, cartoons, quotes, cards, articles, the Internet, personal stories and experiences. Before you go out and invest in any one resource, however, I recommend that you see if it is available in your public library, book store or flea market. Or you could even borrow it from a colleague. Look through the material before you purchase it to make sure that it contains the information you are looking for. Many times, I will purchase a resource for future use and reference. Once you start looking, I think you will be amazed at the unusual places you will find resource materials. Although I could list pages and pages worth, I will share just a few of my own with you:

"Let there be more joy and laughter in your living." – Eileen Caddy

Associations:
- Toastmasters International • P.O. Box 9052, Mission Viejo, California 92690. Or you can look for a local chapter in your area.

Books:
- Antion, Tom. *Wake 'Em Up!*, Maryland: Anchor Publishing, 1997
- Axtell, Roger. Gestures: Do's and Taboos of Body Language around the World, New York: Wiley
- Cousins, Norman. Head First: The Biology of Hope and the Healing Power of the Human Spirit, New York: Dutton, 1989
- Ellenbogen, Glenn C., ed. The Directory of Humor Magazines and Humor Organizations in America, New York: WryBred Press, 1985
- Fry, William F., Jr. M.D. and Waleed A. Salameh, eds. *Handbook of Humor and Psychotherapy* and *Advances in the Clinical Use of Humor*, Florida: Pro Resource, 1987
- Jampolsky, Gerald G. *Love Is Letting Go of Fear*, New York: Bantam, 1981
- Johnson, Eric W. *A Treasury of Humor*, New York: Ivy Books, 1989
- Metcalf, C.W. and Roma Felible. *Lighten Up*, Massachusetts: Perseus Books, 1992
- Perret, Gene. *Comedy Writing Workbook*, New York: Sterling, 1990
- Walters, Lilly. *What to Say When You're Dying on the Platform*, New York: McGraw-Hill, 1995

Publications:
- *The Executive Speaker*, a monthly newsletter. Also publishes the *Quote, Unquote* newsletter
- Executive Speaker Company, P.O. Box 292437, Dayton, Ohio 45429 • (513) 294-8493
- *The Jokesmith*, a monthly newsletter. 44 Queen's View Road, Marlborough, MA 01752

Tapes:
- Metcalf, C.W. *Humor, Risk & Change*, Fort Collins, Colorado: C.W. Metcalf & Co., 1986; *Humaerobics*, Fort Collins, Colorado: C. W. Metcalf & Co, 1986; *Humor Allies*, Fort Collins, Colorado: C.W. Metcalf & Co., 1988
- Antion, Tom. *Make 'Em Laugh*, Maryland: Anchor Publishing, 1997

Videos:
- Antion, Tom. *Make 'Em Laugh*, Maryland: Anchor Publishing, 1997; *Business Lite For Women Only*
- Walters, Lilly and Jeff Dewar. *Games Presenters Play*, California: Royal Publishing
- Jeffries, Michael. *Speaking with Magic*, California: Royal Publishing

Internet:
www.Antion.com
www.humor.com
www.netfunny.com
www.collegehumor.com
www.quotationspage.com

Clip Art Samples:
www.microsoft.com/clipgalleryart
Just give them a topic or name, and they find the clip art for you. I love this site!

Cynthia Hernandez Kolski

"¡Sí puedo!" This is the motto that Cynthia Hernandez Kolski lives by and uses in her interactive workshops. It means: "Yes, I can!" in Spanish. That is her belief and approach to life and she shares it with everyone she meets. Cynthia believes you can achieve what you want, by what you choose! Cynthia is a sought after trainer because her "hands-on approach" reaches both youth and adults. Her company, *Communication Education*, Inc. designs curricula and in-service training on the technology of empowerment as an effective system for problem solving. Cynthia is a passionate speaker who has presented to national and international groups, for public and private sectors alike. Cynthia began her career as a nurse, where she discovered the essential link between mind and body–mental and physical health. Shortly, thereafter, she began to bridge her medical background with the field of training and development. She is committed to making a positive change in this world.

Cynthia Hernandez Kolski
Communication Education, Inc.
835 East Franham Lane
Wheaton, Illinois 60187
Office: (773) 294-0576
Fax: (630) 668-6118
E-Mail: Openhandandheart@cs.com

Chapter 11

Listen Your Way To The Top!

Jolene Carson

Have you ever met someone for the first time and immediately felt "connected?" I'm certain you can recall a number of times in your life when this has happened. It's as if you have known the person all your life even though you are engaged in your very first conversation. You feel exhilarated because the two of you are getting along so well. And the longer you talk, the more you enjoy the conversation. These encounters don't happen often, but when they do, we want them to continue.

Have you ever stopped to think what makes these conversations meaningful? Sometimes a physical attraction causes one to be absorbed by another. More often, however, I believe there is another reason— something the other person is doing and doing well, something most people are not consciously aware of at all—that makes all the difference in how people connect with one another. When practiced well, it can change the dynamics of the workplace and add millions to an organization's bottom line. I'm talking about the art of listening.

Stop for a moment and consider the breadth and scope of business in general. Day in and day out, all around the world, men and women engage in conversations and communications that involve millions, even billions, of pieces of information. Unfortunately, though, much of this information is hidden in the folds of innuendoes, body language, voice inflections, poorly written e-mails and stuttering telephone messages. Bad communication is the bane of business. Conversely, good communication is the lifeblood of business, but the art of listening—which is the foundation of all successful communication—is overlooked or ignored in most organizations around the world.

This chapter will teach you the skills you need to become a better listener. And when actively modeled, your strong listening skills can be passed on to your staff or even your own employer, thus affecting your team and your entire organization.

We'll start out by explaining exactly what listening is (as well as what it is not), then take a look at nine steps to effective listening. We'll then study the nature of nonverbal communication and offer some advice on how to use others' nonverbal cues to enhance the communication process. Finally, we'll take a look at the four different personality styles and how understanding them can help make you both an effective listener and communicator.

Listening is an Active Process

Listening is one of the most important aspects of communication. Studies indicate that it accounts for forty-five percent of communication in the workplace; however, it is the area in which the least amount of workplace training is done. Likewise, it is just as important for creating better relationships with our families and friends.

Many people tell me they believe they are good listeners—that is, until I begin to dig deeper into their listening styles. See if you fit into one of these four categories:

Ignoring

Everyone ignores others from time to time. It is not very subtle. Rather than focusing on the person and the issue at hand, some people just tune the speaker out, not really listening at all.

Pretending

I know many men and women in business who are masters at pretending. They seem to be attentive, nodding from time to time and even commenting occasionally. But it's all a game. Their minds are on other people or projects, and speakers eventually see through them.

Selective Listening

This is the result of people tuning in and out. They hear only certain parts of the conversation. It often happens when conversing with a chatterer such as a young child, spouse or even a friend. People may also use selective listening when their interests lie elsewhere but they are being engaged in conversation. This kind of listening frequently occurs in the home. Everyone can relate to the scene in which a wife is trying to tell her husband something important—right in the middle of a football game on television.

Attentive Listening

With attentive listening, we pay attention and focus on only the <u>words</u> being spoken. But focusing on the words <u>alone</u> is only one small step towards effective listening. We must focus on the total message that's being sent. This means really working to take in the message through words and how they're spoken, and also to "listen" closest of all to what isn't spoken – the non-verbal message. (We'll talk about this in more detail later.)

Effective Listening

<u>Different than all of these</u> is <u>effective listening</u> – an active process. If we actively listen to the total message and use good feedback skills, we will be a good communicator. And that can translate to healthier and happier relationships and a steady climb up the corporate ladder.

First, effective listening requires the intent to really listen. Your intention should be one of the following objectives:

1. Understand the person

2. Enjoy the conversation

3. Learn something

4. Give help or comfort

Effective listening is also an active process, and your understanding of what's really being said will depend upon your participation. It requires not only listening to the total message but using good feedback skills.

A good leader must have good listening habits. Whether in a one on one discussion, a meeting, a teleconference, an e-mail conversation, a negotiation process or an interview, the most successful managers are those who know how to listen and convince the speaker that he has been heard. In today's business climate, superior communication skills are needed to deal diplomatically and assertively with business people from all over the world.

If you want respect from your employees and want to really know what's going on in your department and company, then be an effective listener. Your time may be limited, but your employees need your attention nonetheless. Listen to what they have to say about business issues and personal concerns. Show interest in what they tell you, and acknowledge through verbal and nonverbal feedback that you're listening from their point of view. Offer advice only if asked. Many times, people just want someone to listen.

Remember, though, that communication is a two-way street. Many people do not speak effectively; they take too long to get to the point, and when they finally get to it, the point is often unclear. For example, some employees want to give all the background information first and then build up to the point. This problem is prevalent in every industry.

So while you are developing your top-notch listening skills, you can also help your employees learn how to present their information more effectively. Prior to a meeting, for example, you could ask each person to write down, in one sentence, the point he or she wants to present. If you allow enough time to review this point prior to the meeting, you can determine what you think about it or if any more information is needed. This will be a giant step toward more effective communication with the additional benefits of saving time and showing interest in the employees. It creates a win-win solution and makes it easier for you to listen.

Nine Steps to Effective Listening

Here are nine proven techniques that can not only make you a better listener but improve your overall communication skills:

1. Stay focused.

Have you ever been in a conversation in which there was a long pause, and you knew it was your turn to speak, but you didn't know what had just been said? Your body was there but your mind had temporarily left. Many of us have had this happen because our minds process more quickly than people speak. It also happens when the person talking is speaking more quickly or slowly than we prefer.

Listening with your full, undivided attention means keeping your mind free of other thoughts, such as your own interests and problems. You must make a concentrated effort to eliminate personal thoughts and concentrate one hundred person on the other person.

Actively stay focused by asking yourself continually throughout the conversation, "What does the speaker really mean by that statement? What is he really saying to me? What does he want me to understand or do?"

2. Listen with your whole being.

It's important to give people your full attention, so listen as intently with your eyes as you do with your ears. Body language reveals the most information about what a listener is thinking and feeling. That's why people want to see the listener's eyes and facial expressions when they are speaking—because they want to feel a connection.

For example, if you are listening to someone and doing other tasks at the same time, you will usually fail to achieve effective communication because the speaker will perceive that you're not listening. I was reading the newspaper one evening when my daughter, who was eleven at the time, began telling me something. I continued reading as I listened to her. She said, "You're not listening." I told her that I was and to continue her story. When I went back to my reading, she said again, "You're still not listening." This time, I heard disappointment in her voice. I insisted that I had been listening and repeated back everything she had just told me. "See," I said. "I was listening." I thought she would be impressed that I had heard everything. Instead, she replied, "I don't care. It didn't *feel* like you were listening."

Show interest: Maintain good eye contact and use facial expressions and an alert posture to show that you are truly interested in what the other person is saying. Refrain from doing other things during the conversation.

It's not uncommon for me to hear an employee complain about trying to speak with a manager while he is occupied with other tasks like reading, writing, talking on the phone and checking e-mail or doing annoying things like tapping a pencil or drumming his fingers. The manager may actually hear everything that is said, but the employee doesn't feel that she has been heard. If you have given an employee time to speak with you, make the time count by showing that you're interested in what the person has to say. It goes a long way toward building a good working relationship.

3. Listen from the other person's point of view.

I'm sure there have been times when you have told a speaker that you "know just how he feels," (although you couldn't really know because you had never been in his exact situation). Or maybe you've tried to outdo the person's situation, saying something like, "Oh, you think that's bad. You should have there when I..."

Listening from the other person's point of view, however, requires that you listen empathically. As Steven Covey says, "Seek first to understand, then to be understood." Empathic listening does not mean that you necessarily agree with the other person; it means that you are listening to deeply understand the other person. It requires that you ignore your own life experiences for the time being and not project those thoughts and beliefs onto the current situation.

Listen from the other's point of view by trying to put yourself in his place. Consider who the person is and see things through his eyes. Then you are more likely to understand how he feels emotionally and intellectually. This requires listening with your ears, eyes and heart. You must use your eyes to see what the person's body language tells you and your heart to sense what his true feelings are. Listening from other's point of view also requires that you use both sides of your brain.

4. Be open-minded.

If you have preconceived ideas about something that you're going to discuss with someone, you must put your opinions aside prior to the discussion. Our brains have a way of editing anything another person says that would cause our own opinions to be incorrect. So if you want to take in all the information available, go in with an open mind and really listen.

If you have a different opinion about the subject matter, being open-minded does not necessarily mean that you will change your opinion. It does mean that you're willing to really listen to what the speaker has to say and to take in the information. And if you are truly open-minded, you might be willing to change your mind if you receive information that provides a better answer.

5. Use feedback.

Good feedback skills help people communicate with minimum tension and maximum understanding. You can follow up by rephrasing what the speaker has said, asking questions about what you have heard and then sharing your thoughts or reactions without being defensive.

During this process, be sure to express yourself in a way that holds you responsible. For instance: "Let me be sure that I understood you correctly." Then state what you heard.

Not: "Let me be sure that you said what you intended."

6. Listen to what isn't said.

Although it is important to listen to the spoken words, it is even more important to pay attention to the speaker's tone, pitch, volume and body language. These elements often speak more clearly than the words themselves. Communication experts agree with Albert Mehrabian, PhD, who did extensive communication research and determined that the total impact of a message is divided as follows:

- 7 percent - verbal (words)
- 38 percent - vocal (volume, pitch, tone, rhythm, etc.)
- 55 percent - body movements (mostly facial expressions)

In one-on-one conversations, body language often accounts for ninety percent or more of a message's impact.

For example, if you perceive that something is not right with someone and you ask him what's wrong, he's likely to just say, "Nothing's wrong." If you listen only to the words, you'll miss the real message. But what does the person tell you in the way he speaks the words? What does his body language tell you? If he says, "Nothing's wrong" in a soft, dejected voice, and his shoulders are drooped, he could be suffering from hurt feelings. If he says those same words in a gruff, condescending tone with stiff shoulders and a stern face, then he is probably angry about something you or someone else did.

Listen and watch for incongruence between the nonverbal and the verbal messages. In the above example, there is congruence in the nonverbal communication: The soft, dejected voice fits in with the drooped shoulders, and the gruff, condescending tone, stiff shoulders, and stern face are in line with each other. However, none of these nonverbal messages are congruent with the words that accompany them.

In another example, if someone says, "I have a fantastic idea!" but does not make eye contact with you, that is incongruent. Or if he tells you, "I have a fantastic idea!" and speaks so softly you can hardly hear what he is saying, that is not congruent. This kind of incongruence can be due to conflicting feelings or incomplete communication. For instance, the soft voice could mean the person is lacking in self confidence and that he cannot believe the idea could really be worthwhile. The lack of eye contact could mean the person hopes the listener will not recognize that the idea is self-serving.

An astute listener will recognize the incongruence between the words and the nonverbal communication. This is a signal to dig deeper and try to find out what's really going on. Listening for these contrasts will help you not only find the real meaning in the message but choose the best response to it, which in turn will make a huge difference in the outcome of the encounter.

We'll further discuss the importance of body language later in this chapter.

7. Filter the conversation, and listen for ideas.

Filter out words and information that aren't meaningful. Refrain from focusing on the trivia or details and listen for any information that could produce a good idea. Also try to avoid ruling out an idea because of your previous knowledge, history or experience with the subject. With the passage of time, things change, and ideas that didn't work previously might just work now. Listen with the intent to at least give the information a chance.

I've known some intelligent people who could not express ideas and concepts well. So if someone is presenting you with information in a weak fashion, be careful that you don't miss a good idea because you are prejudging it by its presentation. Filter the delivery, and listen to the content.

8. Control distractions.

We've talked about the importance of controlling internal distractions, but it is equally important to control external distractions. If the person with whom you're conversing is a subordinate, he will need the best possible environment in which to express his thoughts. This can also be true with a peer when discussing an important issue or something he feels strongly about.

If there are loud or disturbing noises going on in adjacent rooms that you can't eliminate, go to a quieter place to talk. (Going outside your office to talk can also create a more friendly environment for the other person, thereby enhancing the communication.) If possible, hold your phone calls during the time allotted to the discussion. Interruptions such as these distract the person who is speaking and can cause the conversation to last longer than it would in the right environment.

9. Keep your cool.

The person speaking may have a much slower pace than you, so be patient. Just because he speaks slowly does not mean that he doesn't have important information to share.

If an employee is upset about something, he may not know how to express himself appropriately, and you may find yourself getting upset at the negative expressions he uses. But keep asking yourself what the other person is really trying to tell you. Try to get the essence of the message. If you can refrain from becoming impatient or upset, you may gain some truthful insights or useful information that would help your department run more smoothly. If you find yourself wanting to refute what the person is saying, coach yourself to refocus and just listen.

To stay cool and think more clearly, one needs to oxygenate the brain. Breathe deeply, using your diaphragm so that you get better oxygen/carbon dioxide exchange. (Be careful you don't make breathing noises as you do this; the other person might perceive you're getting upset.) You might also incorporate some affirmations with this; as you breathe in, think, "I am in control." As you breath out, think, "This anger (frustration or whatever you're feeling) is leaving my body." After doing this two or three times, you'll feel more in control. Also, continue to use "I'm listening to you" body language.

Dealing With An Angry Person

While we're on the subject of keeping one's cool, let's look at some ways we can handle others who have lost theirs. To be sure, dealing with someone who is angry is one of the most difficult situations to manage well. Too often people take the wrong approach:

- They try to tell the other person he shouldn't feel angry.

- They try to remove themselves from being at fault.
- They try to justify the source of the anger.
- They tell him how much worse it could have been.

Most of these responses cause the person to become angrier. Many times an angry person merely wants someone to listen. If he is allowed to vent what he is feeling, often his anger is dissipated.

Melinda was working at her desk when an obviously upset client walked into her office. Mr. X didn't have an appointment, but Melinda chose to treat him as if nothing were more important at the moment than he. She invited him to sit down and make himself comfortable and asked if he wanted a cup of coffee. She said, "Mr. X, I want to hear your story. Please share it from beginning to end." Melinda listened intently and used body language, particularly facial expressions, to show her interest. When Mr. X finished, Melinda said, "If I had been in your position, I think I would feel just as you do. I wish this had not happened, and I'd like to help you. What can I do for you now?" Mr. X smiled slightly, stood up and said, "You just did it." Then he thanked Melinda and left.

Melinda was not at fault regarding Mr. X's complaint. She could have told him he needed to speak to the person who was at fault, but this would likely have made him feel he was getting the run-around and thus, more angry. Melinda knew it would be best for the company if she could turn the situation around and save the client. By simply listening well, she made the difference between having an unhappy person and a satisfied client. She changed a lose-lose situation into a win-win situation.

The next time you find yourself faced with someone who is angry, give him or her the VIP treatment like Melinda did. Keep your cool. Use effective listening skills to hear everything from beginning to end without interrupting. Then tell the person that you understand or that you'd probably feel the same way if the situation had happened to you. This really brings the defensive wall down, and the person will not perceive you as being the enemy but perhaps a friend. Top this off by asking what you can do about the complaint. This usually comes as a pleasant surprise to the person, who will usually ask for less than you expect.

Not all situations will end as favorably as Melinda's, but good effective listening will always make the situation better. Sometimes just being listened to empathically is all that's needed.

Nonverbal Messages (Body Language)

As important as words are to communication, the nonverbal part of a message says even more. In fact, more than fifty percent of a message's impact comes from body movements. And when we add the vocal components (tone, pitch, volume, etc.) and body movements together, they make up approximately ninety-three percent of the communication as illustrated earlier in the chapter.

Body language is a primary part of non-verbal messages. Yet the non-verbal includes more. Sometimes the non-verbal is 100 percent of the message and the sender is not visibly present. For instance, you can be in another room and receive a message in the way someone closes a door, places items on a table, puts his feet to the floor, etc. It is important to be aware of all the non-verbal messages. In this chapter, we will focus on body language and how it can reveal a person's thoughts and feelings in a variety of ways:

- Hands can show fear and anxiety: wet and clammy palms, shaking, gripping the arms of a chair, twitching, clinched fists, etc.
- Eyes can indicate fear by excessive blinking, shifting back and forth and not meeting the other person's gaze.
- The mouth displays fear with a clenched jaw, twitching or biting and licking of lips.
- The body held rigidly and stiffly can mean a deep-seated anxiety as can excessive perspiration or heavy sighs when breathing.

You can learn to interpret another person's body language so you can understand what he's thinking and feeling. He doesn't have to say a word: his hands, body and facial expressions—especially from the eyes and mouth—reveal his true inner feelings.

For example, when you are speaking to someone, watch the way he holds his head. If you're speaking to an employee, he'll usually tilt his head to one side if he is attentive to what you're saying. If you are the more powerful person and you show signs of anxiety while speaking, the less powerful person will soon show signs of anxiety as well.

And as we learned earlier, body language sends a clear message, even when that message runs contrary to the words that are spoken. If someone says, "I am not upset" in a harsh tone, you know that person *is* upset. And if you've asked someone to do something, and he says "yes" while shaking his head "no," which one had you better listen to—the words or the body language? That's right, listen—that is, pay attention—to the body language. It speaks more honestly. Even though the person says "yes," he doesn't really plan to perform the task.

James K. Van Fleet, in his book, *Conversation Power*, speaks of the seven telltale signs that you should watch for when you're listening effectively:

1. Eyes: No matter what the speaker's mouth says, his eyes will tell you what he's really thinking. If the pupils widen, then he's heard something pleasant. You've made him feel good by what you've said. If his pupils contract, then just the opposite is true. He's heard something he dislikes. If his eyes narrow, you've told him something he doesn't believe, so he feels he has cause not to trust you or what you say.

2. Eyebrows: If he lifts one eyebrow, you've told him something he doesn't believe or that he thinks is impossible. Lifting both eyebrows indicates surprise.

3. Nose and ears: If he rubs his nose or tugs at his ear while saying he understands, it means he's puzzled by what you're saying and probably doesn't know what you want him to do.

4. Forehead: If he wrinkles his forehead downward in a frown, it means he's puzzled or he doesn't like what you've told him. If he wrinkles his forehead upward, it indicates surprise at what he's heard.

5. Shoulders: When a person shrugs his shoulders, it usually means he's completely indifferent. He doesn't give a hoot about what you're saying or what you want.

6. Fingers: Drumming or tapping the fingers on the arm of a chair or the top of a desk indicates either nervousness or impatience.

7. Arms: If a person clasps his arms across the chest, it usually means he's trying to isolate himself from others, or he's actually afraid of you and is trying to protect himself.

Keep in mind that someone's body language and nonverbal messages may or may not mean any one specific thing. For instance, when I'm presenting a program in which we discuss body language, one of the comments that I often get from participants is that arms crossed across one's body means that person is closing the other out. And while it can mean that, it can just as easily mean the person is cold or has just formed the habit of folding the arms in this manner. It is important to consider the overall nonverbal message rather than jumping to a wrong conclusion about any one thing. For instance, if a person's arms are crossed, yet he is making good eye contact and using affirming head movements, he is probably not closing you out? The key to reading nonverbal messages is to use all the information available before making an interpretation. That's when nonverbal messages can be used to your advantage.

Recognizing Personality Styles in Communication—An Executive Choice

There are four primary personality styles, which play a big part in communication. Although there are a number of different names used to identify each style, I will refer to them as Analytical, Driver, Amiable and Expressive.

One style is no better than another; they are merely different, just as our physical appearances are different. If you're going to have a better understanding of other people's behaviors, you should have some knowledge of these styles. Style differences often account for conflicts between managers and subordinates, so being familiar with this concept can be very beneficial in the workplace.

None of us has a pure style; we're actually a combination of different styles. Some people strongly represent one style while others show elements of more than one. People may even use different styles in stressful or unfavorable conditions, which is one of the reasons for inconsistencies in behavior. Also, behavior exhibited in one person may have a completely different meaning coming from someone with a different style.

It is not my intention to have an in-depth discussion of personality styles. But if you're not currently making use of them in your communication, I hope to whet your appetite for knowing more about them. I will describe the behaviors, values and concerns associated with the styles and identify some communication approaches that are effective with each.

To use the information effectively, you must know yourself, learn about others' personality styles, then "style flex" to enhance communication. To style flex, you alter your own style and approach others with regard to their style. You adapt to others' styles to make them more comfortable and help the relationship succeed. It means constantly monitoring your behavior and shifting your actions to keep them appropriate for the other person. This does not mean that you are manipulating others but effectively controlling your style and being in control of your part of an interpersonal relationship. The more appropriate your behavior is for the person with whom you are speaking, the more likely you will achieve your goals in a mutually satisfying way.

Because of the variations within each style, the following model should be used only as a guideline.

	Less Responsiveness - Controls Emotions	
L E S S **A S S E R T I V E**	**ANALYTICAL** Asks/Indirect/Slow Paced Task Oriented/Self Contained 　Thinking Oriented 　"Facts"	**DRIVER** Tells/Direct/Fast Paced Task Oriented/Self Contained 　Action Oriented 　"Results"	**M O R E** **A S S E R T I V E**
	AMIABLE Asks/Indirect/Slow Paced People Oriented/Open 　Relationship Oriented 　"Relationships"	**EXPRESSIVE** Tells/Direct/Fast Paced People Oriented/Open 　Intuition Oriented 　"Ideas"	
	More Responsiveness - Shows Emotions	

Personality Style Behavior Model

Direct/Fast-paced people (Driver, Expressive) are typically assertive, forceful, competitive, controlling, outspoken, talkative and dominant.

They start interactions quickly, they express their opinions at meetings, and they're likely to interrupt others. In addition, they see things in terms of black and white and talk loudly, fast and with authority. Also, they are risk takers and want results now; they are impatient. They tend to speak, move and make decisions rapidly.

Style flex: Be brief and concise in what you say; get to the point immediately. Match your communication speed to theirs; e.g., if you speak slowly, increase your speed.

Indirect/Slow-paced people (Analytical, Amiable) are typically nonassertive, compliant, quiet, cooperative and speak slowly and softly. They are less likely to make definite statements, describing things in shades of gray. They seek security and avoid risks. In addition, they don't tend to speak out at meetings; they are cautious, supportive and make good listeners. Indirect/Slow-paced people are less competitive, less demanding and less confrontational than direct people. They take a roundabout approach and tend to ask or speak more tentatively. They may provide more background information and take time getting to the point.

Style flex - Ask these people for their opinions or watch their body language for clues that they have something to say. Pause and look at them to signify your desire for them to speak. Provide background information before getting to the point. Match your communication speed to theirs; e.g., if you speak rapidly, slow down.

Task-oriented people (Analytical, Driver) value the accomplishment of their tasks and goals over people and their feelings, and they keep their distance both mentally and physically. They want the conversation to stay on track and ask questions to keep it to the point. In addition, they do not tell personal stories or share private feelings; they tend to show their emotions less. They are very timely and disciplined.

Style flex - Identify tasks and goals of interest to them, then express your interests and goals in terms of those they are seeking to achieve. Control your emotions, whether positive or negative; speak in an even moderate tone, and restrain your hand gestures.

People-oriented individuals (Amiable, Expressive) express emotions and enter into relationships; they value people and relationships over tasks and duties. They are animated and express their emotional reactions and feelings freely and openly. Also, they are informal and talk about personal and intimate topics. They enjoy physical contact and are not overly time conscious.

Style flex - Talk in terms of how you feel about a situation in addition to the situation itself. Ask others in the conversation what they feel about the situation. Talk about personal as well as professional issues. Be gentle.

As you begin to practice style flexing, watch the other person's body language for signs that you need to alter your style or verbal speed. The greatest challenges usually arise between people of opposing styles: Analytical and Expressive, Driver and Amiable—To overcome, alter (1) the pace and directness in your approach, and (2) your concentration on either people or task. Challenges can also occur with someone with your same style if you both work from the extremes of your styles.

The four styles are further illustrated in the following model by Merrill and Reid, experts on personality styles and authors of *Personal Styles and Effective Performance*. The model outlines each style's attitudes and behaviors. The next section gives examples of words and phrases commonly used by each style. That's followed by more tips for dealing with each type of personality.

ANALYTICAL	DRIVER
Slow Reaction	Swift reaction
Maximum effort to organize	Maximum effort to control
Minimum concern for relationships	Minimum concern for caution in
Historical time frame	relationships
Cautious reaction	Present time frame
Tends to reject involvement	Direct action
	Tends to reject inaction

AMIABLE	EXPRESSIVE
Unhurried reaction	Rapid reaction
Maximum effort to relate	Maximum effort to involve
Minimum concern for effecting	Minimum concern for routine
change	Future time frame
Present time frame	Impulsive action
Supportive action	Tends to reject isolation
Tends to reject conflict	

Says things like:

ANALYTICAL	DRIVER
"I've got to get organized."	"Look, what's the point?"
"Start at the beginning."	"The ball's in your court, get going!"
"Get all the facts."	"This is what I need."

AMIABLE	EXPRESSIVE
"How have you been?"	"Conceptually speaking..."
Uses nostalgic phrases like, "I'll never	"Down the road..."
forget..." and "Remember when..."	"Let's look at the big picture."

Here are some more tips for dealing effectively with the different styles:

Analyticals

Analyticals need a plan and schedule to which both of you will adhere. Show understanding and support for principles and thoughtful approach and refrain from offering solutions and help too quickly. Demonstrate thorough action by preparing a written proposal for their consideration. List pros and cons of any suggestion that you make. Give them plenty of time; they take time to make decisions and to implement, but they stick to commitments. Make sure the "how to" and "what" are clear as well as the "who" and "why." Help them find a balance between data collection and action. Allow them to use logical problem-solving approaches. Provide the opportunity for them to excel by offering continued training and knowledge. Reward achievements by praising the excellence of their planning and strategies.

If you disagree with the Analytical, look for the possibility that you haven't really understood from his point of view. Present a well-thought-out, systematic presentation of your position; a written outline can help.

Drivers

Drivers should be given options. Discover their objectives and find ways to support and help implement them. Ask questions about specifics; stick with "what" questions, not "how," "who" or "why." Deal with the actions that must take place for the Driver to reach the objective. Set high goals for them to measure performance. Agree on performance standards and detail requirements, then give them freedom to work. Keep the relationship businesslike; support the results desired rather than the individual. Make sure that they keep up with daily tasks or they may concentrate all their energies on the big project. Check on their performance in terms of results. Recognize accomplishments with financial rewards.

If you disagree with the Driver, take issue with the facts, not the person. If you can't agree with any objective, state "why" and indicate "what" alternate actions could be taken. Keep the focus on how the results will be affected.

Amiables

Amiables need a detailed and structured environment. Carefully spell out instructions. They like to work jointly to accomplish objectives, so be clear about how much time you can realistically spend with them on a project. Show personal interest. Take time to listen to personal stories as you review their performance. Support their feelings and desire for a personal relationship. When Amiables help to achieve an objective, recognize them with praise and personal thanks.

If you disagree with them, encourage discussions about personal opinions and feelings in the area of difference to keep communication open.

Expressives

Expressive should be given competitive challenges and inspiration. Plan actions that will support their dreams, ideas and intuitions. Ask questions to get their opinions and ideas about people and their efforts to reach future objectives. Then have them tell you what people should do to reach these objectives and what they personally plan to do to achieve them. Initially, the discussion is on the subject of people and their future goals rather than hard facts and realities or results. Keep them on track and organized by regularly reviewing their progress. Reward them for achievement by publicly recognizing their accomplishments in print or at group meetings; praise is appreciated.

If you disagree with Expressives, avoid arguing and look for alternate solutions; they have a strong need to win arguments.

Can you identify the following personality styles? Following are descriptions of behaviors with which you might come in contact. What personality style do you think each one is?

1. Robert has little facial expression, few hand gestures, reserved smiles, speaks rather slowly and asks for more information and details during the conversation.

2. Cindy seldom smiles, has limited animation, uses controlled gestures, uses strong eye contact, appears confident, speaks rather rapidly and shares her ideas.

3. David uses open arm and hand gestures, varied facial expressions, leans forward in his chair and speaks with assurance at a fast pace.

4. Michelle is warm and friendly, smiles, is agreeable, uses occasional hand gestures, is only slightly animated, speaks at a somewhat slow pace and is not quick to speak out and volunteer information.

- Robert - Analytical
- Cindy - Driver
- David - Expressive
- Michelle - Amiable

How did you do? If you were able to determine their styles, you could begin to communicate with them using actions that would create more comfort and harmony for each one.

Be careful not to be deceived. Don't assume that the person who appears warm and friendly likes and respects you more than the person who appears serious and aloof. Likewise, the dynamic, enthusiastic person may not have a better idea than the quiet, non-imposing one. These styles only define aspects of observable behavior—not what a person is thinking or feeling.

We have only touched on some of the ideas management can use to utilize personality styles. Although more detailed information and personality profile forms would be needed to flesh out an in-depth program, I hope this information has piqued your interest enough to begin using the personality style techniques in your communication (if you're not doing so already).

Remember that each style presents different strengths and challenges. People all have different desires and needs; therefore, supervision of employees should be tailored to each style. As a manager, if you approach employees with behavioral flexibility, they will likely be more comfortable, attentive and complying. Style flexing promotes better communication which usually results in increased quality, performance and productivity.

Conclusion

Does effective listening sound like a lot of work? Well, it takes some effort, but the payoff is well worth it. Using the art of listening will help you enhance relationships and connect with people anywhere. Practice active listening by using good feedback skills, listening for the real message in words and how they're spoken, observing the nonverbal message and considering the cues from the speaker's personality style, and you will reap the benefits of better relationships at home and at work.

Just think what could happen in your organization if you began to practice the simple art of listening—the foundation of all successful communication—and others in your organization began to follow your example. You would see immediate results. If you use this skill and change the dynamics in your workplace, you will see morale go up, productivity intensify and quality rise, increasing the organization's bottom line. The simple art of listening yields a big payoff.

Jolene Carson

Jolene Carson, founder and president of SUCCESSabilities, inspires people to take action. She is a national professional speaker, trainer, and author. She is coauthor of *Give Stress a Rest*. Jolene is known for her dynamic, interactive, high-energy programs. With over 25 years experience in administration and education, she draws from personal experience to present practical information that can be used immediately. Jolene, a registered Radiologic Technologist, received her graduate degree in Human Relations and Supervision/Industrial Organizational Psychology from Louisiana Tech University and taught at the University of Louisiana-Monroe. Jolene was on the 2002 "Top Ten" list of trainers for a seminar company with 350 trainers. She is easy to work with and creates a win-win relationship with her clients. She is a member of the National Speakers Association, and has worked as a Graduate Assistant with several Dale Carnegie classes. Clients have turned to Jolene for information, skill-building tools, and relationship strategies. She shares insights and ideas to communicate effectively, build relationships, manage stress, and provide exceptional customer service. Jolene inspires people to "reach for the sky" at work and home. Her messages are personal, professional and powerful!

Jolene Carson / SUCCESSabilities
P.O. Box 426
Hodge, LA 71247
(318) 395-8656
(318) 259-7385
Fax: (318) 259-7385
E-mail: Jolene@JoleneCarson.com
www.JoleneCarson.com

Chapter 12

Peacing It Together:
The Art of Communicating Through Conflict

Mary Ann Ray

I recently visited a friend's home one evening. She was folding laundry while her teenage son sat in the floor watching a television program. She carried the laundry basket back and forth in front of the TV three times, plopped down on the couch with a sigh and banged the basket around waiting for her son to notice her household efforts and offer his assistance with the chores. Help never came. I was intrigued by this display. My friend really wanted her son's help but did not ask for it. And so it is with many human relationships. Have you ever really wanted someone to do something or change a certain behavior, but you were unable to verbalize your request? Maybe you thought that if that person really loved you, he or she would already know what you wanted or needed.

I was teaching a seminar on conflict one afternoon, when a woman approached me with an interoffice dilemma. She said, "I have a co-worker who is so rude. She takes things from my desk without asking. She moves things around. I have labeled all my belongings and have even hidden a few things inside the desk. I am even now locking my desk! She just won't stop taking my stuff! What should I do?" I immediately inquired, "Have you talked to her about this?" "Well—no," was her answer. If we want behavior to change, if we want to effectively work through conflict, if we want strong relationships, we must explore the art of verbal exchange.

So why do we act before we talk? Where does that behavior come from? When we were born, we had to manipulate our environment with our behavior. For example, when our diapers were wet or our tummies were empty, we instinctively cried. Our actions provided an effective outcome. Thus, it was quickly established in our minds that behavior produces desired results. It isn't until children are a year old that they begin to develop the ability to verbally communicate. But because verbal communication is really our secondary mode of relating to our environment, many times the imprinted, innate tendency toward a behavioral response overrides our ability, as adults, to appropriately express ourselves verbally in difficult situations. When a negative situation occurs, our tendency is to try and manipulate outcomes and behaviors with action, as opposed to verbal communication. Usually, human beings try every possible avenue for rectifying a difficult situation before breaking down and approaching the situation verbally.

A majority of the conflict that exists in human relationships could be reduced or eliminated if we were more skilled in our ability to verbally respond. In this chapter, we will explore the emotional roots of our behavior and our communication. We will also look at a constructive formula that can be applied to scenarios in which conflict has reared its ugly head. As we become comfortable with the formula and a new way of looking at conflict, we will become successful at talking through conflict as opposed to inappropriately displaying negative behavior. By extracting negative behavior from communication and utilizing the positive verbal skills outlined within this chapter, you will be able to maintain peace and successfully communicate through conflict situations.

We have already established that human beings have a tendency toward action as opposed to talking when conflict surfaces. But what exactly is conflict? A conflict occurs when two or more parties have opposing needs. For example, if we go to a restaurant and I order spaghetti and you order steak, we have a difference, but not a conflict, because we do not have opposing needs. If I am a vegetarian and you unknowingly order a steak, then a conflict may ensue because my need to express my views and conscience will probably oppose your desire for red meat with your meal. Thus, we have opposing needs.

We all know that there are three primary colors—red, blue and yellow—from which all other colors can be created. Likewise, there are three primary needs—the need for power, the need for control and the need for acceptance—from which all other needs are derived.

Need for Power

All human beings want to be granted respect, a voice and an opinion.

Need for Control

All human beings want freedom of choice as well as leverage in implementing decisions and changes in their lives.

Need for Acceptance

All human beings want to receive love and affection as well as have a peer group with which to identify.

Two motivating emotions drive our behavior—love and fear. Conflict occurs because we have a need that potentially may not be met. The possibility that a need may go unmet produces fear, which, in turn, generates a conflict, and our adrenaline production triggers our fight-or-flight behavioral response. Both of these responses are fueled by fear. We may fear physical or emotion harm. We may fear judgment or criticism. We may fear failure. So we quickly evaluate: Should I run away, or should I fight?

If we choose to run away, we have protected ourselves, but we have failed to communicate or resolve our situation. In fact, when we run, our situations usually fester and become worse. If someone yells at us and we respond by leaving the situation without any further conversation, we still have unresolved conflict, and the other person has indirectly received the message that such communication will be tolerated in the future. Thus our silence is tantamount to our acceptance of the unacceptable behavior. It is said, "We teach people how to treat us." We also teach people what communication is acceptable and expected within our relationships.

On the other hand, if we make that quick decision not to flee the scene and to fight, the outcome takes a new turn. When we choose to fight, our number one weapon tends to be defensiveness. Think about a basketball team. The opposing team has possession of the ball, and they are near the basket and ready to score. The team playing defense engages in a battle of strength and wit to protect the basket and deflect any attempt by the opponents to score. Elbows fly, pushing and shoving ensues. A foul is inevitable. Just as a basketball team may foul to protect its turf, so do individuals in defense mode. If I choose to fight instead of flee, I must protect my position and ward off your attempts to score against my character. Words fly, sarcasm flares. A foul is inevitable. Defensive behavior causes each party involved in the conflict to produce more adrenaline and thus become combative.

We fight and flee based on our fears. We fear losing. We fear being controlled. We fear being wrong. We fear being hurt. We fear being rejected. We fear the loss of power. See if any of these behaviors strike a nerve:

Circle all the fight/flight responses below that you are aware of in your own behavior:

Flight Responses
    Pouting
    Hanging up the phone on someone in mid conversation
    Refusing to respond to e-mail or voice mail
    Avoiding telling the truth
    Ignoring bothersome behavior
    Complaining about someone's behavior to a third party
    Denial
    Holding in your anger

Fight Responses
    Sarcasm
    Finger pointing, hands on hips
    Criticism
    Yelling, shouting, name-calling
    Throwing things, stomping, slamming doors
    Counting past offenses and bringing them up as ammunition
    Intimidation and blame
    Guilt trips

The fight-or-flight response may be innate, based on centuries of survival under various environmental conditions; however, it does not provide us with effective solutions to challenging situations. These behaviors do not promote peace. They generate more conflict. We want more than mere survival when conflict arises. Any time we respond from the flight/fight dyad, we are in survival mode. A survival mentality produces a quick fix without the ability to project down the road and see long-term affects for behavior.

For example, if you walk in the house and do not speak to me, a conflict only erupts if I have a need for your communication, love and interaction. If that need exists and goes unmet, I will probably feel hurt. Let us say that my fear of not having that need met triggers my flight mentality. (You will probably discover that some people are prone to flight tendencies, some people to fight tendencies, and some situations may cause either response based on the situation.) I will probably begin to pout and withdraw from you. There are a number of possible reasons for my flight. I may withdraw to protect myself from a feeling of rejection. I may pout to generate curiosity or intrigue in you. I may keep to myself to save myself from your anger in case I were to speak and you were to decide to unload about your day! Because survival mode does not allow me to project the long-term consequences, I may keep a conflict at bay for the evening, because we are quiet. You go your way in the house, and I go mine. But the long-term affect may be a deteriorating relationship between us because I react with behavior rather that communication concerning my needs and my observations about our situation.

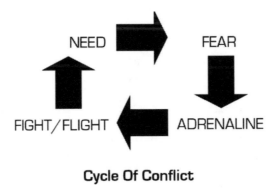

Cycle Of Conflict

When we find ourselves in a situation where we feel a loss of control, power or acceptance, we become fearful. The possibility that our needs will go unmet produces fear. The adrenaline our body produces usually creates anger in response to our fear. Anger is a natural response to fear because it gives us a false sense of power and control—two of our primary needs. A fight mode of response produces visual and obvious expressions of anger (see previous list). There is an assumption that a flight response is not associated with anger. That is simply not true. Though a flight response may not produce outward expressions, the anger exists, and when held in and not expressed, it can manifest itself as stress, depression, illness and even disease.

I was once told that there are two ways to put an airplane on the ground. You can land it or crash it. Either way the plane is on the ground. It is the approach that makes the difference! There is another approach to our communication. As previously stated, there are two motivating emotions—love and fear. Fear generates conflict while love generates peace. If we choose to respond to conflict with love, rather than allowing fear to trigger our fight/flight response, we will automatically generate peace in our communication. To communicate with love, I have developed the following formula:

L: Listen to the message behind the message.

O: Open yourself to all possibilities.

V: Validate yourself.

E: Embrace your choices.

I created this personal formula because it allows you to love yourself and respond to the conflict with openness instead of defensiveness, thus eliminating the need to run away or "foul" the other person.

Let us apply this formula to an actual business situation to see how it works. Let's say you have a co-worker, Margaret, who was recently promoted within your department. The co-worker walks past your desk and initiates the following conversation:

> "I know you have been in your position for six years without a promotion. You really need to take more initiative around the office if you ever expect to get ahead. You are never going to get anywhere if you don't become aggressive like I did."

The hair on the back of your neck is probably standing on end now, and you would either like to crawl under the desk until Margaret walks down the hall, or you would like to come across the desk and punch her lights out! That desire to crawl under the desk and dodge a conversation (even though you are telling Margaret off in your head!) is your flight behavioral response, which suppresses your emotions, and no truth is spoken. You have run away from the situation, and Margaret now has permission to continue to boss you around and offer unsolicited advice in the future!

If you come across the desk and begin to tell Margaret where she can put her criticism, your defensive need to fight and protect yourself will elicit a chain reaction of negative behavior and verbal fouling which serves no purpose in resolving the situation or informing Margaret that her information and its delivery were not positively experienced. The only reason Margaret's comments generated a conflict in the first place was that deep down you had an unaddressed need. Possibilities include: need for success, need to be recognized and respected by co-workers, need to be financially stable and need to be valuable to others, just to name a few.

Rather than allowing fear to dictate the fight/flight response, we will instead apply our L.O.V.E. formula.

Listen to the message behind the message:
What could have been the true motivation for Margaret's remarks? There are several possibilities. Maybe Margaret is really proud of her promotion and couldn't think of any other way to bring up the issue and solicit feedback from you. On the other hand, Margaret may really desire to assist you in your own career advancement but just didn't express herself in a positive way. Another possibility is that Margaret is only capable of feeling empowered when she is criticizing someone else. They say there are two ways to have the tallest building in town: build the tallest building or tear everyone else's down. Some people have a very hard time loving themselves and loving others. They have that need to tear others down in order to falsely build up their own egos. These are frequently the people who initiate conflict!

As you look beyond what was said to why it was said, you are able to step back emotionally and thus take the conversation less personally. In essence, you are applying understanding to the message as opposed to jumping to conclusions and becoming defensive (and we already know defensiveness is all about fear). Einstein said, "The significant problems we face cannot be solved at the same level of thinking which created them."

As you listen to the message behind the message, you begin to shift your level of thinking.

Open yourself to all the possibilities:

Now you quickly cycle appropriate questions through your head: Am I stuck in my position? Am I angry with Margaret because she noticed that I have been overlooked and have not been considered for career advancement? Do I need to become more assertive so that my opportunities in the workforce will increase? Am I jealous of Margaret's promotion?

I find that much of my anger in the midst of conflict is really self-directed. Similarly, it is easier for you to get mad at Margaret for being rude and insensitive than it is to openly acknowledge that you lack assertiveness skills. Blame is a fight response, which not only escalates conflict but also further entrenches us in our own negative behavior.

The other day I was teaching a conflict resolution seminar in Philadelphia. I had a group of people attending the conference who all worked for the same employer. They sat together throughout the day, frequently talking and cutting up during my presentation. Toward the end of the day, I gave instructions for a group activity. I broke the room up into small groups for an exercise, and I allowed these particular people who had come together to work as a group. At the end of the day, I collected the evaluations sheets from the workshop and read through them for feedback and a review of how the day had unfolded for my participants. The evaluation sheet submitted by the "ringleader" of this one particular group really caught my eye. Though the marks were high, there was a note at the bottom of the page indicating that I did not give clear instructions for the exercise and the experience had been very confusing for that group. The author of the evaluation sheet added a few other negative comments about not being able to hear the presentation at times and about being frustrated because she couldn't write fast enough to keep up with what I had said on a few issues. Without my own L.O.V.E. formula, I would have really taken this situation personally! I have a need to please my audience. I want to be perceived as an exceptional speaker and clear communicator. The comments, at first glance, seemed like a personal attack!

As I listened to the message behind the message, however, I recognized the blame. People blame because as long as a situation is someone else's fault, that person doesn't have to change. It is easier to blame than it is to take personal responsibility for one's self and begin to initiate effective behavioral changes. After a little processing, I recognized that this was one of the people who had talked and whispered while I was talking, didn't fully listen and clowned around while I was delivering my presentation. No wonder this person was confused, frustrated and didn't hear all the information! As I opened myself to all the possibilities, though, I realized that I could improve the way I give instructions for the exercise at the end of the day. I appreciated the feedback and released the other negative comments by working through the end of my own L.O.V.E. formula.

Looking again at our previous scenario, if you blame Margaret for the conflict created after her negative comments, you actually trap yourself in the situation. As you blame her, you are giving her the power to control the situation, and you never get to the root of the conflict, which is your own need. You have the power in the situation if you open yourself up to all the possibilities and widen your perspective. What a profound turn the conversation takes when you respond to Margaret in love rather than fear by saying, "Margaret, you are very assertive, and you have a great deal to be proud of. Thank you for encouraging me to continue to improve myself and strengthen my character and abilities." (This is where Margaret's chin hits the desk!!)

Validate yourself:

I firmly believe self-affirmation is the key to handling conflict. If you were to internalize Margaret's statements, you would confirm her message with internal dialogue: "Yes, Margaret is right. I am never going to get out of this position. I am stuck and am a miserable failure. I can't take initiative or speak up; therefore, I am never going to move up!" In the Talmud, there is a verse that says, "Into the well which supplies thee with water, cast no stones." Your inner being is the source of your supply of acceptance, self-worth and support. As you cast stones at yourself, you become your own worst enemy. You have generated more fear, which will continue to spark your fight/flight responses. You will either loathe Margaret from across the room and tell all your co-workers what a horrible person she is without ever having courage to face her, or you will engage in combat every time you see the opportunity to verbally assault her. Your fight/flight response keeps the conflict stirred and steals your peace.

When you choose to validate yourself, you begin self-talk that sounds like this: "I am a capable employee who continually improves on my abilities. I see this as an opportunity to accept who I am and make improvements." I mentioned earlier that conflict only occurs when we have unmet needs. The more we focus on validation of self, the greater attention we are giving each day to our needs and the less attention we are focusing on negativity. As you generate self-validation on a regular basis, you will also notice an increase in your own inner peace. That inner peace will give you strength and courage to communicate positively when conflict surfaces in relationships.

You do not have to believe everything other people tell you! You have every right to dismiss a comment. My sister has a great line. Any time she is the recipient of unsolicited advice and feedback, rather than believing or accepting every comment, she simply says, "I will take that into consideration." She isn't agreeing or disagreeing with the information. She then has every opportunity to process and validate for herself which decisions she wants to make and how she wants to handle the situation. In our example, you could have even responded to Margaret by saying, "I will take that into consideration." You haven't agreed or disagreed with Margaret, and you have bought some time to truly process and think about the situation without allowing the fight-or-flight tendency to kick in and take over. The L.O.V.E. formula is an internal process, which shifts our frame of mind so we can then communicate rather than engage in negative behavior.

Embrace your choices:

At this point, you have a number of choices when it comes to handling Margaret's remarks:

1. You can remain satisfied with you position.

2. You can express to your direct supervisor your interest in a new position.

3. You can search the classified ads for other job opportunities.

4. You can ask Human Resources for constructive feedback.

5. You can ignore Margaret completely and dismiss her hatefulness as her own insecurity.

6. You can sign up for assertiveness training classes.

7. You can see this as the opportunity it is to refine personal skills and formulate a more active approach to your career.

Someone once told me we have three choices in any given situation:

1. We can live with it.

2. We can leave it.

3. We can lobby for change.

When you begin to open up the spectrum of possibilities in your given situation, you release the need to blame, run or interrogate the other person. As you embrace your choices, you take your focus from the conflict and begin to focus on the solution, which is where you will find your peace. In the Chinese written language, crisis and opportunity have the same symbol. You can look at conflict as a crisis, or you can shift and look at it as an opportunity.

You may be looking at this L.O.V.E. formula and saying to yourself, "This is not a realistic approach! How can I just let someone's obnoxious attitude go unaddressed?"

There is a story about two travelers that crossed paths as they were making their way through the Himalayan Mountains. They found themselves facing severe weather conditions, and they realized that their chances for survival increased if they stayed together. The first traveler invited the second to hike with him. The second traveler accepted the invitation but had a harsh and cruel disposition and continued to make snide comments to the first traveler, second-guessing his decisions and arguing with his directions. After three days, the second traveler was outraged. He blurted at the first traveler, "I have walked with you for three days now and have shown you no mercy! Yet you have responded to my harshness and cruelty with kindness and generosity. Why?" The first traveler retorted, "If someone gives you a gift and you refuse the gift, whose gift is it?" The harsh and hateful behavior still belonged to the second traveler because the first traveler never accepted the negativity.

Conflict is only yours if you accept it. The criticism, the judgment, the ridicule are only yours if you embrace it. You can decide what to believe, what to speak, what to accept as truth. When you listen to the message behind the message, you open yourself to all the possibilities, validate yourself and embrace your choices, and you eliminate everything you previously feared. Conflict only occurs if you have an unmet need. With the L.O.V.E. formula, you are caring for your need for power, control and acceptance. You have provided for your need for power by giving yourself permission to look at the choices and possibilities. You have perceived internal control because you only believe and accept the information that you deem true. You have fulfilled your need for acceptance because you are providing your own validation, encouragement and support. The L.O.V.E. formula does not allow fear into communication, thus eliminating the fight/flight response. This in turn alleviates all defensiveness and consequently removes the conflict. Your needs are met. You have peace.

In the above situation with Margaret, you actually gave her all the control in the situation when you allowed your fight/flight response to control your behavior. Though flight keeps the conflict at bay, we still lose. Though fighting is aggressive, we still lose. When we respond with L.O.V.E., we remove all fear, so we empower ourselves, and we retain the control. It is up to us to decide what is right, what is true and what the appropriate response should be.

Take a few moments to reflect upon a current situation in which you are experiencing conflict. Describe the conflict:

What actions have you taken thus far? Have you been willing to verbally communicate about the conflict?

What need has this situation uncovered for you?

Now apply the L.O.V.E. formula:

L. Listen to the message behind the message: What are the possible motives behind the other person's words and behavior? (List at least three.)

1.

2.

3.

O. Open yourself to all the possibilities: Ask yourself if there is any truth in the other person's position. What can you learn from him/her or the situation?

1.

2.

3.

V. Validate yourself: Write at least three positive things about yourself, your position, your opinion in your situation.

1.

2.

3.

E. Embrace your choices: List at least three choices you have available.

1.

2.

3.

Now you are ready to handle your verbal communication in a positive way. You have empowered yourself. You have removed your need to flee the scene and the need to fight to the bitter end. You have dissolved the fear that dictated negative behavior, and you have replaced it with love for yourself and the other person to whom you are relating.

I opened this chapter with a scene from a friend's living room, where she was trying to solicit help from her son in folding the laundry. In fact, she folded the whole load while her son watched television. At the end of his television program, he raced out the front door to meet some friends down the street for an evening of fun. My friend made a remark about how he was insensitive and disrespectful. I inquired about her reason for not asking him for help. She said he was so busy watching TV he would not have even heard her request.

After applying the L.O.V.E. formula, there is one more important act of self-love required in order to communicate effectively and maintain peace in relationships: Ask for what you want and need! The nature of conflict is due to the breach that exists between the involved parties and their respective wants and needs. In order to eliminate that breach, requests (not demands!) must be made. It is an act of love to ask for what you want and need.

One evening, a little boy was playing in the living room while his mother and grandmother cleaned up the evening dishes. Out of the corner of the young boy's eye he saw his grandmother walk through the kitchen with an apple pie. He threw down his toys and ran through the house. "Grandma, Grandma, are you going to cut that pie?" "Yes, I sure am!" She replied. "Grandma, can I have the biggest piece of pie?" asked the little boy. The little boy's mom was standing nearby and sharply scolded the boy: "You can't ask for the biggest piece of pie! How rude! Where are your manners?" The little boy recoiled, and his lower lip began to pucker. He quietly asked, "Well, if you can't ask for the biggest piece of pie, how do you get it?"

Some of us never ask. We walk around feeling undeserving. We have allowed our fears to dictate our ability to voice our needs and wants. We are afraid of being rejected, turned down. Our flight response encourages us to run away from opportunities, risks and new possibilities. We are stuck in life. Much of the conflict we experience is because our needs are unmet; but those needs are unmet due to a lack of action by our own hands. We aren't receiving raises and promotions and recognition because we are not worthy; it is because we don't step up to the plate and ask.

On the other hand, some of us don't ask—we tell! We push and shove and demand. That is the fight end of the fight/flight tendency. After giving a keynote the other day, a person in the audience came up to me and said, "I must disagree with you. I do think we need to fight in this society if we are ever going to get ahead. Situations are tough. Competition is fierce. I was always told, the squeaky wheel gets the oil." I nodded my head, "Yes, the squeaky wheel does get the oil. And eventually, the squeaky wheel gets replaced." Asking for what you want and need is appropriate. "May I have the biggest piece of pie?" is sure to produce more positive results than, "Give me the biggest piece of pie—now!" or standing in the next room hoping someone will offer a piece of pie!

Communication is usually broken into three categories: passive, aggressive and assertive. When we are passive, we are in flight mode. We run away. We don't ask. We do not attend to our own needs. When we are aggressive, we are in fight mode. We are confrontational. We don't ask—we demand. We are so concerned with our own needs that we disregard the needs of others. Assertive communication promotes the following:

- Listening to others
- Asking questions
- Refraining from making demands
- Considering the needs of others
- Validating ourselves
- Recognizing our choices
- Making our needs known

The L.O.V.E. formula empowers you to communicate assertively.

There is a wonderful poem by Jessie B. Rittenhouse that has helped me in my own process of becoming more assertive and asking for what I want and need:

> I bargained with Life for a penny,
> And Life would pay no more,
> However I begged at evening
> When I counted my scanty store;
>
> For Life is a just employer,
> And gives you what you ask,
> But once you have set the wages,
> You must bear the task.
>
> I worked for a menial's hire,
> Only to learn dismayed
> That any wage I had asked of Life,
> Life would have willingly paid.

If you don't ask, you don't get what we need. Even when you ask, you may not receive the results you had in mind. If I ask and my needs are unmet in a situation or unmet by a particular person, I then have a formula in which to empower myself and still maintain peace within. Use the L.O.V.E. formula. Love yourself enough to listen to the message behind the message when someone says something to you. Open yourself to all the possibilities in a situation, including the opportunities presenting themselves. Then as you validate yourself and embrace your choices, you will free yourself of the need to behave in ways that generate or compound conflict. I have learned that there is a difference in resolving or fixing a situation and finding peace with it. By communicating within a loving framework and asking for what you need, you will have "peaced" together a loving relationship with yourself and with those around you!

Mary Ann Ray

Mary Ann Ray began her career in the United Methodist Church in 1986. Since that time she has served nine United Methodist Churches and agencies and is currently pastoring a church in Southwest Missouri. In 1999, after authoring her first book, she started her own professional speaking business, Ray of Light Communications, Inc. to address the important relationship between emotional and spiritual health. Mary Ann received an undergraduate degree in Sociology from Culver Stockton College in Canton, Missouri. In 2000 she completed a program in Christian Counseling from the Center for Biblical Study in Forrest, Virginia. Mary Ann is a member of the American Association of Christian Counselors, the National Speakers Association, and the American Association of Female Executives.

Mary Ann Ray
Ray of Light Communications, Inc.
3237-A E. Sunshine #199
Springfield, MO 65804
(417) 860-6824
Email: ma-ray@juno.com
www.spiritualspeaker.net